Trowels in the Trenches

UNIVERSITY PRESS OF FLORIDA

Florida A&M University, Tallahassee
Florida Atlantic University, Boca Raton
Florida Gulf Coast University, Ft. Myers
Florida International University, Miami
Florida State University, Tallahassee
New College of Florida, Sarasota
University of Central Florida, Orlando
University of Florida, Gainesville
University of North Florida, Jacksonville
University of South Florida, Tampa
University of West Florida, Pensacola

TROWELS in the TRENCHES

Archaeology as Social Activism

EDITED BY

Christopher P. Barton

University Press of Florida

Gainesville · Tallahassee · Tampa · Boca Raton

Pensacola · Orlando · Miami · Jacksonville · Ft. Myers · Sarasota

26 25 24 23 22 21   6 5 4 3 2 1

Names: Barton, Christopher P., 1983– editor.
Title: Trowels in the trenches : archaeology as social activism /
    Christopher P. Barton.
Description: Gainesville : University Press of Florida, 2021. | Includes
    bibliographical references and index.
Identifiers: LCCN 2020022825 (print) | LCCN 2020022826 (ebook) | ISBN
    9780813066738 (hardback) | ISBN 9780813057712 (pdf)
Subjects: LCSH: Social problems. | Social action. | Social movements. |
    Archaeology—Social aspects.
Classification: LCC HN8 .T76 2021 (print) | LCC HN8 (ebook) | DDC
    306—dc23
LC record available at https://lccn.loc.gov/2020022825
LC ebook record available at https://lccn.loc.gov/2020022826

The University Press of Florida is the scholarly publishing agency for the State University System
of Florida, comprising Florida A&M University, Florida Atlantic University, Florida Gulf Coast
University, Florida International University, Florida State University, New College of Florida,
University of Central Florida, University of Florida, University of North Florida, University of
South Florida, and University of West Florida.

University Press of Florida
2046 NE Waldo Road
Suite 2100
Gainesville, FL 32609
http://upress.ufl.edu

CONTENTS

FIGURES

TABLES

PREFACE

I was an activist before I was an archaeologist. I was raised in a devoutly Catholic household, and even though today I am not a practicing Catholic, I still hold on to the lessons my family instilled in me. These are principally that we should care about the world and the people in it. That we should learn from those who came before us, in order to make this a better place for those who will follow us. It was my mom and dad who told me of the connections of people from all different walks of life and that we all possess a goodness inside ourselves; it was my parents who taught me Love. For them this interconnectivity, this love for others, was based on a deep-seated belief in God. For me it is a belief in our species, that we should, that we can, and that we must make this world safer, cleaner, and more humane. Though we differ in our beliefs about what unites us, all of us want to make the world better.

For me, education was the key to using the lessons from my family to effect positive change in the world. Education has always been difficult for me, as I am learning disabled with dyslexia and attention deficit disorder. Like many other young people, I was embarrassed and deeply insecure . because of my difficulties. This led me to shun education at an early age in fear that others would think less of me, that they would think I was dumb. It was my wife who showed me that education was the bridge that could connect the caring I had learned about from my parents with results in the real world. I had always been interested in the past, and as an undergraduate student I majored in history. I remember in my U.S. survey course being introduced to *Narrative of the Life of Frederick Douglass: An American Slave.* Douglass's words and activism resonated with me and led me to pursue a concentration in African Diaspora studies. But I became disillusioned with history, as I felt that a craft based on written sources muted the voices of marginalized people, who have historically been denied literacy. I came to anthropology and archaeology by happenstance. I needed a social sciences course in my sophomore year and the only open seat was in an Archaeology of Native Americans course. The course was needlessly dry, but the fact that it included oral histories and the archaeological record awakened my interest in archaeology. The use of multiple avenues of knowledge addressed my concerns about the representation of marginalized people helping to create a more holistic portrayal of people. I saw archaeology as the connection that united my parents' lessons about Love to my desire to understand the past. From then on, I wanted to be an archaeologist.

My story is similar to that of many other archaeologists, those of us who want to use our power as archaeologists to effect positive change in the world. The contributors to this volume come from diverse backgrounds and have unique experiences. Their topics range from the Himalayas of India to the deserts of Mali; from the Upper Paleolithic to the modern digital age. What unites us all is that we understand that there are important lessons to be learned from the past, that through our knowledge we can better inform people in the present in the hope of making the future brighter.

ACKNOWLEDGMENTS

To my son, Asher, I hope to inspire you to care for the world the way my dad inspired me.

Thank you to my parents, Eileen and Jay, who instilled compassion for my fellow humans in me. I am thankful to the members of the Timbuctoo Discovery Project, particularly Mother Mary Weston and Guy Weston, for their guidance and support. I am indebted to my advisor and dear friend Dave G. Orr for his passion for teaching and for the study of archaeology. Special thanks to Kyle Somerville, Stacey Camp, and all of the contributors for their insights and the valuable chapters they contributed to this reader. I am thankful to Chris Matthews, Carol McDavid, Paul Mullins, Rich Veit, and Charles Orser for their continued support. I also thank Joe Watkins, an activist and archaeologist who has inspired countless archaeologists over the years. I am also grateful to my colleagues at Francis Marion University who have supported my work, and my archaeology kiddos, who have had to endure numerous bad-joke Fridays. Finally, I am forever indebted to my proofreader, best friend, and wife, Jess.

1

Introduction

CHRISTOPHER P. BARTON

Timbuctoo was founded in 1825 by formerly enslaved people who had migrated from Maryland. The community operated as a terminus on the Underground Railroad. In the mid-nineteenth century, several residents of Timbuctoo successfully resisted the attempts of slave catchers to capture them. At least eleven male residents of Timbuctoo served in the United States Colored Troops during the Civil War. Even though most of them were never enslaved, they fought against the system to ensure that people who they had never met would be free. The people of Timbuctoo were poor, not because of any moral failing or because they lacked the will to work but because they lived in a society that limited the opportunities of Black people to accumulate economic, political, and social capital (Barton 2013). In the twentieth century, when New Jersey had an estimated 100,000 residents associated with the Ku Klux Klan (KKK), Timbuctoo residents endured cross burnings, threats, and potential violence from local KKK members. Even in 2017, recruitment flyers for the KKK saying "Stop homosexuality and race mixing" and "Love your race" were distributed in the nearby communities of Cinnaminson and Maple Shade. Despite these historical realities of racism and marginalization, the legacies of which are still felt in the present day, I have frequently been asked after public presentations or meetings with my dissertation committee why I am politicizing the past at Timbuctoo. After one public presentation, a white resident of Burlington County told me that I was a "race baiter" and that the KKK had never been in that area, despite the fact that the KKK had been posting newsletters on people's doors in nearby Shamong (Barton and Markert 2012). I always have had difficulty trying to see the opposite point of view when it comes to repression. How, could the site not be political given its history and the continued subjugation of people of color in the United States? Accusations that I was politicizing the site and that I was being an "activist" were attempts to somehow limit the influences of our work at Timbuctoo. Many people wanted an apolitical narrative of progress that championed racial harmony. At first, as a young graduate student, I was afraid to vocalize my hopes for an activist archaeology, fearing retribution from other professionals and members of the public. But over time, the work at Timbuctoo changed to an understanding that history, archaeology, and politics intersect as we discuss structural problems in the past and their legacies in the present. This brings us to the guiding question of this book: Can archaeology be used for social activism?

Power is the issue at hand. All of us possess power in some way, although our abilities to wield that power can vary due to circumstances and situations. For much of the history of the discipline, in fact, archaeologists have worked for academic institutions, government agencies, and the public sector, and because of this, much of our work has in some way helped to support the networks that have repressed others. While this was often not our intention, archaeology is a product of a society that placed a higher value on some histories at the expense of others. In this regard, archaeology has helped promote some histories while silencing others, all for the sake of those in power in the present.

In this book, we discuss how to use the power of archaeology for social activism. The archaeology of social activism is the use of our craft to generate knowledge about the past in order to use that information to create action in the present and make a more humane future. Activist archaeologists understand that we have a responsibility to the communities we serve to use our craft for their betterment and not to perpetuate systems of repression that have marginalized and hurt people. Similarly, in what he calls "action archaeology," Jeremy Sabloff defines the use of archaeology as activism as the "involvement or engagement with the problems facing the modern world through archaeology" (2008, 17). These definitions force us to understand that although the origins of archaeology are rooted in colonialization, we are not captives to a discipline that aggrandizes the past for the sake of the present. Instead, we can use our craft to challenge social injustice in the present (Atalay 2012, 78–79; Stottman 2010).

The theme of this book is that no matter where in the world, no matter what time period is being studied or what methods are being used, archaeology can be used as social activism. Social activism does not need to be explicitly identified in boldface. Instead, there is power in leaving it to readers to look between the lines, to critically think about what they read. Within these pages you will be introduced to archaeologists studying projects in many locations, and while some are clear about their social activism, others write in a more nuanced way. Yet each of the contributors view their work within the broad spectrum that is archaeology as social activism. Archaeology as a medium for contesting social injustice is not a uniform product; it has no set way of achieving its goals. What may work at one site may not work at another site. This may seem like a copout to some readers, who would argue that the ambiguity and the lack of a clearly defined process somehow diminishes the activist element of archaeology. However, we believe that the democratization of archaeology is not limited to including others in our research designs, our methodologies, and/or our interpretations; it is also about empowering audiences to think critically about our contributions in order to form their own opinions.

Before we dive into the contributors' case studies, it is important to ask several questions about archaeology as social activism. First, can archaeology create positive change in the world? Second, if our goal is to use our craft to make the world a better place, then who are we doing it for? Finally, what is this better world that we are hoping to create?

Can archaeology create positive change in the world? We should not overlook this question: it is the basis for all archaeology. Each of us wants to bring change to the present through our studies of the past, to show how people in the past experienced their world; how they lived, how they viewed themselves in relation to others, and most important, how they are connected to us today. Archaeologists do not uncover the past simply for the sake of exploration; we hope to somehow discover something of ourselves in those who came before us and to use that discovery to define us. Jeremy Sabloff argues that our research "not only can inform us in general about lessons to be learned from the successes and failures of past cultures and provide policy makers with useful contexts for future decisions-making, but it really can make an immediate difference in the world today and directly affect the lives of people at this very moment" (2008, 17). In many ways, social action and activism can be unintended consequences of archaeology.

Not every form of archaeology needs to be directly geared toward social activism to create political action. In fact, since the 1970s and the rise of New Archaeology, there have been concerted efforts to depoliticize archaeology through a push for objective, scientific approaches to our craft. Any quick search for the definition of archaeology will return descriptions featuring the word "science." This is not to say that what we do is not scientific; quite the contrary, many of us pride ourselves on our methods. I believe that archaeologists are scientists, and while some see themselves as "hard scientists" like our friends in biology or geology, others think that we are more like social scientists, as are our siblings in anthropology. But whether you see archaeology as anthropology (Binford 1962) or archaeology as archaeology (Wiseman 1980), the core of our craft is that it seeks to inform the world about the past (McGuire 2008). Even the many people who do not believe that archaeology should be "politicized" or be used to affect social change are creating social action through the ways they use their research to inform the present. Simply put, all archaeology seeks to educate those in the present about the past, and in this way all archaeology is a political act that has power (King 2004, 23–31). The topics we investigate, the sites we dig, the legislation used to protect the past: every process of archaeology is intertwined with social and political networks and thus deals with issues of power. This definition forces us to understand that we are not captives to our past and we can use our craft as a medium for good.

However, over the past few decades there has been a shift in how we use archaeology to explore the past. Some of these changes were not intentional; they were a reflection of how society sees the past and the present lives of marginalized groups. In the United States, much of this new consciousness originated in the 1960s and 1970s in the context of the Civil Rights Movement, the American Indian Movement, the feminist movement, the gay liberation movement, and protests against the Vietnam War (Little and Shackel 2014, 74–75). That is not to say that there were never socially conscious archaeologists before that time period (Patterson and Orser 2004) but that the sociopolitical context of the 1960s and 1970s helped create a consciousness that pushed archaeologists to question their roles in society. However, many archaeologists in the United States feared that if their discipline became overtly political, they would lose social capital and their discipline would be viewed as not an objective science. While archaeologists understood that their craft had power in the context of larger sociopolitical movements, their fear was that their peers and the public would see any interpretations that connected the past to present-day social issues as political bias. These are very real concerns. Economic, political, and social agendas have threatened archaeological sites and archaeologists throughout the world (Colwell [2016]; Newman 2015; see also Keita et al., this volume). These concerns pushed archaeologists to strive for empirically based, purely data-driven research that mirrored the perceived objectivity of the hard sciences (Trigger 2006). Archaeologists began to emphasize the *function* of the archaeological record with a particular focus on past peoples' relationships with the environment at the cost of deemphasizing social interactions between people (Preucel and Hodder 1996; Harris and Cipolla 2017, 29). While some archaeologists understood the connections between the present and their research of the past, few archaeologists sought to directly influence present-day issues.

In my own field of African Diaspora archaeology, most practitioners from the late 1960s to the early 1980s sought to avoid explicitly discussions of modern problems. For example, in 1968, Charles Fairbanks (1974) began excavations at Kingsley Plantation in Florida. Fairbanks is seen as the founder of plantation archaeology in the United States, not because he was the first to excavate at plantation sites but because his focus was primarily on the everyday lives of enslaved people. His work was also distinguished by his interest in uncovering artifacts that showed a direct connection between enslaved people and belief systems in Africa (Fairbanks 1984). While Fairbanks's work at Kingsley was never overtly political, his focus on finding *Africanisms* was in part inspired by the idea that despite the horrors of enslavement and the legacy of slavery, people of the African Diaspora were able to resist assimilation and hold onto a core African identity (Herskovits 1941).

Much historical archaeology in the United States prior to this period had focused on sites that were seen as important to the history of the nation. While Fairbanks was by no means the first archaeologist to look at marginalized peoples (cf. Bullen and Bullen 1945), his work was a watershed moment in American archaeology as the social movements of the 1960s pushed archaeologists to expand their research beyond the traditional topics of their predecessors. While today we do not see a shift from focusing on the plantation's big house to slave cabins as radical, for the archaeologists of the time, the transition to studying past marginalized peoples was revolutionary. I do not believe that anyone would classify much of the archaeological work during this period under the label of "social activist archaeology," but this brief discussion shows that despite our best efforts to appear objective or to present our work as apolitical, the reality is that we are products of our time and every facet of our work has social and political ramifications.

We need to understand that many sites associated with marginalized communities are often poorly documented and overlooked in the present, leading to situations where these sites are developed, excavated, and/ or destroyed with limited or no consultation with the communities that are affected. Such sites have political meaning for diverse communities. As a result, sites like the African Burial Ground in New York City (LaRoche and Blakey 1997); Shockoe Bottom in Richmond, Virginia (Laird 2010); the Cahokia Mound Site (Schuessler 2014); and the Dakota Access Pipeline (Sidder 2016), have become threatened by development even though they have local and national significance. While these projects help us understand the history and archaeology of marginalized people better, their selection for development shows how we often view such sites as expendable or as obstacles that impede the lives of the living. For example, Shockoe Bottom was one of the largest slave-trading districts in the mid-nineteenth century (Deetz et al. 2015). After the end of the Civil War, the area continued to be a historical black community even as sections of Shockoe became vacated or as Virginia Commonwealth University acquired them and turned them into parking lots. From 2005 to 2010, the James River Institute for Archaeology (Laird 2010) excavated the Lumpkin's Jail site in Shockoe which was used as used as a slave auction house until the end of the Civil War and then became a schoolhouse (Mullins 2016). Despite the pleas of scholars and concerned citizens, in 2011, city planners in Richmond, Virginia, unveiled the Shockoe Economic Revitalization Strategy, which included plans for a hotel, over 500 apartments, and a stadium for Minor League Baseball. The city contended that the redevelopment project would not affect the history of the area because the land was underdeveloped and only contained empty parking lots (Berry and Scheeler 2012), despite the detailed historical and archaeological studies that showcased the value of Shockoe. In recent years, the city has slowly backed out of redevelopment plans as it faces mounting pressure from the public. In 2014, the National Trust for Historic Preservation listed the neighborhood of Shockoe Bottom as one of America's 11 Most Endangered Historic Places. Like many other African American sites in the United States, such as Weccacoe Playground (Mooney and Morrell 2013) and the African Burial Ground (LaRoche and Blakey 1997), the archaeology of Shockoe comes at a time when movements such as Black Lives Matter (BLM) are addressing issues of social justice and racism.

BLM originated as a hashtag in 2013 following George Zimmerman's fatal shooting of Trayvon Martin. Since then, BLM has become an international movement and an influential vocal opponent of institutional and everyday forms of racism. Those within archaeology who subscribe to the values and goals of movements such as BLM have sought to highlight Black history by focusing on the issues of redevelopment and neglect. Most notably, the Society of Black Archaeologists (SBA) has become the foremost advocate of using African Diaspora archaeology as a means of social activism. The SBA was formed in 2012 to "promote academic excellence and social responsibility by creating a space for Black archaeologists and other scholars who support SBA's goals and activities." The society's five main goals are:

1. To lobby on behalf [of] and ensure the proper treatment of African and African Diaspora material culture
2. To encourage more people of African descent to enter the field of archaeology
3. To raise and address concerns related to African peoples worldwide
4. To highlight the past and present achievements and contributions that people of African descent have made to the field of archaeology
5. To ensure [that] communities affected by archaeological work act not just as objects of study or informants but are active makers and/or participants in the unearthing of their own history.[1]

The first goals demonstrate that the SBA emphasizes the ethical management of the archaeological record with the much-needed addition of encouraging people of color to become archaeologists. Goals three and five are of particular interest for our discussion of archaeology as social activism. The third goal highlights the need for the SBA to be proponents of the concerns of Black peoples throughout the world. Most important, this goal is not limited to the archaeological record or the past but instead addresses an unlimited range of present-day issues. This places social activism at the very core of the SBA by making knowledge and action in the present a tenet of its mission. In her seminal work on Black feminist archaeology, SBA member Whitney Battle-Baptiste (2011, 70) states that at its core Black feminist archaeology is about changing the ways that people outside (historical) archaeology see the field. She also argues that "artifacts are never just material; they mean more than broken pieces of people's lives buried in the ground. . . . Artifacts can possibly bring forth elements of a more interesting story to communities that would traditionally never see themselves connected with or interested in archaeology as a part of understanding their collective parts" (Battle-Baptiste 2011, 71). Simply put, the importance for socially engaged archaeologists should not be the *things* that we excavate but rather the people in the past and the present who are connected to our archaeology.

This brings us to the SBA's fifth goal: collaborating with other stakeholders. For many practitioners, social activist archaeology is facilitated when we connect archaeological work about the past to contemporary issues that are central to communities in the present (Battle-Baptiste 2011, 71).

If our goal is to use our craft to make the world a better place, then who are we doing it for? The broadest answer to this question is everyone. But we as archaeologists cannot achieve this lofty goal by ourselves. Archaeology and archaeologists are but small nodes in a larger societal network. To broaden our influence and to ensure that we are not working solely for our own needs, we must collaborate with people outside our field. When we pragmatically work with others, including scholars and professionals beyond archaeology, descendant communities and stakeholders, or the public at large, we can begin to understand who this better world is being constructed for. M. Jay Stottman states that "to use archaeology to affect change in and advocate for contemporary communities, not as the archaeologist sees it but as the community itself sees it, defines activist archaeology" (2010, 8). I strongly agree with Stottman that we must collaborate with communities that are related to or find meaning in the sites and topics we research. Although many archaeologists do not have the benefit of collaborating with present-day communities, that does not mean that their work is any less activist than community-based archaeology. However, in my view, some of the most fruitful and meaningful examples of archaeology as social activism emerge from work for local communities (cf. Atalay 2012).

In archaeology, collaboration between people happens at a variety of levels. Some believe that the approach should be a top-down one in which archaeologists and a select group of stakeholders partner to order research, excavate, and interpret the past. Others believe that every voice has something important to say and that all voices should be included in a pragmatic discussion of the past.

Edward González-Tennant (2014) categorizes these forms of public archaeology as participatory and collaborative. Participatory archaeology is the creation of information by archaeologists for others. In this form, stakeholders such as descendants participate in the field and in laboratory work, but they are not fully integrated in every phase of the project, such as planning, archival research, interpretation, and publication. In contrast, collaborative archaeology "seeks to establish a group of co-researchers (professionals and public stakeholders) and a nurturing environment conducive to group learning" (29). McGuire (2008, 146) defines collaboration as "the integration of goals, interests, and practices among the individuals or social groups that work together. . . . It requires humility, patience, listening, careful consultation, equality, and respect." In a collaborative framework, archaeologists and stakeholders discuss the research framework, planning, excavation, analysis, interpretation, and dissemination of information. Collaboration benefits all those engaged in the process and leads to a more holistic interpretation of the past (80–81). While these approaches include people outside archaeology at very different levels, the share a core idea: members of the public, such as descendants, are not simply resources to be mined for information but are research partners whose experiences and knowledge are to be valued.

Some archaeologists fear that they will lose their power when they collaborate, that they will lose their position as authorities when they work on an equal footing with people outside the discipline. However, in a truly collaborative framework the power of the archeologists is not lost, it is merely transformed (McDavid 1997). Archaeologists do not have a monopoly on knowledge or on the meanings of sites. We are not the gatekeepers of the past. When we collaborate, we acknowledge that everyone has their own unique skill set that can benefit the project. Much like the power of descendants, who can have knowledge of genealogy and site history, archaeologists have power that derives from years of learning how to plan, research, excavate, analyze, and interpret—we are craftspeople with a particular set of skills that most people do not have. We are experts in the craft of archaeology, a discipline that has developed over centuries, but we are not the sole proprietors of understandings of the pasts.

I pluralized the noun "past" to highlight the reality that there is not one past, a definitive singular narrative that answers questions about who, what, where, why, and how. Instead, a web of oral and written accounts, archaeological sites, and interpretations exists that weaves together multiple narratives of the past. Objective facts about events, people, and things exist that are realities of the past. However, the often-subjective nature of written documents, oral histories, and archaeology can create alternate interpretations of who, what, where, why, and how. Carol McDavid (2010, 4) refers to these forms of alternative interpretations truth claims. She contends that collaborators must navigate three forms of truth claims. First are archaeological truth claims, interpretations generated by archaeologists that the public may or may not accept.

Second are oral history truth claims, which are both individual and collective accounts about the past. Oral histories have often had a fickle relationship with professional studies of the past. While they have been widely used by scholars, they are often viewed as merely anecdotal when their content runs counter to an authorized public memory. James Delle (2008, 65) defines authorized public memory as a narrative created and reproduced by socially recognized "authorities" such as professionals, academics, and institutions. Many times, they attempt to create a shared identity in the present through monolithic and often celebratory accounts of the past. Sadly, authorized public memories have often distorted and/or silenced the histories of groups that have been marginalized (Delle 2008, 65; Barton and Markert 2012, 88–89). Delle argues that authorized public memory is often contested by social memories such as oral histories, written sources, and material culture that can provide different perspectives regarding a place or person's past. Although oral histories, like any source of information, have potential limitations (Shackel 1993; Barton and Markert 2012), today most archaeologists understand that oral histories and truth claims offer valuable contributions to archaeology.

For example, at Timbuctoo there is an oral history among some of the elders of the community of a "hanging tree" that is often coupled with stories of caves along the nearby Rancocas Creek that still have shackles hanging on the walls from the period of slavery (Barton and Markert 2012). According to oral history, slave catchers hanged runaway slaves from the tree in Timbuctoo. We have been unable to find evidence that the slave trade operated in the community in the documented history of Timbuctoo. In addition, given the geology of the region, there are not any caves along the creek. While there is abundant evidence that slave catchers and their spies terrorized Timbuctoo, there is no evidence that people were hanged in the community; in fact, execution would go against the goals of slave catchers, who wanted to earn a bounty for returning an individual back to the slaver. Although it is unlikely that there ever was a hanging tree or that there are caves with shackles on the walls, these facts do not diminish the contributions these oral histories offer us. These retold stories, passed down from elder to child, conveyed a collective identity of Black experiences. Although in reality there may not have been a hanging tree in Timbuctoo, Black people have endured a history of murder, terrorism, and racism. Additionally, these oral histories and the lessons of shared experiences underscored to children that very real threats and dangers to themselves still existed in their present. Even today, the content of these oral histories directly relates to contemporary issues of police brutality, hate speech, and hate crimes directed at people of color. These oral histories, despite some discrepancies, are still valuable as truth claims in our own research.

The final truth claim McDavid (2010, 4) discusses is community and individual truth claims, or accounts that relate to present-day experiences. Community and individual accounts of everyday lived experiences help inform the goals, research questions, and possible outcomes that develop through collaboration. Through collaboratively answering who, what, where, why, and how questions of the past, we can address their connections to present-day circumstances. When we collaborate, we move beyond the perspective of one archaeologist about the past to a diverse perspective and an understanding of how issues such as classism, racism, sexism, and social justice are still with us today. Sonya Atalay (2012, 3–5) underscores the importance of information and knowledge production created through diverse communities outside and within archaeology. When we work with communities in reciprocal partnerships that value unique traditions and experiences, we can better understand the complexities of the past and address the present-day concerns of the communities we serve (Atalay 2012, 4). Through working together, we can use our craft to make the world a better place.

But what is a better world? It is one based on a framework of unity, equality, and understanding. As McGuire (2008, 4) states, a better, or humane, world is one in which there is less alienation and more emancipation of people. Alienation is "the separation of aspects of the human condition that naturally belong together." Humans are social organisms, and when we work together we can accomplish great things, including our own emancipation. McGuire explains that emancipation occurs when we free ourselves from the social systems that oppress us. Issues such as the uneven distribution of burdens and benefits and the structural and everyday forms of inequality in the contemporary world are not modern phenomena: they are rooted in the past; and if they have origins, they can have endings (Little and Shackel 2014). Archaeology as social activism is not the production of knowledge just for the sake of knowing the past; it is also about using our craft to support universal human rights and dignity (Saitta 2007, 3). Universal rights are unalienable rights that everyone shares regardless of class, creed, gender, nationality, race, and/or sexual orientation.

Barbara Little and Paul Shackel have been at the forefront of the movement to use archaeology to promote social justice. In *Archaeology, Heritage, and Civil Engagement,* they borrow from the "Four Freedoms" speech Franklin D. Roosevelt gave to Congress on January 6, 1941 (Little and Shackel 2014, 53–54). The four freedoms focused on the economic and social needs of everyone: freedom of speech, freedom of worship, freedom from want, and freedom from fear. The first two rights are included in the U.S. Bill of Rights and have been adopted by the United Nations. The last two are particularly interesting, as they touch upon rights that many people see not as universal but as determined by the individual. That is to say, many people regard a human's right to be free from need and fear. While it is not the responsibility of society to provide us with whatever we desire or to keep us free from *all* fears, the freedoms from want and fear simply state that no human should ever have to go hungry or without shelter and that no person should fear harm because of who they are or where they originate. Roosevelt's speech rejected the ideology that issues such as poverty or lack of access to health care are the fault of the individual and instead embraced the concept that these concerns are predominantly the results of systemic and structural inadequacies in modern society. We continue to live in a world that allocates resources, opportunities, and privileges to a select few at the expense of others. As a heterosexual, white, middle-class, male who was born in the United States, I have benefited from this rigid system more than most. I do not fear, I do not want; but others do, and it is our responsibility to ensure that all humans share in these universal rights. In 1948, the United Nations General Assembly approved the Universal Declaration of Human Rights (UDHR), which consists of thirty articles that support the belief that all humans are born free and are equal in rights and dignity; that we all have the right to freedom from oppression, torture, and unjust persecution; that we have the right to the security to live how we want, without fear or threat of harm. The UDHR was the stepping-stone to the creation of the International Bill of Human Rights, which includes the International Covenant on Economic, Social and Cultural Rights (ICESCR), both of which became effective in 1976 and are supported by 169 countries. The ICESCR includes the concept that each participating nation must ensure the rights and obligations of its citizens. The enforcement and recognition of universal human rights has been, and continues to be, fraught with issues of trepidation and an overall unwillingness by many nations to truly enact the UDHR or its latter revisions. Such is the reality when attempting to radically change the ways we see ourselves and each other, but the fact that much of the international community has defined and detailed unalienable rights that we all share demonstrates that there is hope that we can make a more humane world. There are opponents to the concepts of universal human rights who believe that we cannot universalize rights because this could lead to the appropriation of culture and be used as a means of colonization. However, the concept of universal human rights ensures that each of us are able to hold onto the things that make us unique while at the same time understanding that concepts such as freedom from oppression are fundamental rights that should be shared by all peoples.

While the recognition that there are universal human rights offers us a foundation for using archaeology to promote social activism, we must ask a question. Does archaeology have the power to bring about change? On the one hand, to think that one archaeologist at one site will influence social change is a bit naïve; that even a combined effort from an army of archaeologists could sway the world is far out of our reach. Archaeology simply does not have the power to create straightforward, direct change in society. While we can provide commentary on contemporary issues that are drawn from our studies of the past, the reality is that we lack the cultural, political, and social capital to directly influence institutional and everyday practice.

On the other hand, while archaeology has only limited power in society, that power can still be used to make the world better (McGuire 2008, xi; Tilley 1989, 105). Christopher Tilley (1998, 327) argues that "archaeology forms one small but nevertheless significant part of contemporary culture. Changing the nature of archaeology will filter through and have an effect on the other areas, especially through the interaction between professional archaeologists and the public." Archaeology has an observable value to society that we can see in cultural resource legislation, museums, higher education, and popular culture. This worth, although it is limited, suggests that archaeology is important to society and that we can help bring about positive change through our power.

There are many types of power in the world. There is power that can be wielded over others, and there is the power to influence. Not everyone has power over others, but we all have power to influence—and with that power comes the responsibility to help others (Saitta 2008, 23). When archaeologists use their power to change society it is called praxis. McGuire defines praxis is the practice of using the knowledge that we have gained through our studies of the past and consciously acting to create a more humane world (McGuire 2008, 3). Borrowing from Marxist theory, McGuire contends that praxis embraces three goals: to know our world, to critique our world, and to take action to change our world. He (2008, 38–39) further argues that the foundation from which we build praxis is knowing our world. As archaeologists, we must make sure that our knowledge of the past is accurate and rooted in facts. If our knowledge of the world is flawed, then our critiques will also be flawed, and so ultimately will our actions. To ensure that our knowledge is based on fact, we must work with stakeholders within and outside of our discipline. Through many voices we can produce a collective retelling of a more accurate past.

It is important to understand that there is no set way of doing archaeology as social activism. The diversity of approaches is manifested in this book. The SBA, the Society for American Archaeology, and the Society for Historical Archaeology do not provide any definitions of archaeology as social activism. It is a process that entails many options, avenues, and directions. This again brings to a recurring theme in this book: not all archaeology as social activism needs to be overtly radical or explicitly identified as such.

Unlike the majority of other works discussing archaeology as social or political activism (Little and Shackel 2014; McGuire 2008; Sabloff 2008), the contributors in this book study different topics and time periods using a variety of different methods in different parts of the world. While most works associated with socially engaged archaeology are limited to historical archaeology, this book includes studies of the Paleolithic, medieval, and historic periods. In addition, some of the contributors to this volume are from professional spheres of archaeology, highlighting that social activism is not an esoteric practice limited to academia but is thoroughly ingrained in the networks of cultural resource management. Finally, the authors here represent practitioners of archaeology at various stages in their careers, from graduate students to people in the early stages of their career to more senior scholars who have helped shape the field. Despite these differences, all of the contributors share the understanding that we can use archaeology to improve the world.

Chapter 2, by Nathan Klembara, focuses on the use of queer theory in Paleolithic Europe. Klembara argues that alternative interpretations of Upper Paleolithic art can challenge stereotypes of gender roles and perceptions of heteronormativity. Through our knowledge of the realities of sexuality and gender identities in the deep past, we can make the world safer for LGBTQ+ communities today that continue to be persecuted and seen as "abnormal" in the present.

Kyle Somerville, a cultural resources archaeologist, looks at the legacies of interpersonal violence on the colonial American frontier through the study of human remains from Fort Laurens in Ohio. He focuses on the historical, political, and historical networks that resulted in increasing acts of violence based on racial ideologies. His work seeks to use archaeology to understand violence and conflict rooted in social constructs and the ambiguities inherent in understanding violent conflicts.

Daouda Keita, Moussa dit Martin Tessougue, and Yamoussa Fane, archaeologists from Mali, discuss their work to document the destruction to archaeological and heritage sites by the jihadi occupation of Timbuktu in 2012. The archaeologists collaborate with the international community, including UNESCO, to promote preservation and sustainable management of Mali's cultural heritage. Their work seeks to save this heritage in the "Golden Triangle" of Mali and promote heritage tourism to the region.

Tiffany C. Fryer and Kasey Diserens Morgan discuss their work on heritage activism in Quintana Roo, Mexico. They look at the intersections of archaeology, heritage studies, and tourism as ways to challenge economic and social marginalization in a region that is known for the Caste War, or Maya Social War (1847–1901). Fryer and Diserens Morgan's work, which features collaboration with a variety of local communities, embodies archaeology as social activism in the twenty-first century.

Stephen Brighton and Andrew Webster present findings from their work on the archaeology of Skibbereen in County Cork, Ireland. They build on the Archaeology of the Irish Diaspora and Modern Ireland Project, which focuses on the recent past, including the Famine period (1845–1851). Brighton and Webster ask: What is archaeology good for? Who benefits from the knowledge that archaeologists generate? Their central aim is to look at how archaeological knowledge can serve the community to address social justice and heritage production.

My chapter focuses on the racialization of toys in the nineteenth- and early twentieth-century United States. I discuss the intersectionality of class, gender, and race through toys and contend that the toys, such as topsy-turvy dolls, were used to discipline white children into a world view of race, racialism, and racism as an expansion of a social milieu that dehumanized and disenfranchised Black people following the Civil War. The chapter creates connections between the racialized objects of the past to present-day forms of racialized material culture and how these continue to affect children's development.

Bernard Means and Vinod Nautiyal discuss the use of digital technology to save material culture and heritage sites in Uttarakhand, India. Through an international collaboration between their universities, Means and Nautiyal developed a project that digitally documented the material heritage of the region through 3D scanning and printing technologies to raise local, national, and international attention to the richness of Uttarakhand's cultural past. That past has been affected by landslides and earthquakes and by the disturbance of cultural resources as a result of construction projects and limited government funding in India.

Stacey Camp also addresses the importance of technology in archaeology in her chapter on digital databases as powerful tools for the future of our craft. In her case study of the Kooskia Internment Camp, an incarceration camp for Japanese and Japanese Americans in Idaho during World War II, she argues that digital databases can be used to both democratize interpretation and preserve our knowledge for future generations.

Christopher Matthews discusses his work with the Native American and African American community of Setauket, New York, and how the impacts of environmental racism have disproportionally affected people of color. He considers how suburbanization has resulted in contaminated waterways and how pollution as a result of gentrification has impacted the natural environment. Matthews argues that we can address structural and everyday forms of environmental racism using a sociohistorical and archaeological approach.

Kerry Thompson and Ora V. Marek-Martinez discuss cultural resource management regulations and social justice on the Navajo Nation. They argue that the top-down structure of compliance leaves little room for community engagement on heritage issues and that a community-based approach would help the Navajo Nation develop more effective land-use plans.

Finally, Joe Watkins, one of the foremost scholars on issues of social activism in archaeology, offers his insights into the legacies and potential future directions for the field. Watkins argues that we must move archaeology outside of the narrow scope of apolitical science and calls for an activist archaeology. He defines activist archaeology and offers case studies of contemporary research as examples of the importance of an engaged archaeological practice in the twenty-first century.

This book is unique in that while the contributors focus on different topics and varying time periods and use a variety of practices in their research, they all seek to expand their work beyond "traditional" archaeological practice in order to use their craft and their studies of the past to inform the present and make the future brighter. The authors are prehistorians, historical archaeologists, cultural resource management professionals, and academics, but they are all people who see the injustices in the world and use their praxis to promote archaeology as social activism.

Note

1. "About," *Society of Black Archaeologists,* accessed April 22, 2020, https://www.societyofblackarchaeologists.com/about.

References Cited

Atalay, Sonya. 2012. *Community-Based Archaeology: Research with, by, and for Indigenous and Local Communities.* Los Angeles: University of California Press.

Barton, Christopher P. 2013. "Identity and Improvisation: Archaeology at the African American Community of Timbuctoo, Burlington County, NJ." PhD diss., Temple University, Philadelphia.

Barton, Christopher P., and Patricia G. Markert. 2012. "Collaborative Archaeology, Oral History and Social Memory at Timbuctoo, NJ." *Journal of African Diaspora Archaeology and Heritage* 1 (1): 79–102.

Battle-Baptiste, Whitney. 2011. *Black Feminist Archaeology.* New York: Routledge.

Berry, Jack, and Kim Scheeler. 2012. "Time to Act: Build a Ballpark Downtown." *Richmond Times-Dispatch,* August 5.

Binford, Lewis C. 1962. "Archaeology as Anthropology." *American Antiquity* 28 (2): 217–225.

Bullen, Adelaide, and Ripley Bullen. 1945. "Black Lucy's Garden." *Bulletin of the Massachusetts Archaeological Society* 6 (2): 17–28.

Colwell, Chip. [2016]. "How the Archaeological Review Behind the Dakota Access Pipeline Went Wrong." *Conservation.com.* https://theconversation.com/how-the-archaeological-review-behind-the-dakota-access-pipeline-went-wrong-67815.

Deetz, Kelley F., Ellen Chapman, Ana Edwards, and Phil Wilayto. 2015. "Historic Black Lives Matter: Archaeology as Activism in the 21st Century." *African Diaspora Archaeology Newsletter* 15 (1): Article 1.

Delle, James, A. 2008. "A Tale of Two Tunnels: Memory, Archaeology, and the Underground Railroad." *Journal of Social Archaeology* 8 (1): 64–94.

Fairbanks, Charles H. 1974. "The Kingsley Slave Cabins in Duval County, Florida, 1968." *Conference of Historic Site Archaeology Papers* 7: 62–93.

———. 1984. "The Plantation Archaeology of the Southeastern Coast." *Historical Archaeology* 18 (1): 1–14.

González-Tennant, Edward. 2014. "The 'Color' of Heritage: Decolonizing Collaborative Archaeology in the Caribbean." *Journal of African Diaspora Archaeology and Heritage*. 3 (1): 26–50.

Harris, Oliver, and Craig Cipolla. 2017. *Archaeological Theory in the New Millennium: Introducing Current Perspectives.* New York: Routledge.

Herskovits, Melville J. 1941. *The Myth of the Negro Past.* New York: Harper & Brothers.

King, Thomas F. 2004. *Cultural Resource Laws and Practices: An Introductory Guide.* Lanham, MD: AltaMira Press.

Laird, Matthew. 2010. "Archaeological Data Recovery Investigation of the Lumpkin's Slave Jail Site (44HE1053) Richmond, Virginia. vol. 1, Research Report." Report prepared for Richmond City Council Slave Trail Commission by James River Institute for Archaeology, Inc., Williamsburg, Virginia.

LaRoche, Cheryl, and Michael Blakey. 1997. "Seizing Intellectual Power: The Dialogue at the New York African Burial Ground." *Historical Archaeology* 31 (3): 84–106.

Little, Barbara J., and Paul A. Shackel. 2014. *Archaeology, Heritage, and Civic Engagement: Working Toward the Public Good.* Walnut Creek: Left Coast Press.

McDavid, Carol. 1997. "Descendants, Decisions, and Power: The Public Interpretation of the Archaeology of the Levi Jordan Plantation." In *In the Realm of Politics: Prospects for Public Participation in African-American Archaeology,* edited by Carol McDavid and David Babson, special issue of *Historical Archaeology,* 31 (3): 114–131.

McGuire, Randall H. 2008. *Archaeology as Political Action.* Berkeley: University of California Press.

Mooney, Douglas, and Kimberly Morrell. 2013. "Phase IB Archaeological Investigations of the Mother Bethel Burying Ground, 1810–Circa 1864." Site report prepared for the Pennsylvania Horticultural Society. URS Corporation, Philadelphia.

Mullins, Paul R. 2016. "Repressing Repugnant Heritage: Place, Race, and Memory in Shockoe Bottom." Archaeology and Material Culture, January 18. Accessed May 24, 2019. https://paulmullins.wordpress.com/2016/01/18/repressing-repugnant-heritage-place-race-and-memory-in-shockoe-bottom/.

Newman, Conor. 2015. "In the Way of Development: Tara, the M3 and the Celtic Tiger." In *Defining Events: Power, Resistance, and Identity in Twenty-First Century Ireland,* edited by R. Meade and F. Dukelow, 32–50. Manchester: Manchester University Press.

Patterson, Thomas C., and Charles E. Orser. 2004. *Foundation of Social Archaeology: Selected Writings of V. Gordon Childe.* Lanham, MD: AltaMira Press.

Preucel, Robert W., and Ian Hodder. 1996. *Contemporary Archaeology in Theory: A Reader.* Malden, MA: Blackwell Publishers.

Sabloff, Jeremy A. 2008. *Archaeology Matters: Action Archaeology in the Modern World.* Walnut Creek, CA, Left Coast Press.

Saitta, Dean J. 2008. *The Archaeology of Collective Action.* Gainesville: University Press of Florida.

Schuessler, Ryan. 2014. "Suburban Expansion Threatens Prehistoric Sites near St. Louis." *Aljazeera America,* June 28. Accessed May 16, 2019. http://america.aljazeera.com/articles/2014/6/28/prehistoric-sitesstlouis.html.

Shackel, Paul A. 1993. *Personal Discipline and Material Culture: An Archaeology of Annapolis, Maryland, 1695–1870.* Knoxville: University of Tennessee Press.

Sidder, Aaron. 2016. "Understanding the Controversy Behind the Dakota Access Pipeline." *Smithsonian Magazine*, September 14. Accessed December 1, 2018. https://www.smithsonianmag.com/smart-news/understanding-controversy-behind-dakota-access-pipeline-180960450/.

Stottman, M. Jay. 2010. *Archaeologist as Activists: Can Archaeologists Change the World?* Tuscaloosa, AL: University of Alabama Press.

Tilley, Christopher. 1989. "Archaeology as Socio-Political Action in the Present." In *Critical Traditions in Contemporary Archaeology: Essays in the Philosophy, History, and Socio-Politics of Archaeology,* edited by Valerie Pinsky and Alison Wylie, 104–116. Cambridge: Cambridge University Press.

———. 1998. "Archaeology as Socio-Political Action in the Present." In *Reader in Archaeological Theory: Post-Processual and Cognitive Approaches,* edited by D. Whitley, 315–330. New York: Routledge.

Trigger, Bruce. 2006. *A History of Archaeological Thought.* 2nd ed. New York: Cambridge University Press.

Wiseman, James. 1980. "Archaeology as Archaeology." *Journal of Field Archaeology* 7: 149–151.

2

"But I'm a Paleolithic Archaeologist!"

Queer Theory, Paleolithic Art, and Social Justice

NATHAN KLEMBARA

Sit back and imagine a caveperson. Do not think too hard about the image playing in your head. Do not let your "archaeology brain" take over. Focus on the first thing that comes to your mind, the cavepeople you first learned about as a child. What do you see? I assume you're picturing a rather hairy, robust male, perhaps hunched over, with a huge brow ridge and tangled, unkempt hair. His clothing, if there is any, is simple, most likely a simple tunic or a dirty, worn loincloth. It is likely a man doing something "manly." Perhaps he has a club and was hunting or making a fire or some stone tools. If a woman was present in your image, she was doing something passive in the background, such as cooking food or mending clothing for her partner—the image of the ideal heterosexual bonded pair.

We can all generate such images because the stereotypical "caveman" has permeated our media and society, including television shows and commercials, movies, comic strips, video games, lifestyle blogs, and newspapers. In this chapter, I explore these perceptions of the caveman and how these perceptions have become naturalized and have subsequently resulted in the suppression of modern peoples, in particular the LGBTQ+ community. This issue is of great importance to archaeologists because the naturalization of these actions and behaviors are often associated with the peoples of the Paleolithic. For this reason, in this chapter I focus on the Upper Paleolithic in Western Europe.

I argue that an examination of the Upper Paleolithic through a queer lens is an ideal and necessary way to expose the performative nature of the archaeological discourse about the Paleolithic and to denaturalize harmful and problematic normative assumptions about deep prehistory. A queer approach also permits us to see Upper Paleolithic archaeology as a locus for social justice because queer archaeology embraces the political disposition of archaeology (Blackmore 2011; Dowson 2000b). Atalay et al. (2014) define political archaeology as "a form of intellectual activism that analyzes the political nature of knowledge and production by highlighting the intersubjectivity of archaeological research. . . . by championing subaltern groups and deconstructing power" (11) and argue that one of its main goals is "fostering safe spaces for the expression of alternative opinions and practices" (19). The goals of queer archaeology, which is always political, contribute to this larger activist program within archaeology. Following Cobb (2005), I use queer theory "as a political challenge [to] heteronormative world views in the present." Its goals are "to explore and reassess the implications of such heteronormativity within archaeological interpretations and narratives of the past" (631). As is true of all queer archaeology, this chapter is a critique of heteronormative power discourses within archaeological theory. This necessarily involves questions of ontology and epistemology. We cannot unshackle ourselves from heteronormative models of the past unless we deconstruct our understandings of gender, sexuality, and processes of subjectification. Because sexuality "pervades every aspect of culture" (Turner 2000, 140), we must understand it on an ontological basis, rather than simply on an epistemological basis. Too many queer works in archaeology are a critique of the intellectual history of sexuality and queerness in archaeological method and theory rather than a concerted effort to discover and unpack the core, the very nature, of sexuality and queerness. This chapter goes beyond critique. Hopefully it will provide alternative explanations, methods, and ways of thinking based on evidence from the archaeological record. Archaeologies that make real change in the world "embrace the cognitive dissonance of deploying both archaeological sciences and critical archaeology to serve the interests of communities in the world" (Atalay et al. 2014, 8). In the remainder of this chapter I argue that queering the Upper Paleolithic will create a more meaningful and engaging discourse for both our interpretations of the past and our interactions in the present.

People who are not archaeologists commonly believe that the biological and archaeological data indicates that humans "finished" evolving in the Upper Paleolithic. According to this misinterpretation, humans are anatomically and behaviorally adapted to living in Pleistocene conditions and any behaviors from this time are the most "natural" and are the "best" for us even today. According to this belief, our perceptions of Paleolithic lifeways have become naturalized, and any deviation from these behaviors or norms are "unnatural" to our perceived biological state.

Paleolithic archaeology is a performative act; archaeologists quite literally invent human nature (Sterling 2011). In doing so, they unintentionally create privileged identities. Archaeologists who work in deep prehistory, the contexts most distantly removed from written sources (Schmidt 2000), define what it means to be human. In many regards, our work has been hijacked to justify modern people's perception of natural versus unnatural, right versus wrong, and best versus worst. Evidence of such misinterpretations can be as nonsensical as the promotion of the "Paleo" diet in modern society, a fad diet that contends that we should eat like "cavemen," as if there were a homogenized diet that spanned cultures, environments, and time ranges. A nefarious result of the hijacking of archaeology work has been the persecution of LGBTQ+ communities using the argument that any variation from heteronormativity is an affront to the "natural state" of humans (Dowson 2009). By engaging with the public's fascination with the prehistoric past and with these interpretations of archaeology, we can discuss these issues with both archaeologists and those outside the field (Chang and Nowell 2016). Such discussions enable us to use Paleolithic archaeology as an engine for social justice.

I begin with a discussion of the history and major tenets of queer theory in archaeology. I then provide an overview of various androcentric and feminist interpretations of Upper Paleolithic visual imagery, focusing on vulvar images and figurines. I conclude by deconstructing many of these interpretations and reanalyzing Upper Paleolithic visual imagery through a queer lens, contending that a queer Paleolithic archaeology is in important means of social activism.

Queer Theory: Denaturalizing the Past

Queer theory has a robust history in archaeological theory and practice (e.g., Dowson 2000a, 2000b; Blackmore 2011; Geller 2009; Schmidt 2002; Voss 2000). It emerged as a challenge to all normative assumptions about the past and present. The definition of queer archaeology has become broad in order to maintain its identity as inclusive, intersectional, and radically political. The definition of queer scholarship must be left vague so that it does not have a single center (for example, gay and lesbian) but instead has many centers and examines and challenges all normative and nonnormative acts (Giffney 2004). By the 1980s, many people had become dissatisfied with the primacy of gender or sexual identity in the politics of second-wave feminism and gay and lesbian studies. They argued instead for an intersectional approach that would reject the stable, predominantly white identities of feminism and gay and lesbian studies (Sullivan 2003). These stable identities, as Sedgwick (1990, 8) argues, only reproduce heteronormativity in a new form that privileges gender identity, sexual attraction, and the subsequent "sexual orientation." Queer theory enabled scholars to cross gender lines and to reconfigure identity "as a constellation of multiple and unstable positions" (Jagose 1996, 3).

Some academics challenge queer archaeology and queer theory more broadly because, as Halperin (1996) argued, "there is nothing in particular to which [queer] refers" (62). He suggests that queer is anything that is non-normative, that goes against the dominant, the legitimate, or what is perceived as the "good." However, Dowson (2000b) contends that in the context of archaeology, queer theory can be anything and everything. Unlike some theory, queer theory does not attempt to explain macro-phenomena. Instead, it forces us to examine our *positions* within the knowledge production process and the ways that our contemporary identities and politics greatly impact the knowledge we produce and consume. Queer theory is an ever-shifting framework through which we can examine our normative biases and assumptions about the past and present.

In early queer archaeological works, practitioners argued that archaeology is intimately entangled with the politics of homosexuality and heteronormativity (Dowson 1998). She (2000), Claassen (2000), and Rutecki and Blackmore (2016), among others, argue that both explicit and latent heteronormativity in the field of archaeology have deterred queer individuals from having successful careers in archaeology, or, at best, have denigrated the importance or validity of their work. In addition, some have pointed out that heterosexuality is so engrained in the archaeological imagination that archaeologists rarely consider sexuality in prehistory because they do not see it as worth studying because they assume everyone was heterosexual (Dowson 2000a). However, despite its close relationship to those who want to expose heteronormativity in archaeology method and theory, queer archeology is not about "excavating" homosexuality in the past (Dowson 2000b). Over the past twenty years, queer approaches in archaeology have grown in many ways, expanding its theoretical and methodological range beyond its assumed postmodern and theoretical niche. This range now includes a wide variety of themes and approaches, including social constructionism (Alberti 2001), mathematics (Chilton 2008), and the analysis of art or visual imagery (Dowson 2000; Joyce 2000). Queer archaeology has also expanded to include bioarchaeology, burials, and the body (Alberti 2013; Geller 2009; Hollimon 2011; Matic 2012); architecture and space (Eger 2009; Prine 2000; Schofield and Anderton 2000); and cosmology (Schmidt 2000; Solli 2008).

The merging of queer theory and archaeology has enabled people from marginalized communities, including, but not limited to the LGBTQ+ communities, to find a history and a past. Queerness has been viewed and studied as asocial and ahistorical (Dowson 2000b), as if so-called deviant sexual and gendered identities emerged ex nihilo in the latter half of the twentieth century. Archaeology, especially a queer archaeology, can help provide a long-term, collective history for these communities. I contend that because of its immense time depth, a queer theory of the Paleolithic can expose the heteronormative discourse surrounding human nature. Ideologies that claim that heterosexuality is innate or "normal" mask the realities of human sexuality in the past and present. Archaeological studies have helped foster these ideologies by projecting present-day perceptions of heteronormativity onto the past. These studies and a corpus of social structures and everyday practices have created the concept that homosexuality, asexuality, and/or pansexuality did not exist in the past and thus have no place in the present or future. In doing so, archaeology has unwillingly provided "evidence," albeit flawed, to institutions and individuals that have actively repressed LGBTQ+ communities and continue to do so.

Today, some archaeologists are using their work to operate against normative views in the present, including the suppression of LGBTQ+ groups (Rutecki and Blackmore 2016; Dowson 2000a). Queer archaeologists contest traditional interpretations of the archaeological record as a way of challenging these uses of the past and making meaningful change in the present. They are concerned with the practical implications of their work and use archaeology as a tool to combat injustices in the present. Archaeologists working in this line of thought may not be concerned with proving anything about the past, but they are levying critiques of heteronormative discourses in archaeology and how those discourses impact queer individuals and communities in the present.

Attempting to prove or define what it means to be queer in the past is inherently a reflection of modern, western notions of gender and sexuality. Queering the past attains its power not through these kinds of definitions but rather through its ability to expose power differentials and go beyond the simple act of labeling individuals as "queer" (Warner 1999).

In other words, queer archaeologists cannot simply use the word "queer" to label rare or uncommon archaeological finds. Queer becomes a useless term when archaeologists begin to apply it to all nonnormative features and artifacts from the archaeological record without proper regard to the sociopolitical origins of the term.

While "queer" refers to nonnormativity, it is not its direct synonym. If we equate queer with "rare" or "nonnormative" without also deconstructing the power relations involved, we sterilize queer theory. Such practices would make queer theory yet another apolitical approach. They would undermine the ultimate goal of queer theory analyzing the "Hetero/Homosexual figure as a power/knowledge regime that shapes the ordering of desires, behaviors, social institutions, and social relations—in a word, the constitution of the self and society" (Sediman 1997, 150). At their worst, such practices can reinforce (rather than deconstruct) the idea that queer people are (and were) rare to the point of being pathological.

Queer theory has power because it recognizes the power structures that are, or need to be, subverted. As Warner (1993), has noted, "Queer struggles aim not just at toleration and equal status, but [also at] challenging those institutions and accounts" while also "reject[ing] a minoritizing logic of toleration as simple political interest-representation in favor of a more thorough resistance to regimes of the normal" (xiii, xxvi). Queer theory traces the origins of power/knowledge discursive practices, the practices that are seen as "normal," including how heterosexuality came to be seen as natural and unquestioned (Sullivan 2000). It does not reproduce dichotomies, such as the binaries of heterosexual/homosexual or normal/not normal, by simply using the term "queer" instead of "not normal." The term "queer" should be used only when it can help us push against limiting sociocultural norms that are used to oppress minority groups. It should not be used as a tool in which we apolitically and problematically further marginalize these groups by emphasizing a minority status.

While there has been much discussion about applying queer theory to archaeology more broadly, queer theory has been most widely applied to protohistoric and historic contexts (e.g., Eger 2009; Prine 2000; Springate 2017; Voss 2012) and has only been applied as far back as the Mesolithic (Cobb 2005, 2006; Schmidt 2000). Archaeologists of the Upper Paleolithic have begun to challenge the discipline's androcentric origins and history (e.g., Conkey 1991, 1997; Nelson 1990; Owen 2005; Soffer 2004; Sterling 2015) but have yet to directly challenge its heterosexist literature. Thus, Upper Paleolithic archaeologists can look to scholars of the Mesolithic for ideas about how to effectively queer the past. While the Mesolithic differs from the Upper Paleolithic in Europe in many way, there are also many similarities. For instance, communities in both periods pursued hunting and gathering and were relatively nomadic. Groups in the Mesolithic continued to use Upper Paleolithic art forms such as cave painting and carved figurines. The differences matter, but because the practice of applying queer theory to the archaeology of the Upper Paleolithic is so new, scholarly works pertaining to other time periods can offer frameworks for comparative analysis.

Schmidt (2000), who strove to understand sexuality in the late Mesolithic in northern Europe, argues that sexuality should be understood as more than static mating networks. His analysis of Mesolithic cemeteries and of the practice of shamanism suggests that sexuality was an important aspect of lived experience that shaped social identities. Schmidt makes two important points. First, if archaeologists working in deep prehistory are to understand sexuality, particularly nonnormative sexualities, they must be willing to consider a variety of methods and to connect interpretations based on several lines of evidence. Sexuality is difficult to unravel archaeologically and using several kinds of evidence will help archaeologists avoid overly subjective accounts (Wylie 1992, 25–29). Queer theorists argue that all research is undertaken from a particular standpoint (Homfray 2008). This argument often inspires critics to claim that queer theorists are "making things up" or to use the term "biased" in a pejorative way. Multiple lines of evidence enable queer archaeologists to push against the idea of "normal behavior" and deconstruct how this behavior became normalized through historical accidents and circumstances. It is important to base these claims on material evidence from the archaeological record; as Atalay (2014) notes, activist archaeologists should adhere to rigorous research standards. Second, Schmidt's study demonstrates that even in so-called small-scale foraging societies, sexuality is rich and diverse and is an important axis of identity and social formations. We can safely assume that sexuality was also just as diverse and important in the Upper Paleolithic as it was in the Mesolithic.

Cobb (2005), who also focuses on the Mesolithic, also provides some things to consider when queering deep prehistory. She argues that the symbolic nature of material culture from Mesolithic sites suggests that conceptions of gender, sexuality, and the socially constructed body may have been very different from our own. Her work supports that idea of a sexually diverse deep prehistory that extended back into the Upper Paleolithic, a past in which sexual relations and relations to socially constructed bodies differed from our western understandings of sexuality. Relations between people, objects, and bodies were more fluid and contextual in deep prehistory than we think of them today (Cobb 2005, 634). Cobb also notes the importance of feminist critiques of the hunter-gatherer framework in the disciplines of anthropology and archaeology. (For a more comprehensive overview of the feminist critique of hunter-gatherer studies, see Sterling 2014.) However, she suggests that while these feminist critiques tackle androcentric interpretations, they do so using western, heteronormative understandings of sex, gender, and sexuality. She argues that the use of the stereotyped masculine identity in archaeology, which feminist archaeologists have long critiqued, gives "epistemological privilege [not just] to men, but to the heterosexual man alone" (Cobb 2005, 632). For example, archaeologists of the Upper Paleolithic often discuss Paleolithic art as a masculine pursuit. In their assumption that these artists were *heterosexual* men, archaeologists have ignored the possibility that Paleolithic art was produced by artists of a variety of gender and sexual identities. Heteronormativity is not just a semantic issue in Paleolithic and Mesolithic archaeology and deep prehistory. Cobb also argues that commonly held assumptions about men, women, and children in deep prehistory are rooted in the western ideal of the nuclear family. Studies concerning exogamy, endogamy, patrilocal marriage practices, and so forth are all based on heterosexist interpretations of the family unit. The concept of male-female bonded pairs living in strictly monogamous relationships in the ideal nuclear family became naturalized and has precluded the study of other possible family organizations.

Schmidt and Cobb present some theoretical considerations for queer theory in deep prehistory. Given the dearth of queer literature about hunter-gatherer archaeology and anthropology in general, these studies and their critiques of Mesolithic archaeology are immensely valuable for archaeologists interested in deconstructing heteronormative assumptions in archaeological practice.

The Heteronormative "Vulvas" of the Upper Paleolithic

There are several obvious problems with traditional interpretations of Upper Paleolithic parietal art (art on cave walls) and mobiliary art (portable figurines and other art objects). While it is true that explanations that focus on the heterosexual male gaze are inherently androcentric and heteronormative, many critiques of these explanations continue to project an exclusively heterosexual past. In order to reanalyze Upper Paleolithic art through a queer lens, we can turn to the arguments of archaeologists who study the relationship between art and sexuality and queer theorists who study deep prehistory.

Voss (2008) summarizes the challenges and pitfalls of understanding sexuality from prehistoric art. The first challenge is to not assume that what we view as sexual today was viewed as sexual in the past. The second challenge is to not assume that any images are representations of actual bodies or sexual encounters. The images may be idealized, imaginary, or ideological rather than based on lived experience. Voss also notes that prehistoric images are ambiguous and it is challenging to make interpretations about sexuality from artistic representations; it is unclear whether bodies and sexual acts depicted in prehistoric art are a direct reflection of what bodies actually did in the past or whether they were idealized depictions of human bodies and sexuality. The viewer of the art also plays an active role in forming the meaning of these art pieces. Voss calls prehistoric art a kind of "Rorschach test" in which prehistoric archaeologists "see" what they want to see, particularly since the genitalia and sex acts depicted prehistorically are not always obvious (321).

It is this ambiguity, however, that opens up prehistoric art and visual imagery to be queered. Historically, much of this ambiguity has been explained away, ignored, or further obfuscated through heteronormative explanations. If we reintroduce the ambiguity by proposing that these images were not inherently sexual for the heterosexual male gaze, we introduce a space in which heteronormative explanations can be challenged. Once the heteronormative interpretations of these images become unchallenged fact, these images lose their ambiguity and their power to accurately inform archaeologists about prehistoric lifeways. It is possible to use Voss's discussion to analyze Upper Paleolithic art and to critique the heteronormativity of various interpretations of parietal and mobiliary art. I now turn to two examples from the Upper Paleolithic, the so-called vulvar images and Venus and phallic figurines, to illustrate Voss's arguments and the broader arguments queer archaeologists have made.

The Upper Paleolithic in Europe ranges from approximately 40,000 to 10,000 years before the present. While this period is often equated with the last major "Ice Age," the climate of the Upper Paleolithic also varied through time and space. While people in the Upper Paleolithic shared subsistence patterns as mobile foragers, they subscribed to varied and complex belief systems, behaviors, and practices. Contrary to popular belief, Upper

Paleolithic peoples did not live on the edge of death or disaster. They were not slaves to their environment but were socially complex and creative peoples who lived full and meaningful lives. One example of this meaningfulness is visual imagery that we find throughout Europe in the Upper Paleolithic. This art ranged from complex images on cave walls to portable art objects, such as engraved bone and antlers, and the Venus figurines.

One type of art that can be challenged through a queer archaeology lens is the painted or etched "vulvae" in Upper Paleolithic caves in southwestern France and northern Spain. Abri Henri Brueil, a prominent French archaeologist in the early twentieth century, originally interpreted them as vulvae. However, his interpretations of these images were not based on archaeological, anatomical, or scientific analysis, but on an assumption he made when asked about the engravings (Stoliar 1977). In fact, his interpretations may have been based on their similarity to the symbols for female in cuneiform and Egyptian hieroglyphics. That interpretation could have been his attempt to propose universal symbols for the male and female sexes across human cultures, even though such universality did not exist (Delluc and Delluc 1981). Not wanting to be outdone, his rival, Denis Peyrony, another prominent French archaeologist of the twentieth century, began finding vulvae everywhere, even though he had no more reason to recognize them as vulvae than as any other possible symbol. Peyrony even added his own lines to Upper Paleolithic images to complete the vulvae that he believed were the intention of the original artists (Bahn 1986, 100). Archaeologists have continued to use Brueil and Peyrony's initial interpretations in their work, discussing the vulvae in purely sexual terms (Bahn 1986; Hosking 2013). For example, in their discussion of Aurignacian rock art around Les Eyzies in Dordogne, France, Delluc and Delluc (1978) made over 100 references to "*les images vulvaires*," although they also made several references to etched phalluses. They discussed the anatomical referents for these vulvar etches, describing in depth which parts of the female anatomy the various parts of the etches might be depicting. Although Delluc and Delluc stated that they would not attempt to unpack the symbolic meanings of these images (400), they made the unquestioned assumption that these images were analogous to the female anatomy. In doing so, they ascribed meaning to these images, that they were female genitalia.

Upper Paleolithic images from the Dordogne have also been described as "vulvar" more recently (White et al. 2012). Wildgen (2004, 133) states that the two most prominently featured human body parts in Upper Paleolithic art are the human hand and the vulva. He also argues that these vulvar images are often associated with rectangular images, which he states look like huts, which he claims refer "secondarily to the domain of females" (134). Foley (1991) argued that the frequent and broadly distributed presence of these vulvar images indicate that Upper Paleolithic societies were strongly gendered, highly sexual, and heteronormative. This interpretation dates to Leroi-Gourhan's (1965) "sexual symbolism," a theory that claims that vivid sexual images dating back to the Aurignacian (~43,000–28,000 BP) often accompany crudely drawn animals. These sexual images are almost always interpreted as female genitalia. Many criticisms of Leroi-Gourhan's interpretations, such as that of Abadia and Maidagan (2010), push against his chronology but not against his unsubstantiated claims of sexual imagery.

Many feminist archaeologists have criticized these interpretations. They argue that there is no evidence that these V shapes are vulvae and that these interpretations are reflections of the masculine desires of the archaeologists who found the images rather than the intentions of the Paleolithic artists (Kathleen Sterling, pers. comm., March 16, 2016). Hosking (2013) has criticized Brueil's initial interpretation of these images as vulvae. She notes that on unarguably female figurines, the genitalia are not marked, etched, or highlighted in any way and asks why, then, the people of the Upper Paleolithic would etch free-floating female genitalia on walls. Hosking also argues that because archaeologists have uncritically used Brueil's interpretations in their own studies, their analysis misrepresents Upper Paleolithic art. She states that the claims that these were engravings of female genitalia rest on a priori assumptions and that in making such assumptions, "we perpetuate a myth . . . that has become a part of our received common knowledge of prehistory" (196). Hosking asks whether when a new engraved "vulva" is uncovered, is it because the researchers believe it is a vulva, or because similar images have previously been called vulvas (195)? The ascription of these images as "vulvae" is based solely on historical interpretations of our archaeological predecessors rather than on any critical interpretive engagement with the images. Our understanding of symbols is culturally mediated, and Upper Paleolithic archaeologists equate the "V" with the vulva in the same way that the American public equates Valentine's Day hearts with anatomical hearts, or five-pointed stars with actual spherical stars. The interpretive move from images to objects is grounded in cultural expectations and understandings of the world. It is the task of the archaeologist to deconstruct their own (here heteronormative) understanding of the world.

Many archaeologists who assume that these images are vulvar also assume that the Paleolithic artists were male. Fritz, Tosello, and Conkey (2016) argue that archaeologists cannot assume that artists were exclusively male and that there is no evidence to suggest that women or adolescents would have been excluded from producing art in the Paleolithic (1327–1328). Snow (2005, 2013) argues that because men tend to have larger hand sizes, this difference can be used to differentiate male and female artists. Snow analyzed hand stencils from Upper Paleolithic caves in France and Spain in order to determine the sex of the person who created the stencil. He based his estimations on the measurements of modern European populations because genetic testing of the Y chromosome has shown that most Europeans today, with some exceptions such as most Hungarians, have been present in Europe since the Upper Paleolithic. Thus, Snow believes that comparing modern European hands to Upper Paleolithic hand stencils is not problematic. In a later study, Wang et al. (2010) supported this assumption. They argue that when they compared the hand stencils to modern hands, it became evident that sexual dimorphism was more pronounced in the Upper Paleolithic. Wang and colleagues concluded, therefore, that estimating sex from hand print stencils is easier and more accurate for the Upper Paleolithic samples than with modern samples. Snow (2013) examined the hand stencils in two stages. First, they analyzed overall finger length and hand size, and then they measured the ratios between the lengths of the index and ring fingers and the lengths of the index and little fingers. Comparing these to modern European populations, Snow showed that both men and women and at least one subadult, produced cave art. In a follow-up study, in which the sample size was increased from six to thirty-two, Snow (2013) argued that the hand stencils were made largely by females.

If women and possibly some children were also producing Paleolithic art, these V shapes may not be vulvar in nature at all and are likely not sexualized in the way that previous interpretations have claimed. That is, they could still have been sexual; women could have produced these vulvae as sexual images. They could have been a teaching tool for young women, or they could even have been produced by children. However, if women were the artists, they were not the product of the heterosexual male gaze. Other studies suggest that human hand size may vary in modern human populations according to other axes of identity, including sexuality (Grimbos et al. 2010; Kraemer et al. 2006; Lippa 2003; Manning, Churchill, and Peters 2007). There are obvious problems with these kinds of studies. They ignore the fluidity and socially constructed nature of identity while reifying the heterosexual/homosexual identity.

However, they introduce ambiguity and doubt to our understandings of Upper Paleolithic art. The art on cave walls was not predominantly made by men, and thus was not made, or not *only* made, to satisfy male sexual urges but was likely made by a wide variety of individuals, including women and children, for some other purpose. Therefore, androcentric and heteronormative interpretations of these so-called vulvar images lose their epistemic basis. Estimates of hand size is not definitive proof of a variety of Upper Paleolithic artists. It does, however, open up the distinct possibility, especially given the lack of evidence that supports interpretations that leave out women, children, and queer individuals. Proponents of traditional interpretations of Upper Paleolithic art are just as responsible to provide supporting evidence as the feminist and queer scholars who challenge them are. A queer analysis of the Upper Paleolithic can rarely say anything with certainty, for certainty is often "unqueer," but it reopens doors that have previously been closed.

The Venus Figurines and Other Mobiliary Art

Similarly problematic interpretations have been made of mobiliary art, particularly the small Venus figurines of nude females that vary in shape and style. They date to at least 30,000 years ago and were produced most intensively during the Gravettian (approximately 27,000–20,000 years ago). They are found across Europe, extending to Siberia (Nelson 1990). The Venus figurines have been interpreted as objects of male sexual desire, as symbols or female fertility, and as examples of female physical attractiveness. Absolon (1949, 208) was one of the first archaeologists to consider the Venus figurines as pornographic, an interpretation that has persisted in archaeology. For example, Dixson and Dixson (2011) argue that a small group of the Venus figurines that they interpret as "actual" Venus figurines may have represented young females who were sexually attractive to heterosexual men in the past. One of their methodologies was to ask participants to rate each Venus figurine in terms of age, attractiveness, and pregnancy status. All of the participants were heterosexual. For the eye-tracking portion of their study, Dixson and Dixson examined how heterosexual men responded to the Venus figurines (2). Their analyses are based solely on how heterosexual-identifying individuals viewed these figurines and do not take into account the experiences and interpretations of people who identify along the spectrum of queer identities. Interpretations from this study are thus inherently heteronormative. Dixson and Dixson also suggest that Venus figurines that they do not consider to be "true Venuses," which tend to appear to have more body fat, were symbols of hope that the past owners would have enough food and reproduce successfully. Many scholars have focused on the body proportions of the figurines, particularly the waist-to-hip ratios, in order to assess whether these figurines were symbols of beauty and/or fertility (e.g., Colman 1998; King 2013). The unrelenting focus on the Venus figurines and other objects as inherently sexual has limited our ability to use these objects to better understand gender, sexuality, identity, and society in the Upper Paleolithic.

Many scholars have challenged the view that the Venus figurines were exclusively or inherently sexual objects. For example, archaeologists have made arguments that have opened up our understanding of the Venus figurines. Rice (1981) argues that the Venuses are representative of a women's entire lifespan and thus should be seen as signs of womanhood, not fertility. McDermott (1996) argues that the Venus figurines were made by women and that the anomalies in the body proportions were the result of women looking at their own bodies. In this light, the Venus figurines are a result of a perception of "self" in different parts of life and should not be interpreted as a pornographic object for heterosexual males. Soffer, Adovasio, and Hyland (2000) argue that the garments on the Venus figurines were ritual clothing that indicate distinct access to prestige, power, and social standing, thereby offering a nuanced interpretation of the relationships between gender, sexuality, and power in the Upper Paleolithic. Tripp (2015) suggests that there are many similarities between the figurines and toys the Navajo in the American Southwest made and played with. In both cases, the figurines do not have faces or feet, male figurines are rare, and sometimes they have jewelry. The Venus figurines may have been made by children or made by their parents as toys. Bednarik (2008) and Guthrie (2005) argue that a large portion of Upper Paleolithic art may have been produced by children as they learned how to draw, carve, and engrave through play. If these figurines were children's toys, that would rule out many of the sexualized explanations of why they were made.

Nowell and Chang (2014) summarize four critiques of androcentric interpretations of Upper Paleolithic figurines. First, we do not know the gender or age of the makers of the figurines and thus they were probably not exclusively men. Many studies (Chazine 1999; Sharp and Ganvelder 2004; Snow 2006, 2013) suggest that a diverse range of people was responsible for the production of Upper Paleolithic art, even though no studies exist for the figurines themselves. Nowell and Chang (2014) argue that without the contextual evidence to directly indicate that the figurines were made by men, our past interpretations have simply been assumptions based on androcentric norms in the present. Second, both men and women are stimulated by sexual imagery. As discussed throughout this chapter, heterosexuality is not the default, innate, or natural state of sexuality in humans (Katz 1990), and this was also the case in the past. The archaeological literatures contains many examples of various sexual practices in prehistory and history that would not be classified as "heterosexuality" (e.g. Alberti 2001; Casella 2000; Dowson 2000b; Eger 2009; Joyce 2000; Matic 2012; Prine 2000; Reeder 2000; Solli 2008). Thus, it would be incorrect to assume that these items were made exclusively for the heterosexual male gaze—a gaze that has not universally existed throughout space and time and is a cultural invention of our modern sociopolitical circumstances. To sexualize these objects only as sources of pornography for heterosexual males says more about us in the present than it does about past peoples. Modern Euro-American understandings of gendered norms of sexuality privilege active male sexuality and passive female sexuality. Men are viewed as sexually dominant, sexually active, and sexual consumers. Women are seen as none of these things. They are sexually passive and are demonized or slut-shamed for producing or consuming sexual products. In interpreting the Venus figurines as objects of masculine sexual pleasure, archaeologists project these gendered norms and expectations onto the past. In sum, these archaeologists are revealing their own culturally mediated understandings of sexuality instead of critically engaging with the sexualities of the past. Third, not all the figurines are the same. The variations in form and style underscore the individuality of both the object and the creator., Objects have multiple, often intersecting meanings for different users. Variations in the figurines and the vast and varied temporal and spatial ranges where they are found should not be homogenized into a singular interpretation of sexualization.

Finally, not all of the figurines are female. While male figurines are rarer than female ones, phallic art and objects have also been found in a variety of Upper Paleolithic sites, such as the sculptures from Roc de Marcamps (Allain et al. 1985), the phallic drawing from Les Trois-Frères (Bégouën et Bégouën 2013), the deer antler shaped into a phallus from L'Abri du Morin (Deffarge, Laurent, and de Sonneville-Bordes 1975), the arguably male figurine from Brassembuoy (Soffer et al. 2000, 516), and the sorcerer who was drawn with an erect penis from the Grotte du Sorcier (Delluc, Delluc, and Guichard 1987). Phallic batons, which are most common in the Magdalenian (~17,000–12,000 BP) but do appear more rarely in the Gravettian (~33,000–21,000 BP) and Solutrean (~22,000–17,000 BP) (Angulo et al. 2010, 2501), have been interpreted as trophies, ritual objects, arrow or spear straighteners, and harpoon throwers (Bahn 1976; Delluc 2007). These interpretations are inherently hypermasculine and what we call today hyperheterosexuality. The interpretation that these obviously phallic objects were trophies or arrow straighteners perpetuates the myth that phallic images were symbols of masculine power. In other words, according to androcentric and masculinist interpretations, Upper Paleolithic men wanted phallic images on their "manly" objects of war and hunting because of the masculine symbolism; they achieved power through their sex and sexuality. In contrast with interpretations of vulvar images or Venus figurines in which male archaeologists saw everything as pornographic, these objects become symbols of power, not porn. Taylor (1996) notes that women could have used many of these phallic shapes as objects of sexual pleasure by women (128), although there are still very few studies that look at whether phallic images were made and used by women. There is also very little literature on whether men could have made and used these phallic items for sexual pleasure. For example, a rod-like object with two globular nodes from Dolní Věstonice was originally interpreted as a Venus figurine with large breasts. The analysis was that the male artist removed all parts of the female form that he was not interested in. However, could not these globular nodes also be interpreted as testicles? Could this have been a Paleolithic dildo made by a woman (Taylor 1996, 120)? Or even a Paleolithic dildo made for someone else? Even if we were to argue that these figurines were sexual objects, their presence underscores the fact that they may have been made and used by individuals of various gender identities and sexualities. The description of the Venus figurines "as erotic or reproductive is a masculinist construction of the world, in which females are assumed to exist primarily for the use of males, sexually or reproductively" (Nelson 1990, 16). I add a queer perspective to Nelson's feminist critique of this literature, drawing on Cobb's critique that these are assumed to be for adult *heterosexual* males. The problem with these interpretations is the assumptions they make about heteronormative sexuality in prehistory. Masculinist and heteronormative interpretations of the Venus figurines focus on one group of users, heterosexual men, while ignoring perspectives that derive from other gender, sexual, and age identities. As Nelson argues, there is great diversity among the Venus figurines in terms of body proportions, age, body position, and ornamentation. Thus, generalizations about the heterosexual male gaze are inappropriate. A diversity of Venus figurines should lead to a diversity of explanations. This diversity leads to Voss's observation that these are the spaces where archaeologists can queer the past. Some of the Venus figurines may have been objects of heterosexual male desire, but others may have been children's toys, a gynecological tool for a pregnant woman, or an important object to a pansexual, gender-fluid individual. The great diversity among the Venus figurines leads us to explanations that encompass a greater diversity of perspectives and experiences.

Queering Upper Paleolithic Art

The discourse surrounding Upper Paleolithic art can be reanalyzed through a queer theory framework in many different ways. First, queer theory challenges modern stereotypical gender roles. In many of these interpretations, Upper Paleolithic men are sexually active. These interpretations also assume that men are the artists who construct a world that evidences and communicates their sexuality. Such interpretations typically present Upper Paleolithic women as sexuality passive individuals who are incapable of producing important works such as art and never leave material traces of their sexual needs or desires. Artwork that could be the result of female sexuality, such as stone phalluses or depictions of male sexual anatomy, are rarely discussed as objects of female sexual desire. In other heterosexist interpretations, potentially phallic objects have been normatively understood as Venuses made to appeal to men. Queer theory also challenges interpretations of Upper Paleolithic imagery that assume that there are only two genders and that women and men engaged in exclusively heterosexual relationships. In many interpretations, men produce art, both parietal and mobiliary, that sexualizes women for the heterosexual male gaze (Dowson 2001). Such interpretations also perpetuate the false narrative that men are producers and consumers of art and women are merely the passive objects of imagery. Interpretations of Upper Paleolithic art have been androcentric and heteronormative. Challenges to the masculinist, androcentric interpretations of Upper Paleolithic often exclude any considerations of queer artists. For example, as Dowson (2009, 283) argues, artistic representations of the vulvae are anatomically incorrect. Instead of reinterpreting these images as symbolizing something else or even suggesting that the artists were homosexual men who would not have been intimately familiar with female sexual anatomy, scholars have instead been proposed that the makers of these "vulvar" images were sexually inexperienced adolescent teenage boys.

I do not argue that these examples of visual imagery in the Upper Paleolithic were definitively sexual or that they were evidence of homosexuality in deep prehistory. As Voss (2008, 321) warns us, these images and objects may not have been sexualized at all: what is considered attractive or sexual varies widely across time and space. In contexts where we do not know the identities of prehistoric artists with any degree of definitiveness (Fritz, Tosello, and Conkey 2016), we must be careful not to project a western, heteronormative view of sexuality and gender into the past. We must always be open to the possibility of homosexual and homoerotic visual imagery and art in the past.

While a definitive explanation of these objects is impossible, opening up the possibility that the Upper Paleolithic artists were queer has two primary advantages. First, it offers us another avenue through which to analyze Upper Paleolithic identities. As Schmidt (2000) argues, sexuality is important to the shaping of human social identities. Thus, it is important that we consider Upper Paleolithic sexualities from an interpretive stance instead of relying exclusively on evolutionary theory. Human sexuality is never static; it is always changing and in flux through the interactions between sociocultural influences and embodied being-in-the-world. Contemporary evidence underscores that it exists along a spectrum of desires. Why should we assume that this spectrum of sexuality was not present in the deep past? What evidence do we have for heteronormative assumptions? While there is no *definitive* evidence for queer identities in deep prehistory, there is also a severe lack of evidence to support heteronormative interpretations. There is no epistemic foundation for heteronormativity in Paleolithic archaeology. As archaeologists, we should take care to incorporate the relational and contextual nature of sexuality—and identity more broadly—into our analyses of deep prehistory. This is not to suggest that sexuality manifested itself in Paleolithic societies in the same socially constructed way it does today. However, projecting contemporary Western heteronormative biases restricts our understanding of prehistoric sexuality and of prehistoric social identity more broadly. Because identity and sexuality are entwined, additional scholarship on the relationship between art and sexuality in the Upper Paleolithic is necessary.

Second, the queering of the Upper Paleolithic enables us to challenge heteronormativity in the past and present. Allowing for the possibility of queer individuals in deep prehistory denaturalizes sexuality, particularly heterosexuality, in the present. No longer can the past be used to argue that heterosexuality alone is the natural state or that heterosexuality is "right" because that is the way it has always been. It is not necessary to prove that some of these Paleolithic artists were queer, just as it is not necessary to prove that some Upper Paleolithic artists were women. It is more important that we deconstruct interpretations of the past that are predicated on exclusive and naturalized perceptions of heterosexuality. We must always be wary of explanations such as those of Lovejoy (1981) and Lancaster and Lancaster (1987), who argue that the heterosexual nuclear family was an important evolutionary development that led to the success of our early human ancestors, particularly when everything from evolutionary theory (Hill, Barton, and Hurtado 2009, 194) to Marxism (Davis 1983, 414) refutes these claims. Hill, Barton, and Hurtado argue that among the Ache and Hiwi, hunting and gathering nuclear families were not able to produce enough food to support their children, challenging the idea that nuclear families developed because that structure was the most efficient way to gather resources and ensure the survival of the next generation. Davis points out that according to classic Marxist theory, the nuclear family was not supposed to emerge in pre-class societies. Similarly, arguing that Upper Paleolithic art was made exclusively for the heterosexual male gaze, or even flipping the argument to the heterosexual female gaze, risks naturalizing heterosexuality in the present. If art, as Voss (2008) argues, is always ambiguous, then we can use this ambiguity. We can provide alternative explanations that are just as likely to be true as heteronormative explanations.

Conclusion

Because a queer lens focuses on social and political engagement, analyzing the Upper Paleolithic using queer theory creates meaningful and relevant work that can be shared outside academic journals, that transcends academia and matters to people, and that is of benefit to all peoples, particularly those that are marginalized. When we engage with the contemporary political atmosphere, we are not "snowflakes" and we are not doing bad science. All science is subjective because scientists are enmeshed in sociopolitical and economic systems (Wylie 1997). All science and all archaeology is political, and it is up to each individual scientist to recognize the political nature of their work or to allow the politics to fester or be locked away (Latour 1999). I am not slighting science; science continues to have great explanatory power. I am advocating for a more reflexive and engaged science.

Queering and challenging norms in Upper Paleolithic archaeology is necessary because Upper Paleolithic archaeology naturalizes and privileges certain identities and embodiments in the present. The time depth of this work does not absolve Upper Paleolithic archaeologists from responsibility for thinking about the social consequences of their work. It is because of this time depth that Upper Paleolithic archaeologists must be concerned with archaeology as an engine for social justice.

Heteronormative interpretations of the past based on static sexual and gendered identities and the nuclear family risk naturalizing those lifeways in the present. These interpretations are not based on direct scientific evidence and project present-day heteronormative, androcentric values onto the past. Feminist scholars of the Upper Paleolithic have critiqued androcentric bias and have demonstrated the contributions and roles of women in prehistory. Queer theory allows us to expand upon the feminist critique by emphasizing that androcentrism often implies only heterosexual men and omits queer men. Queer theory also enables archaeologists to explore the fluidity and contextual natures of gender and identity.

This analysis of queer archaeology in Upper Paleolithic art has brought up some key issues. First, we must be cautious not to assume there were only two genders in deep prehistory. While an archaeology of gender that focuses on the role of women is important and necessary work, it risks naturalizing a two-gender system. Second, we should ask whether any suggestion that universalizes human sexuality is myopic. Men are not always sexually active and women are not always sexually passive. Individuals were and are not always exclusively heterosexual or homosexual. Finally, archaeologists in the Upper Paleolithic should continue to challenge problematic foundational normativity in their theory and practice.

As a modern invention of the late nineteenth century, heterosexuality is only one way of categorizing, interpreting, and analyzing the interactions and relationships between people we call "men" and "women" (Halperin 1989; Katz 1990). When we do not take the time to examine the history, of heterosexuality as an organizing and analytic concept, we continue to privilege heterosexuality as "normal" over queerness as "abnormal" (Katz 1990). This is particularly salient in our current political climate. Sexuality is always political, and its political nature is emphasized in times of social and political upheaval (Rubin 1984). The rise of the far right in many countries around the world has brought sexuality, sexual identity, and sexual relations back into the foreground of conservative politics that seek to roll back decades of social justice victories. Moreover, heterosexuality is a social institution that involves more than just "sex." It is also intimately entangled with normative perspectives on domestic vs. public space, kinship, couple forms, property, citizenship, and the nation-state itself (Berlant and Warner 1998). Queer scholarship and activism have far-reaching consequences that go beyond sexual relations and identities. Denouncing sexual oppression and injustice is a key component of political activism and liberatory social reform. Archaeology and archaeologists cannot be removed from this political climate (Rutecki and Blackmore 2016), and have a key role to play in eliminating the presumed time depth of heterosexuality and challenging monolithic, normative notions of human nature. Examining the Upper Paleolithic through a queer lens, as I have argued in this chapter, is part of a larger, transformative political and social project.

It is time that Upper Paleolithic archaeologists start to take queer theory, its critiques, and its contributions more seriously. In the past, proposing that the Dolní Věstonice phallus was a gay sex object would have been met with ridicule; making such a comment would have elicited laughs in a graduate seminar before it moved on to more "serious" matters. Queer scholars learn early in their academic careers that their identities and experiences are invalid and unimportant, that their mentors and colleagues think that their ideas and works are excuses to say "penis" in a professional setting rather than a rigorous and important contribution to our knowledge of the past. Queer scholarship is not respected in a heterosexist field like archaeology, and thus queer scholars themselves are not respected because of their sexualities and gender identities. In fact, all of the ways that we as archaeologists see the world are grounded in the dominant aspects of society, including race, gender, sexuality, class, and any other identity. However, as I hope I have demonstrated, the discussion presented here is important because it can impact our understanding of Upper Paleolithic identities and contribute to the continued liberation of the LGBTQ+ community in the present.

In this chapter, I have focused on Upper Paleolithic visual imagery. However, there are many avenues for further research. A queer analysis of stone tools, the most ubiquitous artifact type in the Upper Paleolithic archaeological record, is sorely needed. Reanalysis of other kinds of visual imagery, burials, social structures, gender roles, and the nuclear family can all greatly contribute to our understanding of the Upper Paleolithic.

In addition, an expansion of what queer theory is and does will continue to create a more inclusive and diverse discourse about the Upper Paleolithic. In this chapter I have taken a rather traditional approach to queer theory and focused primarily on homosexuality. Transgender (see Weismantel 2013) and asexual perspectives, as just two examples, will broaden our archaeological imaginations and help us rethink what is possible in archaeological interpretation.

Archaeologists too often project modern conceptions of identity, gender, and sexuality onto the past and then use that imagined past to reinforce and naturalize those same norms in the present. Queer theory exposes and critiques this process and points to the many-faceted political and social ramifications this naturalization of ideas conjures in the present. Minority groups, including the LGBTQ+ community, exist in a constant state of instability and suppression. Violent acts are often committed against queer bodies and the rights of queer individuals are often in flux. The archaeology of the Upper Paleolithic can contribute to this violence because we provide the oppressors of queer bodies with misinterpretations of a heteronormalized past that they then use as false fodder for their hatred. Through looking at the Upper Paleolithic through a queer lens, we can actively deconstruct these views and denaturalize the heteronormative past and present. For all of these reasons, Upper Paleolithic art can and needs to be queered.

References Cited

Abadía, Oscar Moro, and Diego Gárate Maidagán. 2010. "The Beginnings of European Upper-Paleolithic Art: A Critical Review." *North Atlantic Archaeology* 2:1–18.

Absolon, Karel. 1949. "The Diluvial Anthropomorphic Statuettes and Drawings, Especially the So-Called Venus Statuettes, Discovered in Moravia: A Comparative Study." *Artibus Asiae* 12 (3): 201–220.

Alberti, Benjamin. 2001. "Faience Goddesses and Ivory Bull-Leapers: The Aesthetics of Sexual Difference at Late Bronze Age Knossos." *World Archaeology* 32 (2): 189–205.

———. 2013. "Queer Prehistory: Bodies, Performativity, and Matter." In *A Companion to Gender Prehistory,* edited by Diane Bolger, 86–107. New York: John Wiley and Sons.

Allain, Jacques, René Desbrosse, Janusz K. Kozlowski, and André Rigaud. 1985. "Le Magdalénien à Navettes." *Gallia Préhistoire* 28 (1): 37–124.

Angulo, Javier C., Marco García-Díez and Marc Martínez. 2010. "Phallic Decoration in Paleolithic Art: Genital Scarification, Piercing and Tattoos." *Journal of Urology* 186: 2498–2503.

Atalay, Sonya. 2014. "Engaging Archaeology: Positivism, Objectivity, and Rigor in Activist Archaeology." In *Transforming Archaeology: Activist Practices and Prospects,* edited by Sonya Atalay, John R. Welch, Randall H. McGuire, and Lee Rains Clauss, 45–60. Walnut Creek, CA: Left Coast Press.

Atalay, Sonya, Lee Rains Clauss, Randall H. McGuire, and John R. Welch. 2014. "Transforming Archaeology." In *Transforming Archaeology: Activist Practices and Prospects,* edited by Sonya Atalay, John R. Welch, Randall H. McGuire, and Lee Rains Clauss, 7–28. Walnut Creek, CA: Left Coast Press.

Bahn, Paul G. 1976. "Les bâtons percés réveil d'une hypothèse abandonnée." *Bulletin de la Société Préhistorique de l'Ariège* 31: 47–54.

———. 1986. "No Sex Please, We're Aurignacians." *Rock Art Research: The Journal of the Australian Rock Art Research Association* 2: 99–102.

Bednarik, Robert G. 2008. "Children as Pleistocene Artists." *Rock Art Research* 25 (2): 173–182.

Bégouën, Éric, and Marie-Brune Bégouën. 2013. "Découverte d'un grand phallus gravé Magdalénien dans la grotte des Trois-Frères (Ariège)." *Bulletin de la Société Préhistorique Française* 110:127–129.

Berlant, Lauren, and Michael Warner. 1998. "Sex in Public." *Critical Inquiry* 24: 547–566.

Blackmore, Chelsea. 2011. "How to Queer the Past without Sex: Queer Theory, Feminisms, and the Archaeology of Identity." *Archaeologies* 7 (1): 75–96.

Casella, Eleanor Conlin. 2000. "'Doing trade': A Sexual Economy of Nineteenth-Century Australian Female Convict Prisons." *World Archaeology* 32 (2):209–221.

Chazine, Jean-Michel. "Prehistoire: Découverte de grottes ornées à Bornéo." *Archéologia* 352: 12–19.

Claassen, Cheryl. 2000. "Homophobia and Women Archaeologists." *World Archaeology* 32 (2): 173–179.

Chang, Melanie L., and April Nowell. 2016. "How to Make Stone Soup: Is the 'Paleo Diet' a Missed Opportunity for Anthropologists?" *Evolutionary Anthropology* 25: 228–231.

Chilton, Elizabeth. 2008. "Queer Archaeology, Mathematical Modeling, and the Peopling of the Americas." Paper presented at the 48th annual meeting of the Northeastern Anthropological Association, Amherst, MA.

Cobb, Hannah. 2005. "Straight Down the Line? A Queer Consideration of Hunter-Gatherer Studies in North-West Europe." *World Archaeology* 37 (4): 630–636.

———. 2006. "(Dead) Bodies that Matter? Examining Prehistory from a Queer Perspective." In *Proceedings of the UK Postgraduate Conference in Gender Studies—Thinking Gender—the NEXT Generation,* epaper 8. Accessed July 12, 2020. https://genderstudies.leeds.ac.uk/wp-content/uploads/sites/53/2013/02/epaper8-hannah-cobb.pdf.

Colman, Eric. 1998. "Obesity in the Paleolithic Era? The Venus of Willendorf." *Endocrine Practice* 4 (1): 58–59.

Conkey, Margaret W. 1991. "Contexts of Action, Contexts for Power: Material Culture and Gender in the Magdalenian." In *Engendering Archaeology: Women and Prehistory,* edited by Joan M. Gero and Margaret W. Conkey, 57–92. Cambridge: Basil Blackwell.

———. 1997. "Mobilizing Ideologies: Paleolithic 'Art,' Gender Trouble, and Thinking about Alternatives." In *Women in Human Evolution,* edited by Lori D. Hager, 172–207. London: Routledge.

Davis, Richard S. 1983. "Theoretical Issues in Contemporary Soviet Paleolithic Archaeology." *Annual Review of Anthropology* 12:403–428.

Deffarge, René, Pierre Laurent, and Denise de Sonneville-Bordes. 1975. "Art mobilier du Magdalénien supérieur de l'abri Morin à Pessac-sur-Dordogne (Gironde)." *Gallia préhistoire* 18 (1): 1–64.

Delluc, Brigitte, and Gilles Delluc. 1978. "Les manifestations graphiques Aurignaciennes sur support rocheux des environs des Eyzies (Dordogne)." *Gallia préhistoire* 21 (2): 333–438.

———. 1981. "Les plus anciens dessins de l'homme." *La Recherche* 118:14–21.

Delluc, Brigitte, Gilles Delluc, and Francis Guichard. 1987. "La grotte ornée de Saint-Cirq (Dordogne)." *Bulletin de la Société préhistorique française* 84: 364–393.

Delluc, Gilles. 2007. *Le sexe au temps des Cro-Magnons.* Périgueux: Pilote 24.

Dixson, Alan F., and Barnaby J. Dixson. 2011. "Venus Figurines of the European Paleolithic: Symbols of Fertility or Attractiveness?" *Journal of Anthropology* 2011:1–11.

Dowson, Thomas. 1998. "Homosexualitat, teoria queer i arqueologia." *Cota Zero* 14:81–87.

———. 2000a. "Homosexuality, Queer Theory, and Archaeology." In *Interpretive Archaeology: A Reader,* edited by Julian Thomas, 283–289. London: Leicester University Press.

———. 2000b. "Why Queer Archaeology? An Introduction." *World Archaeology* 32 (2): 161–165.

———. 2001. "Queer Theory and Feminist Theory: Towards a Sociology of Sexual Politics in Rock Art Research." In *Theoretical Perspectives in Rock Art Research,* edited by Knut Helskog, 312–329. Oslo: Novus.

———. 2008. "Queering Sex and Gender in Ancient Egypt." In *Sex and Gender in Ancient Egypt,* edited by Carolyn Graves Brown, 27–46. Swansea: Classical Press of Wales.

———. 2009. "Queer Theory Meets Archaeology: Disrupting Epistemological Privilege and Heteronormativity in Constructing the Past." In *The Ashgate Companion to Queer Theory,* edited by Noreen Gifney and Michael O'Rourke, 277–294. Burlington, VT: Ashgate.

Eger, A. Asa. 2009. "Architectures of Desire and Queered Space in the Roman Bathhouse." In *Que(e)rying Archaeology: Proceedings of the Thirty-Seventh Annual Chacmool Conference, University of Calgary,* edited by Susan Terendy, Natasha Lyons, Michelle Janse-Smekal. Calgary: Archaeological Association of the University of Calgary.

Foley, Robert. 1991. "Hominids, Humans, and Hunter-Gatherers: An Evolutionary Perspective." In: *Hunters and Gatherers: History, Evolution, and Social Change,* edited by Tim Ingold, David Riches, and James Woodburn, 201–221. New York: Berg.

Fritz, Carole, Gilles Tosello, and Margaret W. Conkey. 2016. "Reflection on the Identities and the Roles of the Artists in European Paleolithic Societies." *Journal of Archaeological Method and Theory* 23 (4): 1307–1332.

Geller, Pamela. 2009. "Bodyscapes, Biology, and Heteronormativity." *American Anthropologist* 111 (4): 504–516.

Giffney, Noreen. 2004. "Denormatizing Queer Theory: More than (Simply) Lesbian and Gay Studies." *Feminist Theory* 5 (1): 73–78

Green, Sarah F. 1997. *Urban Amazons: Lesbian Feminism and Beyond in the Gender, Sexuality, and Identity Battles of London.* New York: St. Martin's Press.

Grimbos, Teresa, Kenneth Zucker, Khytam Dawood, Robert P. Buriss, and David A.

Puts. 2010. "Sexual Orientation and the Second to Fourth Finger Length Ratio: A Meta-Analysis in Men and Women." *Behavioral Neuroscience* 124 (2): 278–287.

Guthrie, R. Dale. 2005. *The Nature of Paleolithic Art*. Chicago: University of Chicago Press.

Halperin, David M. 1989. "One Hundred Years of Homosexuality." In *One Hundred Years of Homosexuality, and Other Essays on Greek Love*, edited by David M. Halperin, 15–40. Routledge: New York.

———. 1996. *Saint Foucault: Towards a Gay Hagiography*. Oxford University Press, New York.

Hill, Kim, Michael Barton, and A. Magdalena Hurtado. 2009. "The Emergence of Human Uniqueness: Characters Underlying Behavioral Modernity." *Evolutionary Anthropology* 18: 187–200.

Hollimon, Sandra. 2011. "Sex and Gender in Bioarchaeological Research: Theory Method and Interpretation." In *Social Bioarchaeology*, edited by Sabrina C. Agarwal and Bonnie A. Glenncross, 147–182. Malden, MA: Wiley-Blackwell.

Homfray, Mike. 2008. "Standpoint, Objectivity, and Social Construction: Reflections from the Study of Gay and Lesbian Communities." *Sociological Research Online* 13 (1).

Hosking, Nada. 2013. "The Mind in the Vulva: Deconstructing the Androcentric Interpretation of Prehistoric Images." *UC Berkeley Undergraduate Journal* 26 (3): 193–201.

Jagose, Annamarie. 1996. *Queer Theory: An Introduction*. New York: New York University Press.

Joyce, Rosemary. 2000. "A Precolumbian Gaze: Male Sexuality among the Ancient Maya." In *Archaeologies of Sexuality*, edited by Robert A. Schmidt and Barbara L. Voss, 263–286. New York: Routledge.

Katz, Jonathan N. 1990. "The Invention of Heterosexuality." *Socialist Review* 20 (1): 7–34.

King, Robert J. 2013. "Baby Got Back: Some Brief Observations on Obesity in Ancient Female Figurines: Limited Support for Waist to Hip Ratio Constant as a Signal of Fertility." *Journal of Obesity and Weight Loss Therapy* 3: 159.

Kraemer, Bernd, Thomas Noll, Aba Delsignore, Gabriella Milos, Ulrich Schnyder, and Urs Hepp. 2006. "Finger Length Ratio (2D:4D) and Dimensions of Sexual Orientation." *Neuropsychobiology* 53:210–214.

Lancaster, Chet S., and Jane B. Lancaster. 1987. "The Watershed: Change in Parental Investment and Family-Formation Strategies in the Course of Human Evolution." In *Parenting Across the Life Span*, edited by Jeanne Altmann, 187–205. New York: Aldine.

Latour, Bruno. 1999. *Pandora's Hope: Essays on the Reality of Science Studies*. Cambridge, MA: Harvard University Press.

Leroi-Gourhan, André. 1965. *Préhistoire de l'art occidental*. Paris: Citadelles et Mazenod.

Lippa, Richard A. 2003. "Are 2D:4D Finger-Length Ratios Related to Sexual Orientation? Yes for Men, No for Women." *Journal of Personality and Social Psychology* 85 (1): 179–188.

Lovejoy, C. Owen. 1981. "The Origin of Man." *Science* 211 (4480): 341–350.

Manning, John T., Andrew J. G. Churchill, and Michael Peters. 2007. "The Effects of Sex, Ethnicity, and Sexual Orientation on Self-Measured Digit Ration (2D:4D)." *Archives of Sexual Behavior* 36 (2): 223–233.

Matic, Uros. 2012. "To Queer or Not to Queer: That Is the Question: Sex/Gender, Prestige, and Burial No. 10. on the Mokrin Necropolis." *Dacia* 56:169–185.

McDermott, LeRoy. 1996. "Self-Representation in Upper Paleolithic Female Figurines." *Current Anthropology* 37 (2): 227–275.

Nelson, Sarah Milledge. 1990. "Diversity of the Upper Paleolithic 'Venus' Figurines and Archaeological Mythology." *Archaeological Papers of the American Anthropological Association* 2 (1): 11–22.

Nowell, April, and Melanie L. Chang. 2014. "Science, the Media, and Interpretations of Upper Paleolithic Figurines." *American Anthropologist* 116 (3): 562–577.

Owen, Linda. 2005. *Distorting the Past: Gender and the Division of Labor in the European Upper Paleolithic*. Tubingen: Kerns Verlag.

Prine, Elizabeth. 2000. "Searching for Third Genders: Towards a Prehistory of Domestic Space in Middle Missouri Villages." In *Archaeologies of Sexuality*, edited by Robert A. Schmidt and Barbara L. Voss, 197–219. New York: Routledge.

Reeder, Greg. 2000. "Same-Sex Desire, Conjugal Constructs, and the Tomb of Niankhhnum and Khnumhotp." *World Archaeology* 32 (2): 193–208.

Rice, Patricia. 1981. "Prehistoric Venuses: Symbols of Motherhood or Womanhood?" *Journal of Anthropological Research* 37 (4): 402–414.

Rubin, Gayle. 1984. "Thinking Sex: Notes for a Radical Theory of the Politics of Sexuality." In *Pleasure and Danger*, edited by Carole S. Vance, 267–319. New York: Routledge.

Rutecki, Dawn, and Chelsea Blackmore. 2016. "Towards an Inclusive Queer Archaeology: An Overview and Introduction." *SAA Archaeological Record* 16 (1): 9–11.

Schmidt, Robert A. 2000. "Shamans and Northern Cosmology: The Direct Historical Approach to Mesolithic Sexuality." In *Archaeologies of Sexuality*, edited by Robert A. Schmidt and Barbara L. Voss, 220–235. New York: Routledge.

———. 2002. "The Iceman Cometh: Queering the Archaeological Past." In *Out in Theory: The Emergence of Lesbian and Gay Anthropology*, edited by Ellen Lewin and William L. Leap, 155–184. Urbana: University of Illinois Press.

Schofield, John, and Mike Anderton. 2000. "The Queer Archaeology of Green Gate: Interpreting Contested Space at Greenham Common Airbase." *World Archaeology* 32 (2): 236–251.

Sedgwick, Eve Kosofsky. 1990. *The Epistemology of the Closet*. Berkeley, CA: University of California Press.

Sediman, Steven. 1997. *Difference Troubles: Queering Social Theory and Sexual Politics*. New York: Cambridge University Press.

Sharpe, Kevin, and Leslie Van Gelder. 2004. "Children and Paleolithic 'Art': Indications from Rouffignac Cave, France." *International Newsletter on Rock Art* 38: 9–17.

She. 2000. Sex and a Career. *World and Archaeology* 32 (2): 162–177.

Snow, Dean R. 2005. "Sexual Dimorphism in Upper Palaeolithic Hand Stencils." *Antiquity* 80: 390–404.

———. 2013. "Sexual Dimorphism in European Upper Paleolithic Cave Art." *American Antiquity* 78 (4): 746–761.

Soffer, Olga. 2004. "Recovering Perishable Technologies through Use Wear on Tools: Preliminary Evidence for Upper Paleolithic Weaving and Net Making." *Current Anthropology* 45 (3): 407–413.

Soffer, Olga, James M. Adovasio, and David C. Hyland. 2000. "The 'Venus' Figurines: Textiles, Basketry, Gender, and Status in the Upper Paleolithic." *Current Anthropology* 41 (4): 511–537.

Solli, Brit. 2008. "Queering the Cosmology of the Vikings: A Queer Analysis of the Cult of Odin and the 'Holy White Stones.'" *Journal of Homosexuality* 54: 1–2.

Springate, Megan. 2017. "'Archaeology? How Does That Work?' Incorporating Archaeology into the National Park Service LGBTQ Heritage Initiative as Community Engagement." *Journal of Community Archaeology and Heritage* 4 (3): 173–185.

Sterling, Kathleen. 2011. "Inventing Human Nature." In *Ideologies in Archaeology*, edited by Reinhard Bernbeck and Randall McGuire, 175–193. Tucson: University of Arizona Press.

———. 2014. "Man the Hunter, Woman the Gatherer? The Impact of Gender Studies on Hunter-Gatherer Research (A Retrospective)." In *The Oxford Handbook of the Archaeology and Anthropology of Hunter-Gatherers*, edited by Vicki Cummings, Peter Jordan, and Marek Zvelebil, 151–176. New York: Oxford University Press.

———. 2015. "Black Feminist Theory in Prehistory." *Archaeologies* 11 (1): 93–120.

Stoliar, A. D. 1977. "On the Sociohistorical Decoding of Upper Paleolithic Female Signs." *Soviet Anthropology and Archaeology* 16 (2): 36–77.

Sullivan, Nicole. 2003. *A Critical Introduction to Queer Theory*. New York: New York University Press.

Taylor, Timothy. 1996. *The Prehistory of Sex*. New York: Bantam Books.

Tripp, Allison J. 2015. "Paleolithic Art." In *The International Encyclopedia of Human Sexuality*, edited by Patricia Whelehan and Anne Bolin, 1–4. New York: Wiley-Blackwell.

Turner, Michael B. 2000. *A Genealogy of Queer Theory*. Philadelphia, PA: Temple University Press.

Voss, Barbara L. 2000. "Feminisms, Queer Theories, and the Archaeological Study of Past Sexualities." *World Archaeology* 32 (2): 180–192.

———. 2008. "Sexuality Studies in Archaeology." *Annual Reviews of Anthropology* 37:317–336.

———. 2012. "Sexual Effects: Postcolonial and Queer Perspectives on the Archaeology of Sexuality and Empire." In *Archaeology of Colonialism: Intimate Encounters and Sexual Effects*, edited by Barbara L. Voss and Eleanor Conlin Cassela, 11–28. Cambridge: Cambridge University Press.

Wang, James Z., Weina Ge, Dean R. Snow, Prasenjit Mitra, and C. Lee Giles. 2010. "Determining the Sexual Identities of Prehistoric Cave Artists Using Digitized Handprints." In *MM '10, Proceedings of the 18th ACM International Conference on Multimedia*, 1325–1332. New York: ACM.

Warner, Michael. 1993. "Introduction." In *Fear of a Queer Planet*, edited by Michael Warner, vii–xxx. Minneapolis: University of Minnesota Press.

———. 1999. *The Trouble with Normal: Sex, Politics, and the Ethics of Queer Life*. New York: The Free Press.

Weismantel, Mary J. 2013. "Towards a Transgender Archaeology: A Queer Rampage through Prehistory." In *The Transgender Studies Reader 2*, edited by Susan Stryker and Aren Aizura, 319–354. New York: Routledge.

White, Randall, Romain Mensan, Raphaëlle Bourrillon, Catherine Cretin, Thomas F. G. Higham, Amy E. Clark, Matthew L. Sisk, Elise Tartar, Philippe Gardère, Paul Goldberg, Jacques Pelegrin, Hélène Valladas, Nadine Tisnérat-Labordek, Jacques de Sanoit, Dominique Chambellan, and Laurent Chiottim. 2012. "Context and Dating of Aurignacian Vulvar Representations from Abri Castanet, France." *Proceedings of the National Academy of Sciences* 109 (22): 8450–8455.

Wildgen, Wolfgang. 2004. "The Paleolithic Origins of Art, Its Dynamic and Topological Aspects, and the Transition to Writing." In *Semiotic Evolution and the Dynamics of Culture,* edited by Marcel Bax, Barend van Heusden, and Wolfgang Wildgen, 117–153. Bern, Switzerland: Peter Lang.

Wylie, Alison. 1992. "The Interplay of Evidential Constraints and Political Interests: Recent Archaeological Research on Gender." *American Antiquity* 57 (1): 15–35.

———. 1997. "Good Science, Bad Science, or Science as Usual? Feminist Critiques of Science." In *Women in Human Evolution,* edited by Lori D. Hager, 29–55. New York: Routledge.

3

Bodies for Evidence

The Fort Laurens Ambush and Archaeological
Perspectives on Legacies of Interpersonal Violence
on the Colonial American Frontier

KYLE SOMERVILLE

On the morning of February 23rd, 1779, a work party of soldiers left Fort
Laurens (pronounced "Lawrence"), a small Continental Army fortification
on the Ohio frontier, to gather firewood and stray packhorses. After pass-
ing beyond the effective range of the fort's defenses, a group of Indians and
British soldiers ambushed the party. The dead were gathered up the following month and buried in a mass grave (Gramly 1999). A museum and
memorial to the garrison are now located on the site. Previous archaeological studies of the Fort Laurens cemetery focused on the skeletal trauma
suffered by the ambush victims and the ideological factors underlying
colonial frontier warfare (Gramly 1999; Pansing 2007; Sciulli and Gramly
1989; Williamson et al. 2003). This research demonstrated that the physical
trauma the soldiers at the fort suffered was not unusual on the American
frontier during the mid-eighteenth century (Herrmann n.d.; Liston and
Baker 1996).

How can an event that happened nearly 250 years ago help us understand violence and promote social justice in the present? Anthropological
research has demonstrated that there are no known forms of social organization, modes of production, or environments that are free of violence.
This means that evolutionary, ecological, or materialist explanations are
not sufficient to explain violent encounters (Otterbein 1999; Thorpe 2003;
Walker 2001). Anthropology (and by extension archaeology) is best able
to contribute by exposing the forgotten or unexpected linkages between
violence and power, what González-Ruibal and Hall (2017, 25–26) describe

as "bring[ing] to light not only the glorious but [also] the abject and violent" (see also Scheper-Hughes and Bourgois 2003; Fujii 2013; Hume 2008;
Staudigl 2007). An anthropology of violent events connects moments,
links material culture to the social relations and historical circumstances
that constitute them (Hoffman and Lubkemann 2005, 321; Wurst and
Mrozowski 2014, 221). Historical archaeology's value to social activism lies
in its ability to marshal a variety of data sources to explain how behaviors in multiple, often competing pasts have given rise to the conditions of
modern life (Crist 2006). Because social contexts influence which weapons
assailants use, the trauma these weapons inflict reflects social and cultural
values and which practices of war a society deems acceptable (Walker 2001,
574–584). Interpreting the nature of skeletal trauma may reveal an attacking
agent's motivations, whether the injurious action was considered socially
acceptable, and how social relationships and material constraints mediate
different expressions of violence. When supported by other forms of evidence, skeletal traces of violence and trauma can be explained by examining their frequency, location, severity, and context, while indirect evidence
of violence can be extrapolated from historical documentation (Boyd 1996,
230–233).

Violence between and among social groups is a fundamental element of
human interaction and thus a core component of what it is to be human.
Archaeological and anthropological research has clearly demonstrated that
physically violent encounters were common among many indigenous societies, including those in the northeastern United States, prior to European
contact (Milner 1999; Otterbein 1979, 1999). Evidence for these encounters includes skeletons with embedded arrowheads and skeletons that bear
signs of torture and execution (Keener 1999; Lekson 2002; Sempowski et
al. 2001; Williamson 2007; Wray et al. 1991). Indirect evidence for violence
includes evidence for palisaded settlements in defensible positions and the
development of stone arrowhead technologies (Birch 2010; Engelbrecht
2003, 2009; Engelbrecht and Jamieson 2016). However, violence is never a
totally isolated act and is always part of other, often broader, historical processes that are circumscribed by material constraints and incentives, by the
social structures in which it occurs, and by cultural representations of these
conditions. Violence thus must be examined as an extension of existing
social relations between groups. The Fort Laurens ambush is a minor foot-
note in the Revolutionary War, but the nature of that event, the social relations that constituted and directed it, and the circumstances that differentiate it from other events are meaningful (Hoffman and Lubkemann 2005).

Understanding that interpersonal violence between American settlers and Native Americans was an outgrowth of competition over land illustrates how a violent event from the past can help us see how social inequality in the present day has roots in the past. This suggests that frontier violence was rooted in competition for land, which meant access to food crops and game. However, such an approach underplays the social and cultural roots of violence. Understanding the geographic contours of violence requires examining the social relations that circumscribe a space (Blomley 2003, 129). The interpersonal violence between Euro-American settlers and Indians at the time of the Revolutionary War was an outgrowth of structural and political violence as an outgrowth of growing liberal property regime towards arable land that was both a cause of physical and legal violence in broader, competing cultural ideas of property rights, masculinity, and status normalized brutal, everyday physical violence (Farmer 2004, 320). Interpreting the deaths of the soldiers at the fort requires an understanding of the ideological motives of the killers and the killed, the regional social and cultural context in which they lived, and the social, ideological, and economic structures of violence that provided the context for the ambush (Adelman and Aron 1999; Farmer 2004, 309–312; Knouff 1994; Reid 2008).

Violence is an extension of existing social relations between groups that has long-term, unanticipated consequences (Crist 2006, 109; Wurst and Mrozowski 2014). Whether it is physical, structural, or psychological, it is a pervasive part of human social interaction and has social, environmental, material, and demographic consequences (Jackman 2002; Lowell 2007; Lubkemann 2005; Milner 2005). Examining the power relations inherent in structural violence at a local level enables us to learn how structural violence is enacted through routines of daily life are created and reproduced by local tensions, factions, and contradictions (Farmer 2004, 320). Archaeological perspectives on violence in the past become a powerful political device when they challenge social memory at colony-wide (in this case) and local scales. That is why understanding the physical wounds suffered by those who died in the Fort Laurens ambush can clarify the cultural and ideological factors that gave rise to them, the different forms of violence on the frontier, and which effects of that violence have seeped into the present.

What Is Violence?

Most scholars who research violence point out that it is a difficult concept to define. The term "violence" has taken on meanings in anthropology beyond physical trauma (Bourgois 2001; Pike et al. 2010; Riches 1991). In the past, archaeological research on violence typically referred to damage to the human body during raids and larger-scale conflict, but the definition has grown to encompass symbolic, structural, and psychological violence (Farmer 2004; Jenkins 1998, 124). These latter forms have gained traction in the literature as anthropologists have recognized that studies of violence must expand to include the conflicts over self-respect, the law, autonomy, and personhood that give violence its force and meaning (Bourgois 2001, 2002; Blomley 2003; Scheper-Hughes and Bourgois 2003). This broadening of the scope of the study of violence has led to more nuanced reflections on the relationships of social actors because interactions may result in the alienation of an actor or group of actors (Krohn-Hansen 1994). Thus, studies of violence now include the study of desecrated churches and mosques (Lahiri 2003). Researchers have begun to frame violent actions along a continuum from physical attacks to symbolic violence in which actors acquire and maintain domination over others by manipulating moral and emotional commitments in the service of practical and economic ones. They also study how the dominated contribute to their own domination by misrecognizing power structures as natural and self-evident (Bourdieu 1977; Bourgois 2001; Krohn-Hansen 1994). Psychological violence includes, for example, witchcraft and other spiritual terror (MacGaffey 2000), the use of the threat of physical violence to accomplish goals (Blomley 2003; Riches 1991), and forms of structural violence that legitimize and recreate oppression that is obscured through everyday action (Blomley 2003; Farmer 2004; Given 2002; Springer and Le Billon 2016). Riches (1991) suggests that violence may be manifested in other forms such as ritual violence and violence against animals, but the focus here will be on physical and structural forms.

Violence may also be defined as a goal-oriented behavior to maintain or contest unbalanced social relations through struggle (Ball-Rokeach 1980, 47). MacGaffey (2000, 71) points out that casting violent encounters in terms of contestation means that it is always a political act in one form or another. Riches (1991, 293) cautions that framing violence as informed by economic constraints implies that violence exists in every human social interaction, reducing violence to an inevitability with little analytic value. It is more fruitful to frame violence in the context of social systems that make impositions on some actors but not others. Another strategy is to view violence as inherent in social roles that organize and direct physical injury. For example, a government soldier shooting at enemies implies a political-economic structure that legitimizes and sanctions the shooting.

However, this view overlooks the soldier's motivations for fighting and the constraints on his/her behavior, such as rewards/punishments for fighting that other actors mete out, which are derived from ideas of authority and resources. Such an analysis would move beyond understanding the specific physical harm of violence (Riches 1991, 293).

Violent encounters are also a tripartite relation that includes the agent(s) performing the acts(s), a victim or victims, and those who witness the act and judge the legitimacy of the violent act (Jackman 2002, 404; MacGaffey 2000, 71). Victim compliance may affect whether actions are considered violent. Researchers may define actions as violent and injurious and the "victim" as unwilling when injury is noticeable, but these definitions become ambiguous when resistance is unclear or when the recipient willingly endures injuries or is complicit by participating in their own injury (Korbin 2003; Traphagan 2008, 3). The legitimacy of the performance of violence may be contested, but basic understandings of physical hurt are often shared among the parties involved (Krohn-Hansen 1994).

Violent acts can used both for practical purposes (that is, to transform social relations) and for symbolic purposes (that is, to dramatize ideas) (MacGaffey 2000; Sutterlüty and Blauhut 2007). These two motivations often intersect. The content of violence conforms to cultural traditions, often local ones (MacGaffey 2000; Sutterlüty and Blauhut 2007). Distinguishing how violence is manifested in different cultural contexts provides insights into social structures. Violent encounters are part of broader social and historical processes. Violence is thus not epiphenomenal or senseless (Jackman 2001, 405–408). It becomes chronic when it becomes characterized as a part of everyday life and perpetuates itself (Pike et al. 2010, 48). Everyday violence includes daily practices on a microlevel of interpersonal, domestic and delinquent acts that become routine and normalize brutality and terror (Bourgois 2001; Pike et al. 2010).

A Case Study in Frontier Warfare

Fort Laurens is located in Bolivar, Ohio, approximately 75 miles south of Cleveland. The fort was constructed in November 1778 by a Continental Army detachment from Fort Pitt (present-day Pittsburgh). In the summer of 1778, a force of 1,200 men left Fort Pitt to attack British positions at Detroit and to protect American and Christianized Wyandot Indian settlements in Ohio.[1] This force included companies from the 8th Pennsylvania Regiment (which consisted of men from western and south-central

Pennsylvania), the 9th and 13th Virginia Regiment (men from southwestern Pennsylvania and northwestern West Virginia), and a contingent that consisted of soldiers from North Carolina, militia from western Virginia, and allied Delaware Indians, French officers, and auxiliary personnel (Pieper and Gidney 1976).

Impending winter weather compelled the detachment to construct a one-acre quadrangular fort around a fortified house the British had built in 1764 next to the Tuscarawas River (Heldman 1979; Kellogg 1916). The fort was to function as a base to attack Detroit and to protect Christian missionaries and allied Delaware Indians. More important, the fort was built to control the territory between American Fort Pitt and British Detroit and facilitate American settlement in the Ohio country (Heldman 1974). With winter approaching, most of the soldiers from the North Carolina and militia units withdrew on December 9th, leaving behind a token garrison of 150 to 181 men (most of whom were from Pennsylvania). The fort attracted the notice of the British and their Wyandot, Shawnee, and Mingo allies, and in January 1779, 180 Indian warriors and British soldiers lay siege to it (Kellogg 1916, 210).

On the night of February 22nd, the Indians managed to catch the garrison's horses and lead them to a deeper part of the woods. The Indians took the bells off the horses and concealed themselves in long grass along the path leading to the fort (Mitchener 1876, 133; Withers 1895, 262). As a small work detail left the fort the next morning to gather firewood and collect the stray horses, they passed outside the fort's defenses, "allured by the sound of the bells." They "kept along the path where the Indians lay in wait . . . until they found themselves unexpectedly in the presence of an enemy, who opened fire" (Mitchener 1876, 133). All but two of the work detail were killed in the ambush. The survivors were taken prisoner; one was later released and the fate of the other is unknown (Withers 1895, 262). Historical accounts vary regarding both the size of the work party and the number killed. Some sources claim that nineteen men left the fort, while others place the number at sixteen or seventeen. Sources vary about the number of casualties; the range of fatalities claimed is fourteen to eighteen. Most sources agree that two were taken prisoner (Mitchener 1876, 133; Kellogg 1916, 241, 257; Pansing 2007, 1–3; Withers 1895, 262). Sciulli and Gramly (1989) note that only thirteen bodies were found in the mass grave associated with the ambush victims. This figure does not include two men who were killed as they attempted to retrieve the bodies. The remaining garrison believed that the besieging force was larger than it was and left the fallen men to exposure and scavenging wolves until a relief force arrived on March 23rd (Pansing 2007). The dead were buried in a mass grave to the west of the fort. The garrison suffered six additional deaths from combat and illness. American officials believed that the fort was too far from Detroit to launch effective attacks and too difficult to keep supplied. The fort was abandoned in August 1779 and Indians burned it the following year (Pieper and Gidney 1976; Sciulli and Gramly 1989). For the rest of the war, the Continental Army had no further presence in eastern Ohio and western Pennsylvania, which left local militiamen responsible for protecting settlers in the area.[2]

Outlines of the fort's bastions were visible as late as 1850, although the site was partially destroyed by farming and by the construction of the Ohio and Erie Canal in 1832 (Mitchener 1876, 129). The state of Ohio designated the site a state memorial in 1915 even though the exact location of the fort was uncertain, and in 1970 additional remains of the fort were discovered during construction of the current museum and interpretive center. Excavations in 1972–1973 uncovered the fort's cemetery, and additional excavations in 1986–1987 outlined portions of the palisade walls and structures within the fort. A total of twenty-one to twenty-seven people are buried in the cemetery. Seven individuals were interred in individual graves and at least fifteen individuals were placed in a single mass grave outside the fort (Gramly 1999; Sciulli and Gramly 1989; Williamson et al. 2003). The remains varied in levels of preservation; some individuals retained the small bones of the hands and feet while others were represented only by the denser bones of the legs, arms, and skull (Gramly 1999; Sciulli and Gramly 1989; Williamson et al. 2003, 114). Four features contained single individuals and one contained two individuals. The mass grave contained approximately fifteen individuals; thirteen who were buried in a cluster were the victims of the ambush, while two buried in an extended position side by side just north of the cluster were the individuals who were killed as they tried to recover the bodies of the ambush victims. One individual interred in the fort's Tomb of the Unknown Patriot was not available for study (Williamson et al. 2003, 114).

Sciulli and Gramly (1989), Gramly (1999), and Williamson et al. (2003) conducted analyses of the general health and skeletal trauma of the individuals in the fort cemetery. Although some of skeletons in the cemetery are fragmentary, it does not appear that women were among the dead. Dental eruption data indicated that the average age of death was 23.5 years and perhaps as low as 16 years for some individuals. Skeletal pathologies indicated diets and mechanical stress consistent with agricultural lifestyles. All of the skeletons in the fort cemetery had trauma consistent with wounds made with a tomahawk or hatchet, common close-quarters weapons that Indians in the Eastern Woodlands carried during the Revolutionary War. The archaeological evidence revealed that the ambush victims all suffered substantial head trauma, often from more than one blow and in several cases from more than one attacker and from weapons likely used by American Indians. All of the victims were scalped and in some case the attackers had stripped them of their uniforms as trophies (Gramly 1999). The archaeological evidence is clear that the soldiers in the Fort Laurens cemetery suffered horrific injuries and deaths. Although ambushes were by no means unprecedented on the colonial American frontier, physical evidence for this violence is comparatively rare and few frontier burials dating to the eighteenth century have been examined. A few studies have reported similar injuries (Herrmann n.d.; Liston and Baker 1996) and documentary evidence suggests that similar incidents occurred at other places along the colonial frontier (Beatty [1779] 1893, 245; Clark 1879; Peck 1908; Seaver 1918, 72–73).

Anthropological Perspectives on Violence on the American Frontier

Frontiers are loci of culture contact that emerge from particular historical circumstances and processes. In these areas, social interactions are influenced by geographic, political, and cultural factors that result in dynamic, variable, but often unstable zones of interaction (Parker 2006). The American frontier at the time of the Revolutionary War was already the site of a long history of violence before 1779. In June 1754, the Six Nations Iroquois sold 7 million acres in what is now western Pennsylvania to the British, opening lands in the Ohio Valley to white settlement. The Delaware Indians who claimed those lands were not consulted, which strained relations among Indians and Euro-American whites (Denaci 2007, 309–310). Violence between Euro-Americans and Indians in the colonial period became increasingly common as white settlers moved west (Kruer 2017). It is estimated that in the period 1754–1758, over 2,000 white settlers and an unknown number of Indians died on the Virginia and Pennsylvania frontiers during the French and Indian War (1754–1763), or almost 1 percent of the total white population of those colonies and 3 percent of the entire white population on the colonial frontier (Mahon 1958; Ward 1995). Reid (2008, 9) suggests that during the Revolutionary War, 7 percent of Kentucky's white settler population was killed during combat between settlers and Indians, compared to the 1 percent killed in the other thirteen colonies combined in other theaters of the war. Settlers on the frontier resisted religious and colonial establishments that threatened to disrupt their land claims, but these conflicts stemmed from differing political and class hostilities, not race (Martin 1971; Knouff 1994:57; Ousterhout 1993; Taylor 1993; Whittenburg 1977; see also Sharfstein 2012).

My focus is conflicts between whites and Indians. These hostilities were the result of several interrelated factors. Competition over arable land and other natural resources was one of the central issues underlying violence on the American frontier in the eighteenth century (Knouff 1994; Lee 2007; Martin 1971; Taylor 1993). British territories expanded into Ohio after the defeat of the French during the French and Indian War. Before 1781, just six of the original thirteen colonies had defined boundaries (Viele 1882). In 1763, British colonial officials established that the Appalachian Mountains formed the borders of its colonial territories. They later extended that boundary to include most of West Virginia and prohibited white settlement on the lands of Indian nations allied with the British (Rice 2008). White settlers ignored this limitation, and by 1768, over 50,000 people had moved onto or near these new borderlands in the Ohio Valley and the lower Great Lakes region (Adelman and Aron 1999, 822). This pushed Delaware, Shawnee, Mingo, and Cherokee peoples who had ancestral and legal claims there out of their lands (Aron 1992; Rice 2008). In response to increasing encroachment, Indian groups on the Ohio frontier banded together to drive out white settlers (Ward 1995). According to one account, the besieging Indians at Fort Laurens presented that reason for the attack:

On the evening of the day on which [the ambush] took place, the Indian army . . . painted and equipped for war, marched in single file through a prairie near the fort and in full view of the garrison, and encamped on an adjacent elevation on the opposite side of the river. From this situation, frequent conversations were held by them with the whites, in which they deprecated the longer continuance of hostilities and hoped for peace, but yet protested and were much exasperated at the Americans for attempting to penetrate so far into their country and against the encroachment made upon their territory by the whites, the erection of a fort and the garrisoning soldiers within their country, not only unpermitted by them, but for some time before they knew anything of it. For these infringements on their rights, they were determined on prosecuting the war, and continued the investure of the fort. (Withers 1895, 263; see also Mitchener 1876, 134)

Indian concepts of masculinity were based on an individual's prowess in warring and hunting. Successful warriors had significant social prestige, increased prospects in marriage, and leadership opportunities because they replenished the community's spiritual power through taking captives (Danvers 2001; Richter 1983; Traphagan 2008). Colonial officials were aware of these beliefs and used them to recruit Indian warriors for colonial ends by appealing directly to warriors with promises of military glory and material plunder (Danvers 2001, 192). Euro-American ideas of masculinity differed by class. Elite males valued virtue and emotional control, which differed from the masculinity backcountry farmers exhibited. This set the "stage for the emergence of the American nation as an 'empire of liberty,' a state whose citizens deliberately valorized violence while professing to pursue humanitarian aims" (Eustace 2008, 30–33). The practice of scalping Indians, which religious leaders encouraged, had become so common that in 1763 a military chaplain wrote, "the general cry and wish is for what they call a Scalp Act. . . . Vast numbers of Young Fellows who would not chuse to enlist as Soldiers, would be prompted by Revenge, Duty, Ambition & the Prospect of the Reward, to carry Fire & Sword into the Heart of the Indian Country. And indeed, if this Method could be reconcil'd with Revelation and the Humanity of the English Nation, it is the only one that appears likely to put a final stop to those Barbarians" (quoted in Axtell and Sturtevant 1980, 471). These ideological bases were supported by through various practices that directed killing. For example, both Indians and whites perpetrated revenge killings (Milner 1999). Native American societies practiced blood revenge, which was predicated on the notion that the killing of a person, either accidentally or on purpose, created an obligation on the part of the dead person's kin to exact revenge on the killer and/or his people. Any member of the killer's people, either himself or one of his relatives, would suffice as a target. If there was no expectation that the killer's relatives would stop supporting him, the killer's individual identity stopped mattering (Lee 2007, 714–715). Although Indian political structure lacked much coercive power and (in most cases) limited the scale of most warfare between Indian peoples, large forces of warriors sometimes formed to gain material benefits in territories or to force a restructuring of relationships between groups (Lee 2007). The blood-debt system could spiral into endemic conflict as various parties sought redress, but such conflict could be ended with peace rituals (Lee 2007, 738–739). The composition of the war party sometimes made it difficult to "balance blood" in tit-for-tat killings; such parties were often filled with young men who participated in the hope of raising their own personal status through scalping and taking prisoners and who would not necessarily limit their attacks to the perpetrator and/or his kin. This conflicted with European ideas of vengeance, which could be large in scale and broad in target but occurred under certain circumstances. Euro-American settlers believed that all Indians, regardless of group, were responsible for attacking their property, family, and friends (Knouff 1994). White settlers thus justified their taking of land and indiscriminate killings by referring to Indian "treacherousness" (Lee 2007, 716).

 European warfare tactics differed from traditional Indian methods, although there is debate about whether Indian methods of warfare arose in reaction to the Europeans' practice of total and indiscriminate destruction (Abler 1992; Knouff 1994; Lee 2007; Martin 1971). American Indians used warfare to replenish demographic populations and spiritual power but they strongly preferred to avoid loss of life in the process and used ambushes and tactical retreats to minimize causalities. Their white opponents considered these practices to be cowardly (Otterbein 1979; Richter 1983, 1985). The two sides also differed in their practices regarding taking prisoners. Indians took prisoners to adopt them or for later torture and execution, while Europeans took them for later exchange. However, for Indians, letting prisoners go just to have to fight them again was a foreign concept (Lee 2007; Parmenter 2007).

Both Indians and whites practiced scalping on the frontier. The removal of body parts was a tangible sign of victory, expressing a warrior's prowess and disdain for fallen enemies (Milner 1999, 111). Indians in the Eastern Woodlands believed that taking an enemy scalp restored spiritual power to the community (Abler 1992; Richter 1983, 1985). Europeans mutilated and tortured criminals in public spaces, but they generally did not use these practices against combatants or civilians (Abler 1992). By the mid-eighteenth century, whites on the American frontier had adopted scalping as a routine practice (Axtell and Sturtevant 1980, 470–472). Colonial governments encouraged settlers to kill Indians by paying for Indian scalps and by serving in expeditions against Indian enemies. This practice jeopardized white settlers' relationships with their allies. For example, in western Pennsylvania in 1763, when militia soldiers scalped the Indian dead after the Battle of Bushy Run, part of Pontiac's War, their British allies were surprised and abhorred. British peace negotiations with the Shawnee the next year were jeopardized after a Pennsylvania militiaman murdered and scalped a Shawnee hostage (Abler 1992, 8).

When two groups with differing conceptions of warfare practices fight each other, as was the case with Native Americans and Europeans in the eighteenth century, the battlefield can become a site of cultural and ideological change in how warfare is conducted as each side reacts to the behavior of the other (Abler 1992, 6). Taking prisoners was a central component of Indian warfare, both to replenish village populations and replace dead relatives and for torture and execution (Abler 1992; Kolodny 1993; Richter 1983). Europeans were horrified by the latter practices, while Europeans' practice of total war, which included killing women and children and destroying crops and entire villages, angered many native groups (Lee 2007). This misunderstanding of warfare practices was part of the ideological justification for racial violence on the frontier and, combined with the competition for land, contributed to failure of restraint on both sides and served as the justification for increasing numbers of revenge killings (Abler 1992; Sandberg 2006). These opposing cultural attitudes made it difficult to limit violence between Euro-Americans and Indians on the frontier. Captivity narratives, which were popular reading among white colonists, stoked hatred for Indians and support for raising troops for defense (Denaci 2007, 318). Colonial militia units and Indian war parties accepted the routine use of excessive violence, which became a routine part of life on the frontier (Sandberg 2006). Soldiers from the western colonial frontier tended to be ambivalent about fighting the British in distant places on the eastern coast because they did not see the British as a direct threat to their livelihoods, farms, or families (Knouff 1994, 55–65; see also Rice 2008, 83). Many men from the Pennsylvania backcountry fought against the British in the eastern theaters of the Revolutionary War only when they were drafted or otherwise forced, but they eagerly enlisted in volunteer militia units to fight Indian and loyalist opponents (Knouff 1994). It is also a reason, perhaps, why the garrison at Fort Laurens consisted of men from Pennsylvania and western Virginia (Gramly 1999). Those were the men who had the most to gain by serving on the frontier.

Both white settlers and Indians also used psychological violence throughout the frontier. Leaving bodies unburied, displaying scalps as warnings and signs of fighting prowess, making armed demonstrations of fighting numbers, and mutilating opponents all defined frontier warfare in a way that was not seen in other areas of the colonies during the Revolutionary War (Reid 2008).

Of the many cultural differences between white settlers and Indians was a fundamental disparity in how whites and Indians viewed the physical landscape. For American Indian groups in the northeastern United States, the material and spirit worlds were closely intertwined. Humans shared the natural world with animate and inanimate entities, all of which had inherent spiritual power and were considered as sentient beings that possessed humanlike qualities (Berres et al. 2004; Engelbrecht 2003:4; Hamell 1992; Hamell and Miller 1986). The Indian village was "the world in microcosm," a threshold for ritual encounters between humans and other-than-human beings (Hamell 1992, 454). For white settlers, engagement with the land was bound up with ownership of private property. This was embodied in the Euro-American "homesteader ethic," which was based on the idea that ownership of land was synonymous with freedom and that land was owned only if it was cultivated (Aron 1992; Hofstra 1998). This ideology was a driving force for white settlers, most of who came from middling economic backgrounds. For those people, the vast amount of land that was apparently available for the taking meant that they could become independent and free by cultivating land. This concept of earning a right to land through working it put whites into conflict with the various native peoples they encountered. Although Indians in the Northeast had practiced agriculture for centuries before European contact, many whites did not or would not distinguish the differences among native practices and assumed that all Indian peoples hunted only to provide for themselves because of their "willful idleness" (Kolodny 1993, 191). Because whites viewed Indians as living off the land without investing their labor, they believed Indians did not have legitimate claims to land (Perdue 1995). This belief set the precedent for future dealings with Indian groups as the United States expanded westward (Faragher 1998; Williams 1980).

Blomley (2003, 129) suggests that land systems are forms of disciplinary power because they regulate who and what has the rights to the land. Maps, fences, grids, tracts, and other surveying tools were disciplinary powers backed by property owners who were backed by the law. This is an example of violence manifests itself in both material and nonmaterial forms. Although these lands were surveyed, they were not under British authority and settlers developed informal laws to lay claim to these lands that were known as the "right of the woods." Under this informal code, white hunters claimed the forests through hunting and sharing meat with the community and those in need and through their participation in the peltry trades (Aron 1998). They believed that their labor gave them a right to the backcountry wilderness. This contrasted with how people acquired the gridded, parceled, and surveyed lands colonial officials created in more settled areas (Blomley 2003, 129).

The fact that whites built numerous military forts on the frontier is evidence that they expected violent encounters. Of course colonial powers attempted to map holdings in the New World long before Fort Laurens was established. Map-making delineates and solidifies space. Maps are a kind of text that codifies the landscape by naturalizing spatial information (Johnson 2007; Myers 1999; Schein 1997). Structural violence was also present in how these lands were apportioned beyond the established colonies. British colonial officials viewed predominantly white, Protestant, yeoman farmers as an advantage in terms of securing the frontier. The establishment of county courts in these areas, which functioned as both criminal courts and courts of land records, and the clearing of roads between properties also defined the rights and routes by which settlers could communicate, further cementing colonial control of these lands (Hofstra 1998).

Ordering the world through maps, property boundaries, captivity narratives, and racism harmed American Indian social institutions as much as guns and knives did (Snead 2011; Staudigl 2007). The contrast between white peoples' belief that they gained rights to land by making improvements on it and Indians' concepts of ancestral and legal rights formed the ideological basis of competition for land on the colonial frontier and spurred much of the extreme violence between and among settlers, Indians, and colonial governments.

Modern American values of personhood linked to individuality and land ownership are rooted in these bloody encounters between whites and Indians. Sharfstein (2012, 655–656) observes that the concept of private property is the central component of the American Dream and forms the foundation for how modern Americans think of communities, democratic government, and liberty itself. Whites and Indians had their own distinct motivations for and expectations about violence that contributed to the social nature of the emerging United States. The roots of that new country included violent racism, a determination to expand, a suspicion of authority, and a commitment to community. These are the values that shaped modern American cultural attitudes that link personal identification and liberty to property ownership (Knouff 1994; Sharfstein 2012). Thus, "the backcountry Revolution left an important, if not always positive, legacy" (Knouff 1994, 69).

Conclusion: The Fort Laurens Ambush and Legacies
of Frontier Violence

Violence is an extension of existing relations between groups. Warfare on the American frontier after European contact was not just the result of anger about violations of expectations about warfare or the pursuit of economic gain (Lee 2007). Instead, fundamental differences in rules about restraint in warfare shaped violence on the frontier. Neither Europeans nor Indians understood or participated in war according to the other group's rules. Physical violence was the result of gunshots, taking scalps, and revenge killings; the symbolic violence of unburied bodies left to rot in the elements as warnings to enemies; impersonal colonial policies that encouraged displacement; maps that subsumed Indian understandings of the landscape; and bounties on scalps. White settlers and Indians had their own distinct motivations for and expectations about violent encounters. This framework offers a new view of violence on the American frontier at the time of the American Revolution (Knouff 1994).

The soldiers at Fort Laurens suffered injuries that were common for the time and place in which they occurred. How does an understanding of the skeletal trauma on the soldiers at Fort Laurens is a reflection of violence in the past help us achieve social justice in the present? One way, as Wright (2010, 99) observes, is in the presence of the bodies themselves:

> Without the bodies as material evidence of events . . . those who wish to deny that they happened can—and have tried hard to—set up a contest where we argue about how to interpret words in historical documents, and about the integrity of the characters and memories of those who claim to remember. Of course historical scholarship and memories are critical, but the powerful evidence of the bodies themselves, especially in conjunction with documentary evidence and witness memory, is difficult to contest. If bodies with gunshots are there in the ground, then somebody shot them. The bodies demand an explanation.

Bodies serve as material evidence of violence by providing evidence for the historical and cultural context in which those injuries occurred. The Fort Laurens cemetery offers evidence for numerous lines of commentary on how historical archaeology can be used to promote social activism. Perhaps most obviously, it provides a perspective on physical violence in the past. Lubkemann (2005, 504–505) suggests that analyzing how violence is shaped by social organization and ideology at the local level provides information about social relationships that cannot otherwise be understood at broader levels of analysis: "What the war 'was about' in one area of the country had little to do with what it was about elsewhere." As Knouff (1994) points out, the American Revolution was a war people experienced at the local level, and understanding the deaths of the Fort Laurens soldiers requires both an understanding of the ideological motives of the killers and the killed and an understanding of the social and cultural contexts of the region. Archaeological perspectives on violence must go beyond delineating physical and skeletal trauma, even though doing so is difficult.

Because violence is part of broader social and historical processes that are often local in character, it is possible to interpret violence in relativist terms. Thus, an activist archaeology must also negotiate issues of cultural relativism because unbiased accounts of violence do not exist (Hume 2008; Zechenter 1997). On the one hand, uncovering the historical and structural roots of violent actions is often seen as an exercise in making excuses (Farmer 2004). On the other hand, framing violent actions as endemic in some societies but not others "threatens to set up a hierarchy of societies and inform the international community's response to acts of violence by individual states and peoples" as another form of structural violence (Bourgois 2002; Sundar 2004). Casting the physical trauma the skeletons in the Fort Laurens cemetery exhibit as the outcome of long-standing racial tensions spurred by cultural and political differences between Euro-American settlers and Indian peoples moves us closer to understanding how local instances of violence are the outcomes of structural conditions. That, in turn, moves us closer to understanding their legacies in the present. To paraphrase the medical anthropologist Paul Farmer (2004, 311), while the colonial powers of England, Spain, and France may be gone, the transnational political and economic structures that maintained them are still in place and are still inflicting harm.

Expressions of violence are historically contingent actions that are circumscribed by the material constraints, material incentives, social structures, and cultural representations in which they occur. In many ways, the study of violence in the past is difficult for precisely the same reasons that it is difficult in the present. Although violence is an inseparable component of the human condition, archaeologists must be careful to avoid labeling all human interactions as violent and to avoid categorizing all violence, even structural violence that is legally sanctioned, in negative terms (Blomley 2003; Riches 1991; Staudigl 2007). Given the unique historical and cultural circumstances in which violence is enacted, archaeologists must consider whether cross-cultural studies of violence are feasible. Riches (1991, 295) suggests that such studies entail a sense of ethnocentrism because they imply that similarities and differences between cultures can be determined, a conclusion that is based on qualities of the nature of the social world as determined by the researcher. Analysis of competing ideas about perpetrators and victims, social organization, the world, and even linguistic categories of what violence is and what counts as violence (which are rooted in western ideas of causality) may devolve into cultural relativism. The defenders of Fort Laurens, who were from Pennsylvania and western Virginia, may have seen their service in the Continental Army as one way to defend their families and friends. No doubt the Wyandot, Shawnee, and Mingo warriors who participated in the ambush saw their actions as one way of achieving the same goals.

It must not be forgotten that the suffering and death of our ancestors or someone else's ancestors is the raw material archaeologists use to fashion explanations of violence in the past and articulate the politics that underlie our visions of social activism. People on the colonial American frontier often suffered brutal deaths at the hands of others in front of their spouses, children, and friends. Historical accounts of colonial frontier battles suggest that Indians and whites experienced feelings of terror, survivors' guilt, anger, betrayal, and racially motivated hatred (Abler 1992; Beatty [1779] 1893; Egle 1890; Eustace 2008; Hurt 1996; Martin 1971; Reid 2008; Rice 2008; Seaver 1918). Analyzing the deaths of both whites and Indians on the basis of measurements of lesions and bone landmarks glosses over the pain and fear the victims went through in their final moments, as do explanations that point to social institutions that promoted violence or economic motives such as competition for land (Seeman 2011; Tarlow 2012).

Historical archaeology contributes valuable perspectives on different forms of violence in the past by deconstructing pervasive myths about senseless violence to reveal the social relations that validate violence against others. If social situations involving violence are characterized at a basic level by conflicting ideas, then the Fort Laurens ambush was an illustration of the physical, cultural, and structural conflicts that led to frontier warfare in microcosm (Adelman and Aron 1999, 815; Krohn-Hansen 1994, 374). The archaeological and historical evidence are clear that the ambush at Fort Laurens was a brutal but not unprecedented event in the bloody history of the American frontier. The roots of that violence began long before that February morning in 1779 and its effects continued long after the event.

The ambush is also a reminder that the historical roots of the current social issues that archaeologists wish to affect are deep and entangled. Bones or other material evidence of violence force us to interrogate our assumptions and reconsider the available evidence in light of which groups will be most affected by the outcome of our work (Bourgois 2001; Novak and Kopp 2003; Whitehead 2007; Wright 2010). Archaeologists should not valorize or demonize actions in the past or determine who was "right" or "wrong." Instead, we should make clear the unseen structural, political, and symbolic linkages that lead to and shape the expressions of physical violence in everyday life and the consequences such linkages have for the future.

Acknowledgments

I am grateful to Mike and Barb Zimmerman, Kate Babbitt, and the anonymous reviewers for their helpful comments on this chapter. As always, my deepest gratitude goes to Marie-Lorraine Pipes, George Hamell, and Paul Powers.

Notes

1. "Fort Laurens," *Ohio History Connection*, n.d., accessed May 2, 2017, http://www.ohiohistorycentral.org/entry.php?rec=710.
2. "Fort Laurens."

References Cited

Abler, Thomas S. 1992. "Scalping, Torture, Cannibalism and Rape: An Ethnohistorical Analysis of Conflicting Cultural Values in War." *Anthropologica* 34 (1): 3–20.

Adelman, Jeremy, and Stephen Aron. 1999. "From Borderlands to Borders: Empires, Nation-States, and the Peoples in between in North American History." *American Historical Review* 104 (3): 814–841.

Aron, Stephen. 1992. "Pioneers and Profiteers: Land Speculation and the Homestead Ethic in Frontier Kentucky." *Western Historical Quarterly* 23 (2): 179–198.

———. 1998. "Pigs and Hunters: 'Rights in the Woods' on the Trans-Appalachian Frontier." In *Contact Points: American Frontiers from the Mohawk Valley to the Mississippi, 1750–1830*, edited by Andrew Cayton and Fredrika J. Teute, 173–197. Chapel Hill: University of North Carolina Press.

Axtell, James, and William C. Sturtevant. 1980. "The Unkindest Cut, or Who Invented Scalping." *William and Mary Quarterly* 37 (3): 451–472.

Ball-Rokeach, S. J. 1980. "Normative and Deviant Violence from a Conflict Perspective." *Social Problems* 28 (1): 45–62.

Beatty, Erkuries. (1779) 1893. "Journal of Lieut. Erkuries Beatty in the Expedition against the Six Nations under Gen. Sullivan." In *Journals and Diaries of the War of the Revolution*, edited by William Henry Egle, 219–254. Harrisburg, PA: E. K. Myers.

Berres, Thomas E., David M. Stothers, and David Mather. 2004. "Bear Imagery and Ritual in Northeast North America: An Update and Assessment of A. Irving Hallowell's Work." *Midcontinental Journal of Archaeology* 29 (1): 5–42.

Birch, Jennifer. 2010. "Coalescence and Conflict in Iroquoian Ontario." *Archaeological Review from Cambridge* 25 (1): 29–48.

Blomley, Nicholas. 2003. "Law, Property, and the Geography of Violence: The Frontier, the Survey, and the Grid." *Annals of the Association of American Geographers* 93 (1): 121–141.

Bourdieu, Pierre. 1977. *Outline of a Theory of Practice*. Cambridge, UK: Cambridge University Press.

———. 2001. "The Power of Violence in War and Peace: Post-Cold War Lessons from El Salvador." *Ethnography* 2 (1): 5–34.

———. 2002. "The Violence of Moral Binaries: Response to Leigh Binford." *Ethnography* 3 (2): 221–231.

Boyd, Donna C. 1996. "Skeletal Correlates of Human Behavior in the Americas." *Journal of Archaeological Method and Theory* 3 (3): 189–251.

Breckenridge, Keith. 1998. "The Allure of Violence: Men, Race and Masculinity on the South African Goldmines, 1900–1950." *Journal of Southern African Studies* 24 (4): 669–693.

Clark, John S. 1879. *The Journal of Lieut. John Hardenbergh of the Second New York Continental Regiment from May 1 to October 3, 1779 in General Sullivan's Campaign against the Western Indians*. Auburn, NY: Knapp and Peck.

Crist, Thomas A. 2006. "The Good, the Bad, and the Ugly: Bioarchaeology and the Modern Gun Culture Debate." *Historical Archaeology* 40 (3): 109–130.

Danvers, Gail D. 2001. "Gendered Encounters: Warriors, Women, and William Johnson." *Journal of American Studies* 35 (2): 187–202.

Denaci, Ruth Ann. 2007. "The Penn's Creek Massacre and the Captivity of Marie Le Roy and Barbara Leininger." *Pennsylvania History: A Journal of Mid-Atlantic Studies* 74 (3): 307–332.

Egle, William H., ed. 1890. *Journals and Diaries of the War of the Revolution*. Harrisburg, PA: E. K. Meyers.

Engelbrecht, William E. 2003. *Iroquoia: The Development of a Native World*. Syracuse, NY: Syracuse University.

———. 2009. "Defense in an Iroquois Village." In *Iroquoian Archaeology and Analytic Scale*, edited by Laurie E. Miroff and Timothy D. Knapp, 179–187. Knoxville: University of Tennessee Press.

Engelbrecht, William, and Bruce Jamieson. 2016. "St. Lawrence Iroquoian Projectile Points: A Regional Perspective." *Archaeology of Eastern North America* 44: 81–98.

Eustace, Nicole. 2008. "The Sentimental Paradox: Humanity and Violence on the Pennsylvania Frontier." *William and Mary Quarterly* 65 (1): 29–64.

Faragher, John Mack. 1998. "More Motley than Mackinaw: From Ethnic Mixing to Ethnic Cleansing on the Frontier of the Lower Missouri, 1783–1833." In *Contact Points:*

American Frontiers from the Mohawk Valley to the Mississippi, 1750–1830, edited by Andrew Cayton and Fredrika J. Teute, 304–321. Chapel Hill: University of North Carolina Press.

Farmer, Paul. 2004. "An Anthropology of Structural Violence." *Current Anthropology* 45 (3): 305–325.

Fujii, Lee Ann. 2013. "The Puzzle of Extra-Lethal Violence." *Perspectives on Politics* 11 (2): 410–426.

Given, Michael. 2002. "Maps, Fields, and Boundary Cairns: Demarcation and Resistance in Colonial Cyprus." *International Journal of Historical Archaeology* 6 (1): 1–22.

González-Ruibal, Alfredo, and Martin Hall. 2007. "Heritage and Violence." In *Global Heritage: A Reader*, edited by Lynn Meskell, 150–170. Malden, MA: Wiley-Blackwell.

Gramly, Richard M. 1999. *Fort Laurens 1778–9: Pictorial Record of Excavations*. Buffalo, NY: American Society for Amateur Archaeology.

Hamell, George R. 1992. "The Iroquois and the World's Rim: Speculations on Color, Culture, and Contact." *American Indian Quarterly* 16 (4): 451–469.

Heldman, Donald P. 1979. "Review: Fort Laurens 1778–9: The Archaeological Record by Richard Michael Gramly." *Archaeology* 32 (4): 67–69.

Herrmann, Nicholas P. N.d. "A Report on the Human Burial Recovered from Logan's Fort (15LI95), Lincoln County, Kentucky." Unpublished report, University of Tennessee, Knoxville.

Hoffman, Danny, and Stephen Lubkemann. 2005. "West-African Warscapes: Warscape Ethnography in West Africa and the Anthropology of 'Events.'" *Anthropological Quarterly* 78 (2): 315–327.

Hofstra, Warren R. 1998. "'The Extention of His Majesties Dominions': The Virginia Backcountry and the Reconfiguration of Imperial Frontiers." *Journal of American History* 84 (4): 1281–1312.

Hume, Mo. 2008. "The Myths of Violence: Gender, Conflict, and Community in El Salvador." *Latin American Perspectives* 35 (5): 59–76.

Hurt, R. Douglas. 1996. *The Ohio Frontier: Crucible of the Old Northwest, 1720–1830*. Bloomington: Indiana University Press.

Jackman, Mary R. 2002. "Violence in Social Life." *Annual Review of Sociology* 28: 387–415.

Jenkins, Janis H. 1998. "The Medical Anthropology of Political Violence: A Cultural and Feminist Agenda." *Medical Anthropology Quarterly* 12 (1): 122–131.

Johnson, Matthew. 2007. *Ideas of Landscape*. Oxford, UK: Blackwell.

Keener, Craig S. 1999. "An Ethnohistorical Analysis of Iroquois Assault Tactics Used against Fortified Settlements of the Northeast in the Seventeenth Century." *Ethnohistory* 46 (4): 777–807.

Kellogg, Louise Phelps, ed. 1916. *Frontier Advance on the Upper Ohio 1778–1779*. Madison: State Historical Society of Wisconsin.

Knouff, Gregory T. 1994. "'An Arduous Service': The Pennsylvania Backcountry Soldiers' Revolution." *Pennsylvania History* 62: 45–74.

Kolodny, Annette. 1993. "Among the Indians: The Uses of Captivity." *Women's Studies Quarterly* 21 (3–4): 184–195.

Korbin, Jill E. 2003. "Children, Childhoods, and Violence." *Annual Review of Anthropology* 32: 431–446.

Krohn-Hansen, Christian. 1994. "The Anthropology of Violent Interaction." *Journal of Anthropological Research* 50 (4): 367–381.

Kruer, Matthew. 2017. "Bloody Minds and Peoples Undone: Emotion, Family, and Political Order in the Susquehannock-Virginia War." *William and Mary Quarterly* 74 (3): 401–436.

Lahiri, Nayanjot. 2003. "Commemorating and Remembering 1857: The Revolt in Delhi and Its Afterlife." *World Archaeology* 35 (1): 35–60.

Lee, Wayne E. 2007. "Peace Chiefs and Blood Revenge: Patterns of Restraint in Native American Warfare, 1500–1800." *Journal of Military History* 71 (3): 701–741.

Lekson, Stephen H. 2002. "War in the Southwest, War in the World." *American Antiquity* 67 (4): 607–624.

Liston, Maria A., and Brenda J. Baker. 1996. "Reconstructing the Massacre at Fort William Henry, New York." *International Journal of Osteoarchaeology* 6: 28–41.

Lowell, Julia C. 2007. "Women and Men in Warfare and Migration: Implications of Gender Imbalance in the Grasshopper Region of Arizona." *American Antiquity* 72 (1): 95–123.

Lubkemann, Stephen C. 2005. "Migratory Coping in Wartime Mozambique: An Anthropology of Violence and Displacement in 'Fragmented Wars.'" *Journal of Peace Research* 42 (4): 493–508.

MacGaffey, Wyatt. 2000. "Aesthetics and Politics of Violence in Central Africa." *Journal of African Cultural Studies* 13 (1): 63–75.

Mahon, John K. 1958. "Anglo-American Methods of Indian Warfare, 1676–1794." *Mississippi Valley Historical Review* 45 (2): 254–275.

Martin, James Kirby. 1971. "The Return of the Paxton Boys and the Historical State of the Pennsylvania Frontier, 1764–1774." *Pennsylvania History: A Journal of Mid-Atlantic Studies* 38 (2): 117–133.

Milner, George R. 1999. "Warfare in Prehistoric and Early Historic Eastern North America." *Journal of Archaeological Research* 7 (2): 105–151.

———. 2005. "Nineteenth-Century Arrow Wounds and Perceptions of Prehistoric Warfare." *American Antiquity* 70 (1): 144–156.

Mitchener, C. H. 1876. *Historic Events in the Tuscawaras and Muskingum Valleys, and in Other Portions of the State of Ohio.* Dayton, OH: Thomas W. Odell.

Myers, James P., Jr. 1999. "Mapping Pennsylvania's Western Frontier in 1756." *The Pennsylvania Magazine of History and Biography* 123 (1–2): 3–29.

Novak, Shannon A., and Derinna Kopp. 2003. "To Feed a Tree in Zion: Osteological Analysis of the 1857 Mountain Meadows Massacre." *Historical Archaeology* 37 (2): 85–108.

Otterbein, Keith F. 1979. "Huron vs. Iroquois: A Case Study in Inter-Tribal Warfare." *Ethnohistory* 26 (2): 141–152.

———. 1999. "A History of Research on Warfare in Anthropology." *American Anthropologist* 101 (4): 794–805.

Ousterhout, Anne M. 1993. "Frontier Vengeance: Connecticut Yankees vs. Pennamites in the Wyoming Valley." *Pennsylvania History* 62 (3): 330–363.

Pansing, Linda. 2007. "Fort Laurens Musket Ball Concentration: Evidence of a Fight or Fiasco?" *Ohio Archaeological Council Newsletter* (December): 1–2.

Parker, Bradley J. 2006. "Toward an Understanding of Borderland Processes." *American Antiquity* 71 (1): 77–100.

Parmenter, Jon. 2007. "After the Mourning Wars: The Iroquois as Allies in Colonial North American Campaigns, 1676–1760." *William and Mary Quarterly* 64 (1): 39–76.

Peck, William F. 1908. *History of Rochester and Monroe County, New York, from the Earliest Times to the Beginning of 1907.* Chicago, IL: Pioneer Publishing Company.

Perdue, Theda. 1995. "Women, Men and American Indian Policy: The Cherokee Response to 'Civilization.'" In *Negotiators of Change: Historical Perspectives on Native American Women,* edited by Nancy Shoemaker, 90–114. New York: Routledge.

Pieper, Thomas I., and James B. Gidney. 1976. *Fort Laurens, 1778–1779: The Revolutionary War in Ohio.* Kent, OH: Kent State University Press.

Pike, Ivy L., Bilinda Straight, Matthias Oesterle, Charles Hilton, and Adamson Lanyasunya. 2010. "Documenting the Health Consequences of Endemic Warfare in Three Pastoralist Communities of Northern Kenya: A Conceptual Framework." *Social Science & Medicine* 70: 45–52.

Reid, Darren. 2008. "Soldiers of Settlement: Violence and Psychological Warfare on the Kentucky Frontier, 1775–1783." *Eras* 10: 1–20.

Rice, Connie Park. 2008. "Letters from William Haymond to His Nephew, Luther Haymond, Recalling the Settlement of Western Virginia and Conflict with Native Americans between 1773 and 1794." *West Virginia History: A Journal of Regional Studies* 2 (2): 79–98.

Riches, David. 1991. "Aggression, War, Violence: Space/Time and Paradigm." *Man* 26 (2): 281–297.

Richter, Daniel K. 1983. "War and Culture: The Iroquois Experience." *William and Mary Quarterly* 40 (4): 528–559.

———. 1985. "Iroquois versus Iroquois: Jesuit Missions and Christianity in Village Politics, 1642–1686." *Ethnohistory* 32 (1): 1–16.

Sandberg, Brian. 2006. "Beyond Encounters: Religion, Ethnicity, and Violence in the Early Modern Atlantic World, 1492–1700." *Journal of World History* 17 (1): 1–25.

Sempowski, Martha L., Lorraine P. Saunders, Kathleen M. S. Allen, Annette W. Nohe, Gene Mackay, Ralph Brown, and Dale Knapp. 2001. *Dutch Hollow and Factory Hollow: The Advent of Dutch Trade among the Seneca.* Part 1. Charles F. Wray Series in Seneca Archaeology. Rochester, NY: Collections Dept. of the Rochester Museum and Science Center.

Schein, Richard H. 1997. "The Place of Landscape: A Conceptual Framework for Interpreting an American Scene." *Annals of the Association of American Geographers* 87 (4): 660–680.

Scheper-Hughes, Nancy, and Philippe I. Bourgois. 2003. *Violence in War and Peace: An Anthology.* Hoboken, NJ: Blackwell.

Sciulli, Paul W., and Richard M. Gramly. 1989. "Analysis of the Ft. Laurens, Ohio Skeletal Sample." *American Journal of Physical Anthropology* 80: 11–24.

Seaver, James E. 1918. *A Narrative of the Life of Mary Jemison.* Canandaigua, NY: J. D. Bemis and Company.

Seeman, Erik R. 2011. "Teaching the History of Death in Colonial North America." *OAH Magazine of History* 25 (1): 31–34.

Sharfstein, Daniel J. 2012. "Atrocity, Entitlement, and Personhood in Property." *Virginia Law Review* 98 (3): 635–690.

Snead, James E. 2011. "The 'Secret and Bloody War Path': Movement, Place and Conflict in the Archaeological Landscape of North America." *World Archaeology* 43 (3): 478–492.

Staudigl, Michael. 2007. "Towards a Phenomenological Theory of Violence: Reflections following Merleau-Ponty and Schutz." *Human Studies* 30 (3): 233–253.

Sundar, Nandini. 2004. "Toward an Anthropology of Culpability." *American Ethnologist* 31 (2): 145–163.

Sutterlüty, Ferdinand, and Adam Blauhut. 2007. "The Genesis of Violent Careers." *Ethnography* 8 (3): 267–296.

Tarlow, Sarah. 2012. "The Archaeology of Emotion and Affect." *Annual Review of Anthropology* 41:169–185.

Taylor, Alan. 1993. "Agrarian Independence: Northern Land Rioters after the Revolution." In *Beyond the American Revolution: Explorations in the History of American Radicalism,* edited by Alfred Fabian Young, 200–226. DeKalb: Northern Illinois University Press.

Thorpe, I. J. N. 2003. "Anthropology, Archaeology, and the Origin of Warfare." *World Archaeology* 35 (1): 145–165.

Traphagan, John W. 2008. "Embodiment, Ritual Incorporation, and Cannibalism among the Iroquoians after 1300 C.E." *Journal of Ritual Studies* 22 (2): 1–12.

Viele, Egbert. 1882. "The Frontiers of the United States." *Journal of the American Geographical Society of New York* 14: 166–204.

Walker, Philip L. 2001. "A Bioarchaeological Perspective on the History of Violence." *Annual Review of Anthropology* 30: 573–596.

Ward, Matthew C. 1995. "Fighting the 'Old Women': Indian Strategy on the Virginia and Pennsylvania Frontier, 1754–1758." *Virginia Magazine of History and Biography* 103 (3): 297–320.

Whittenburg, James P. 1977. "Planters, Merchants, and Lawyers: Social Change and the Origins of the North Carolina Regulation." *William and Mary Quarterly* 34 (2): 215–238.

Williams, Walter L. 1980. "United States Indian Policy and the Debate over Philippine Annexation: Implications for the Origins of American Imperialism." *Journal of American History* 66 (4): 800–816.

Williamson, Matthew A., Cheryl A. Johnston, Steven A. Symes, and John J. Schultz. 2003. "Interpersonal Violence between 18th Century Native Americans and Europeans in Ohio." *American Journal of Physical Anthropology* 122: 113–122.

Williamson, Ronald F. 2007. "'*Otinontsiskiaj ondaon*'—'The House of Cut-Off Heads': The History and Archaeology of Northern Iroquoian Trophy-Taking." In *The Taking and Displaying of Human Body Parts as Trophies by Amerindians,* edited by Richard J. Chacon and David H. Dye, 1–47. New York: Springer.

Withers, Alexander. 1895. *Chronicles of Border Warfare.* Glendale, CA: Arthur H. Clark Company.

Wray, Charles F., Martha L. Sempowski, Lorraine P. Saunders, Gian Carlo Cervone, and Patricia L. Miller. 1991. *Tram and Cameron: Two Early Contact Era Seneca Sites.*

Charles F. Wray Series in Seneca Archaeology. Rochester, NY: Rochester Museum and Science Center.

Wurst, LouAnn, and Stephen A. Mrozowski. 2014. "Toward an Archaeology of the Future." *International Journal of Historical Archaeology* 18 (2): 210–223.

Zechenter, Elizabeth M. 1997. "In the Name of Culture: Cultural Relativism and the Abuse of the Individual." *Journal of Anthropological Research* 53 (3): 319–347.

4

The Archaeology of Recovery in the Golden Triangle of Mali

Salvage Archaeology following Jihadist Occupation

DAOUDA KEITA, MOUSSA DIT MARTIN TESSOUGUE,
AND YAMOUSSA FANE

In 2012, Mali experienced a crisis from which it is trying to recover. The northern portion of the country was occupied by armed jihadists who preached a radicalized form of Sharia. Among the many crises the occupation inflicted was damage to the cultural heritage of the region. Timbuktu, a renowned medieval city of higher learning, was particularly targeted, as were hundreds of archaeological and heritage sites located in the region. The jihadists destroyed archaeological sites, buildings, mausoleums, and manuscripts. As a result of this occupation and the destruction of cultural heritage, tourism has been greatly affected in Mali. The chapter focuses on collaborations among Malian scholars and UNESCO to document the destruction and analyzes the mechanisms that have been instituted to sustainably manage endangered cultural heritage in the region.

Introduction

Mali, which celebrated the fiftieth anniversary of its independence in 2010, became the scene of a major international crisis in 2012. Armed jihadists invaded and occupied the northern regions of Mali, including the ancient city of Timbuktu. The situation worsened when a coup d'état of the Malian government on March 22, 2012, plunged the country into an unprecedented political, social, and economic situation. The jihadists' destruction of material culture and their desire to institute Sharia had a major impact on tourism in the Djenné-Bandiagara-Timbuktu region, also known as the Golden Triangle of tourism. Because the jihadists targeted the economic resources of the region for destruction, the occupation went beyond a security and government crises. Widespread insecurity has led to a suspension of tourism, a vital sector for the local economy, and a halting of scholarship in the region as European and American governments have forbidden their citizens to travel there.

The jihadists occupied northern Mali until January 2013, when an international military operation freed the region. That same year, the Malian government, in collaboration with UNESCO, drew up the "Action Plan for the Rehabilitation of Damaged Cultural Heritage and the Implementation of Measures to Safeguard Timbuktu Manuscripts." The aim of this plan was to inventory the cultural heritage that was destroyed during the occupation and to offer recommendations for future preservation.

Methodology

The action plan used the methodologies of field surveys, literature reviews, and documentation conducted by preservation teams. The literature reviews focused on works that describe the cultural heritage in the region. This phase helped provide historical and cultural context for the next stages of the plan. Another part of our research focused on the geopolitics and cultural diversity of the region as a way of better understanding the varied meanings assigned to archaeology and heritage sites. This phase was particularly important because the rich cultural and ethnic diversity of the region, specifically at Timbuktu, was a primary reason for the jihadists' occupation. Finally, we consulted the site reports of the National Directorate of Cultural Heritage and the National Directorate of Tourism and Hotels and the reports UNESCO had commissioned in Mali. This phase helped our team understand the myriad ways that the jihadi destruction was influencing not just heritage sites but also the local economy and everyday lives of people in the region.

For the stages of field observations and documentation, the Ministry of Culture mobilized our technical team to assess the extent of the damage to the material culture of Timbuktu. Our team's first directive was to research sacred mausoleums that the jihadists had targeted. As a result of our reporting on the situation in Timbuktu, the Ministry of Culture commissioned us to conduct further work elsewhere in the Golden Triangle. Our goal was to create an inventory of material culture that was destroyed in the larger region, including identifying archaeological sites that had been looted during the occupation. However, this chapter focuses primarily on the destruction that took place at the archaeological and heritage sites of Timbuktu.

The Destruction of Heritage

According to the jihadists, they destroyed material culture and heritage sites in the region because they viewed any veneration or memorial as unfaithful to their dogmatic view of Islam. They saw sites such as mausoleums as glorifying or sanctifying an individual, which they considered to be sacrilege. The presence of sacred sites in the region is one of the main reasons that the jihadists sought to challenge the practice of Islam in Mali that they considered impure (Keita et al. 2017) by persecuting people and destroying sites. Fourteen mausoleums (Table 4.1) and the door of the Sidi Yahia mosque, all of which are on UNESCO's World Heritage List, were vandalized and/or destroyed. From the ninth to the nineteenth century, Timbuktu, known as the city of 333 Saints, has been home to residents who have been extolled as leaders in the community because of their knowledge of Islamic studies and/or their piety. At the time of their death, these faithful were buried and elevated to the title of "Saint." Saints are supposed to be intermediaries between Allah and the present world. In order to preserve the memory of these Saints, their places of burial were covered by mausoleums and consecrated as sanctified spaces.

The mausoleums are ancient earthen constructions of various forms, often covered with stones. According to local tradition, residents believe that these sacred sites offer the city protection against misfortune (Keita et al. 2018). Some mausoleums have only one burial, while others have several. In many cases, several burials of "apostles," or faithful followers of the Saints, surround the mausoleums. These burial sites are found throughout the city, in streets, near mosques, in private homes, and even on a military base (Keita et al. 2017). Additionally, the mausoleums showcase the cultural diversity and religious history of the city. Among the honored deceased are people who belonged to Songhoy, Arab, and Fulani ethnic groups of the region, underscoring the significance of the city as a sacred place to a variety of peoples.

The jihadists specifically targeted these sacred sites as a means of terrorizing and demoralizing the city's residents. Their justification for this destruction was that these sites and their associated artifacts were blasphemy.

Table 4.1. Dates Timbuktu mausoleums were destroyed

DATE OF DESTRUCTION: JUNE 30–JULY 1, 2012
Sheik Sidi Mahmoud
Sheik Sidi El Moktar el Kounti
Sheik Alpha Moya
Sheik Sidi Amar ben Amar
Sheik Sidi Mohamed el Miky
DATE OF DESTRUCTION: JULY 10, 2012
Sheik Baber Baba Idjié
Sheik Mahamane Al Fullani
Sheik Mahamane Tamba Tamba
DATE OF DESTRUCTION: OCTOBER 18, 2012
Sheik Nou
Sheik Ousmane El Bekir
Sheik Mohamed el Fulani al Macina
DATE OF DESTRUCTION: DECEMBER 23, 2012
Sheik Mahamane Askia
Sheik Sidi Mohamed Boukko
Taleb Abdallah and his disciple

Within their world view, venerating and memorializing anyone other than Allah is an idolatrous, unholy act. The vandalism of mausoleums typically entailed the use of sledgehammers and/or blunt weapons (Keita et al. 2018). The jihadists destroyed sacred sites for reasons that went beyond their radicalized world view. At a deeper level, they performed these acts to erase the history, heritage, and cultural diversity of the region. Through doing so, jihadists sought to replace the varied pasts of Timbuktu with a dogmatic, homogenized, singular narrative that promoted the jihadi mission; they wanted the region to submit to their interpretation of Islam.

The erasure of history and heritage was not limited to the destruction or mausoleums. The jihadists also burned thousands of historic documents. Timbuktu was renowned as a university city until the Moroccan invasion of the sixteenth century. The city hosted one of the most comprehensive library collections in the medieval world. While many of these collections have been lost or destroyed through the centuries, an assortment of manuscripts remained pertaining to Islamic studies, science, mathematics, and philosophy. From 2012 to 2013, jihadists burned some 4,203 manuscripts that belonged to the Ahmed Baba Institute of Higher Learning and Islamic Research (IHERI-AB). Thankfully, the Association for the Protection and

Promotion of Manuscripts and the Defense of Islamic Culture (SAVAMA-DCI) moved an estimated 370,000 manuscripts to the Bamako region for safekeeping before the jihadi threat. Nevertheless, the cultural heritage of Timbuktu has been so seriously affected that the entire city was put on the List of World Heritage in Danger in 2012 (Keita et al. 20187).

Tourism and Terrorism

Heritage tourism has long been one of the main industries of Mali and Timbuktu is of particular interest for tourists. According to statistics collected from Mali's Office of Tourism and Hospitality and the National Directorate of Tourism and Hospitality; the number of international tourist arrivals to the country in 2011 was slightly less than 200,000. In 2012, the number of tourists dropped to below 50,000, and in 2015, it was only 35,000 (Tessougué et al. 2016; OMATHO 2015). The tourist industry in Timbuktu has been decimated. Hotels, restaurants and other businesses that cater to tourists have closed, leading to high unemployment rates in the region. Additionally, due to a mixture of poverty and the breakdown of the Malian government's ability to protect cultural resources during and immediately after the jihadi occupation, several of the archaeological sites in the region were looted and their artifacts were apparently sold on the black market.

Strategies for Rehabilitating Damaged Cultural Heritage

Before the mausoleums in Timbuktu were reconstructed, our team documented and photographed evidence of the destruction inflicted during the occupation. This plan included help from UNESCO and from the National Directorate of Cultural Heritage, in partnership with its technical and financial partners. Our action plan included:

Establishing a national committee for reconstructing damaged material heritage in northern Mali that was charged with drawing up a national plan and coordinating the reconstruction and rehabilitation efforts.

Creating a technical unit to supervise and document all activities of reconstruction.

Holding a national seminar on the protection of World Heritage sites in Mali.

Holding a workshop on strategies for documenting and rebuilding mausoleums and other damaged sites.

The second phase of the action plan relates to the implementation of fieldwork, including

Documenting the damage incurred at each site and making architectural surveys of the mausoleums.

Excavating the mausoleums so we can understand the building techniques used in construction in order to ensure that reconstructions are as close to the original as possible.

Finally, begin reconstructing the mausoleums and other affected sites.

The results of this two-phased action plan are still being fully assessed. Here we offer some details about the documentation, excavation, and interpretation drawn from archaeological fieldwork at Timbuktu.

Excavations were carried out at eight mausoleums. Investigations of the mausoleums have found that the walls consist of several layers with thicknesses that range from 0.5 to 1.5 meters. These different layers are the result of additions made during regular maintenance over the course of centuries. The additions, which were intended to buttress an original wall, sometimes changed the initial architectural form so that some mausoleums took on a pyramidal appearance This was the case at the Alpha Moya mausoleum.

To identify the original wall, a cross-section was made during excavation. The original wall was made with two types of bricks, *kamba ferey* (handmade bricks) and *kohira ferey* (bricks of the city), which were locally produced. These mud bricks were made by hand and were of varying dimensions and oblong shapes. During a second phase of construction, other materials were used as facings to reinforce the walls, including bricks made of limestone (*alhor*) that was quarried not far from Timbuktu. Being able to identify the two phases of construction helped us develop an action plan for reconstruction (Keita et al. 2017). However, given the extent of the destruction and continued security concerns in the region, we have yet to initiate a full reconstruction plan.

The damage to Mali's cultural heritage is reprehensible. Beyond the act of destroying heritage sites, the jihadists also desired to desecrate the spirits of the dead and demoralize the living. Their vandalism of heritage was meant to erase the history of religious tolerance and cultural diversity in Timbuktu.

Figure 4.1. Reclaimed beads that were looted during the occupation. Photo by Daouda Keita, 2015.

The looting of archaeological sites and the illegal sale of cultural property is another developing crisis in the region. In the time leading up to the jihadi occupation and during and after that event, a number of sites were pillaged. Some looters were emboldened by the absence of government protection at sites. Given the decimation of the local economy due to a lack of tourism, looters likely used the money from the sale of pillaged artifacts to support their families in times of desperation. This is a sad reality in places that are affected by security and economic concerns. The return of peace and the stabilization of the economy should mean that there is no longer a shred of a reason to justify the looting and sale of cultural heritage artifacts on the black market (Keita et al. 2018).

However, the illegal trade continues in Timbuktu. Without the participation of local people, protecting heritage sites and fighting against the trafficking of material culture will continue to be issues. In order to limit the continued looting, the government, local peoples, and archaeologists need to collaborate. This would require the involvement of residents in supervising, managing, and preserving their own cultural heritage. Consideration should be given to the development of a substantial awareness program, the regular monitoring of this program, the dissemination of laws

Figure 4.2. Reclaimed artifacts that were looted during the occupation. Photo by Daouda Keita, 2015.

and regulations governing cultural heritage, and, finally, the creation of relay structures and training of their members.

Conclusion

Now that relative peace has returned, some tourists are coming back to the country, repairs to sites and monuments have commenced, and archaeological research programs have slowly resumed in Timbuktu, but more could always be done. In times of conflict, cultural heritage always suffers damage, whether it is done intentionally or unintentionally. These losses are detrimental to the local, national, and international community. Cultural property embodies the social, cultural, and historical values that characterize our societies. Heritage and heritage sites tell us where we came from and who we are. War, economic, and political insecurities adversely affect the past, the present, and the future—so much so that histories and heritage can be erased. Thus, safeguarding measures should be taken before, during, and after conflicts to minimize damage to heritage sites. This involves the participation of all parties concerned, including local, national, and international communities. Local communities in particular must play

locals

an important role in this process as they are the ones on the ground that can make the most meaningful impacts. Protecting human life should always be the top priority, but when local communities and archaeologists are in safe conditions, they should seek to protect heritage sites. Although it is often impossible to protect heritage without the threat of losing one's life during wartime and violent occupations, local communities and local archaeologists should make efforts to limit postwar destruction and looting to the best of their ability. The crisis in Mali underscores the need for a socially conscious archaeology that works on multiple levels locally, nationally, and internationally to quickly—and safely—record, preserve, and rehabilitate heritage sites that are adversely affected by conflict. For without heritage, we lose what we are fighting for.

References Cited

Keita, D., M. M. Tessougue, and Y. Fane. 2018. "Patrimoine culturel malien sabordé au nom d'un islam puritain." *Annales de l'Université de Ouaga I Prof. Joseph KI-ZERBO.* Série A, vol. 25: 1–27.

Keita, D., M. M. Tessougue, and Y. Fane. 2017. "Menaces des conflits armés sur le patrimoine: Cas de l'occupation djihadiste de la ville de Tombouctou." *Revue Ivoirienne de Géographie des Savanes* 3 (December): 225–251.

OMATHO. 2015. *Analyse quantitative des données statistiques sur le tourisme au Mali: Annuaire 2014.* Bamako, Mali: Ministère de l'artisanat et du tourisme, Office malien du tourisme et de l'hôtellerie (OMATHO).

Tessougue, M. M., and D. Keita. 2016. "Instabilité géopolitique au Sahel et crise du secteur touristique au Mali." *Cahiers du CBRST* 9 (June): 422–433.

Mexico

5

Heritage Activism
in Quintana Roo, Mexico

Assembling New Futures
through an Umbrella Heritage Practice

TIFFANY C. FRYER AND KASEY DISERENS MORGAN

The Tihosuco Heritage Preservation and Community Development Project (hereafter Tihosuco Project) works to combat economic and social inequalities through multimodal approaches to heritage, including the creation of community-organized initiatives related to identity, the economy, and the future (Leventhal et al. 2014). The continued legacy of the Caste War of Yucatan (or Maya Social War, 1847–1901) anchors the project's collaborative work in the town of Tihosuco, Quintana Roo, Mexico. Although the Caste War was arguably one of the most successful anticolonial indigenous insurrections in the Americas (Bricker 1984, 88), it remains largely absent from national and (to some extent) regional historical narratives. The war began in the nineteenth century parish of Tihosuco, a southern frontier region of the Yucatan Peninsula, and persisted in various forms for at least fifty-four years. Although the war itself will not be the focus of this chapter, it is important to bear in mind that it permanently altered the geopolitical landscape of the Yucatan Peninsula. A major consequence was the creation of the Mexican state of Quintana Roo. The reflections we offer here have emerged from over seven years of partnership with Tihosuqueños (residents of Tihosuco).

Our project advocates an umbrella heritage model that pushes beyond conventional archaeology by recognizing the centrality of both colonialism and modern globalization for how communities—in this case

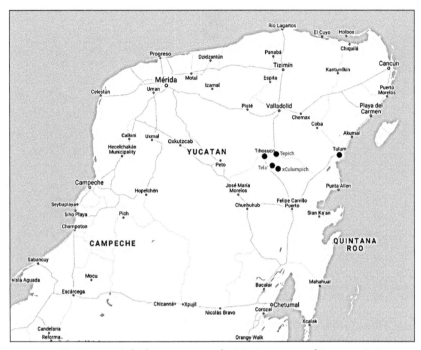

Figure 5.1. The Yucatan (which encompasses the Mexican states of Yucatan, Quintana Roo, and Campeche), showing key locations mentioned in chapter. Map by Tiffany C. Fryer.

predominantly Yukatek Maya–speaking communities across Quintana Roo—negotiate and assert their collective identities and agendas. "Umbrella" here refers to the overarching structure of the heritage initiative and the integrated approach to what are typically considered disparate forms of heritage practice (e.g., archaeology, museum development, oral histories). Contemporary politics are not, as some have implied (Stump 2013), an ancillary concern for archaeological heritage practice. Rather, incorporating our activist agendas and multimodal thinking in our research designs ultimately enriches both the overall quality of the archaeological research and the value of that research to particular communities. Our umbrella heritage model uses grassroots initiatives that use wide-ranging methods, engage a multiplicity of heritage narratives, and exercise a self-representative process of heritage management. We place our work in the context of heritage and tourism in the Yucatan Peninsula more broadly, as tourism is increasingly intertwined with and commodified by the heritage industry.

We begin with an overview of the current state of affairs regarding tourism, heritage management, and Maya self-representation in the Yucatan. We then offer an analysis of two heritage assemblages that are connected by their roles in the narratives surrounding settler colonialism and the Caste War in the area. We use the concept of assemblage to break down the methodological and temporal barriers that often undergird heritage projects. The first assemblage we address consists of the colonial-era structures in the town center of Tihosuco. We focus on how the regulations that govern the preservation of these structures complicate their status as heritage assets. The second assemblage zooms out to think about how documenting the historic properties located outside town on Tihosuco's ejido (federally recognized land commune) has provided another complex but potentially promising resource for the community. Finally, we reflect on how attention to these assemblages can shift our practices away from heritage management toward heritage activism that bolsters the effectiveness of past-centered research in marginalized communities such as Tihosuco, whose members face very real, present-day problems. We both began working with the Tihosuco Project as graduate students, and we seek to encourage and train junior scholars who want to advance an activist anthropology for the future (Hale 2007; Atalay, Clauss, McGuire, and Welch 2014; Berry et al. 2017).

Although our arguments are specific to Tihosuco and the conditions we work in, the examples we highlight here will likely resonate with others working under similar circumstances. We hope that what we discuss will provoke self-reflection about the potential for broad-reaching heritage programs to create spaces from which effective change—however fragile—may develop.

Heritage, Tourism, and Maya Self-Representation

In Mexico, the forces of the global tourism industry situate heritage and culture as exploitable commodities. Tourism is one of the largest industries in Mexico, second only to agriculture (Ely 2013). The processes of heritage management and tourism in Mexico are highly regulated and top heavy. Government programs and private agencies set the terms and tone of heritage discourse, especially with respect to the management of historical landscapes and archaeological sites (Clark and Anderson 2015).

Although tourism to the Yucatan Peninsula is dominated by beach vacationing and ecoparks, heritage tourism is a significant secondary draw. Cultural tourists, as the industry calls them, are thought to be seeking novel experiences that will facilitate a deeper connection with a culture that is not their own (McKercher and du Cros 2002). Heritage destinations that target cultural tourists include historic cities, museums, towns, and archaeological sites (Visit Mexico 2018). Sites such as the ruins at Chichen Itza, Coba, and Ek Balam draw millions of foreign and domestic tourists annually. For example, the town and archaeological park of Tulum, a main attraction in Quintana Roo's coastal "Riviera Maya," grew from around 3,000 residents in 1995 to 28,000 in 2010. In 2016, they received over 738,000 tourists (Instituto Nacional de Estadística y Geografía 2010; Secretaría de Turismo del Estado de Quintana Roo 2017). Ana Juárez (2002) concluded that the shift toward an economy based largely on tourism in Tulum limited the amount of control that local, primarily indigenous residents have over economic and environmental resources which has increased both distributive and social inequalities. She noted that this increase also contributes to the loss of Maya cultural autonomy in Mexico. For instance, the spike in Tulum's population severely disrupted customary fishing and swidden agricultural practices. The residents of Tulum whose families have been there for generations (they reoccupied the site during the Caste War) shifted to larger-scale farming and ranching to support the growth in their town and the resort areas surrounding it. Job seekers in places such as Tihosuco must move closer to these new tourism centers or must be bussed in and out for fifteen-hour workdays. This can disrupt familial structures and local economies (though it may also open opportunities for already marginalized groups such as single mothers). The forces of global capitalism that are bound up in the development of transnational tourism are quickly transforming social relations across the peninsula (Re Cruz 1996; Castañeda 2009; Castellanos 2010; Wynne 2015; Taylor 2018).

In order to streamline the rapidly expanding cultural tourism industry, private and government agencies seek to present a standardized, consistent, and thereby static past as their primary cultural product (Castañeda 1996). The industry seems perfectly content to misrepresent Maya heritage as a relic of a lost culture (Ardren 2004; Torres and Momsen 2005). Limited value gets placed on how the peninsula's majority-Maya communities want to represent themselves (cf. Hawn and Tison 2015). Instead, cultural promoters emphasize a palatable, exotic, homogenized culture that can be packaged, marketed, and eventually sold to tourists (Castañeda 2004; Taylor 2009; Little 2004).

Heritage certainly has consequences outside the realm of tourism. Across Mexico, there are several often-competing frameworks for protecting historical and/or archaeological sites. Principal among these are the rules set by the Instituto Nacional de Arqueología e Historia (INAH) under federal law. Other frameworks operate at different scales: at UNESCO World Heritage sites, in national archaeological parks, on smaller-scale archaeological and ecological reserves, and through Pueblos Magicos ("magic towns," a brand used to promote and link sites around the country). Multiple entities may vie for the right to own and manage these sites, their objects, their histories, and the economic opportunities they bring. Like the cultural tourism industry, the heritage conservation industry only grudgingly includes local indigenous communities in decisions made about heritage management plans (Breglia 2006).

Like other indigenous groups across the Americas, Maya communities continue to face estrangement from their pasts and their cultural practices by the processes of colonialism and modern state making (McAnany and Parks 2012). Archaeologists have played and continue to play a significant role in this estrangement (Vázquez León 2003; Watkins 2005; Bueno 2016). In the Yucatan, the relationships between archaeologists and indigenous communities are often acknowledged as contentious or ambivalent (Castañeda 1996; Juárez 2002; Breglia 2006; Magnoni, Ardren, and Hutson 2007; Armstrong-Fumero 2009), but in our experience are rarely construed as positive or substantively beneficial to the community (cf. Ardren 2002; Hutson, Can Herrera, and Chi 2014). This subpar relationship exists at least in part because "while [anthropological] scholars have long found Maya cultures worthy of attention, their agendas, and conclusions have not always coincided with current Maya politics and priorities" (Watanabe 1995, 33). Under the pressure "to be considered 'authentic Maya,'" people find themselves in a complicated web of relationships that values the "the real Mayas of the past" while disavowing, dehumanizing, and devaluing present-day Maya peoples (Cojti Ren 2006, 12). Archaeologists and other Mayanist scholars may undertake research that meets the standards of their professional organizations, but many remain deeply out of touch with the current needs of the communities they work with (or—more often—who work for them). In turn, these practices feed into a system that perpetuates unjust racial geographies characterized by historically embedded social hierarchies and paternalism (Saldaña-Portillo 2016).

A social activism agenda in Maya archaeology, then, requires that practitioners exercise epistemic deference, by which we mean the humility to understand that researchers' self-perceived expertise is unlikely to be exclusive or more relevant in the contexts they find themselves in. Epistemic deference is necessary for effectively decentering non-Maya researchers' independently designed agendas and making space for collaborative research decisions made in concert with their community partners (who are researchers in their own right). We support practicing what Llanes-Ortiz (2019, 178) outlines as the Yukatek Maya notion of "e'esaj-ing," or "showing, demonstrating, and partnering in," a given task—in this case, collaboratively designed research agendas. E'esaj is an orientation toward learning and cooperation that maintains open dialogue in the partnerships we seek to construct. We applaud programs such as the well-known Maya Area Cultural Heritage Initiative (MACHI) that are beginning to change the frameworks of Maya archaeology by adopting "an activist stance in reference to mitigating the rapid destruction of archaeological heritage in the Maya region and addressing the centuries-old pattern of heritage distancing" (McAnany and Parks 2012, 85). These initiatives are still too rare. Moreover, they tend to emerge as an afterthought to the priority that archaeological research objectives take at these sites. Indeed, these shifts frequently result from what archaeologists recognize as a threat to the archaeological record rather than the belief that one can both practice archaeology in an academically rigorous way and work alongside communities to address local social justice concerns. As McAnany (2016, 101) notes about the successful Maya Area Cultural Heritage Initiative, "I was concerned about social justice intellectually but at the time did not feel compelled to link that concern with the practice of archaeology—a space within which I sense many of my colleagues dwell today." The foundations archaeologists and heritage professionals who received conventional training but continue to seek more from their work have set enable us to alter the ways we design our research agendas. Instead of treating local social concerns as auxiliary, we may begin incorporating more equitable practices such as sharing power and epistemic deference in our research aims.

The Tihosuco Heritage Preservation and Community Development Project

A primary aim of the Tihosuco Project has been to take seriously the interests members of the Tihosuco community express. The idea is simple: when confronted by neocolonial practices such as the mega-tourist industry in Quintana Roo (Scher 2011), communities such as Tihosuco might be able to use localized heritage practices to subvert repression and design a more desirable future for themselves, based in part on tourism but set on their own terms. Determining who we call "the community" in any collaborative project can be difficult and is usually far less static than is suggested by the way scholars may sometimes talk about it (Agbe-Davies 2010; Crooke 2010). In our case, we began by identifying the community with members of three local representative bodies: the ejido, the *alcaldía* (mayor's office), and El Museo de la Guerra de Castas (a state-funded, locally run Caste War Museum). As the project has grown, the community has expanded beyond these initial gateway organizations to include a broader group of interested Tihosuqueños. Together with researchers from the University of Pennsylvania's Penn Cultural Heritage Center, the members of the Tihosuco Project have developed a grassroots initiative centered on a localized Maya heritage that departs from, although it does not ignore, the more common emphasis on the precolonial past encountered in heritage and cultural tourism work across the peninsula.

The Tihosuco Project combines multiple subprojects that highlight a variety of approaches to co-creating heritage, each of which is in some way linked to the town's involvement in the Caste War (Diserens Morgan and Leventhal 2020). We see this blending of subprograms as forming the necessary spokes for an activist, engaged, unashamedly political umbrella heritage project. Together, we study the history and legacy of the Caste War as an anticolonial movement through archaeology and historic preservation. We focus on the material remains of the towns, haciendas, ranches, houses, churches, and convent associated with Tihosuco from roughly the eighteenth to the twentieth centuries. Additionally, we engage the more recent history of Tihosuco's postwar repopulation through oral histories, museum development, archival exploration, the reclamation of Yukatek Maya language among Tihosuco's youth (including the production of a bilingual comic book series), the digital archiving of the community's historic photos and documents, and a biographical portrait project. Through our collaborative work, we seek not only to understand the history of the war but also to help Tihosuqueños tell their history to outsiders in a way that reflects their experiences. By doing so, we celebrate the power of self-representation in a heritage economy that would prefer to market a standardized historical narrative that is more aligned with the essentialized tropes of Mayaness that pervade it.

The story of the Caste War is one that in both its proclamations and silences constructs both identity and contemporary sociopolitical consciousness across the peninsula. Nonetheless, the pride and solemnity that is connected to the history of Maya oppression and resistance, as exemplified by the war, is readily apparent in towns such as Tihosuco (although that history is more nuanced than its description as "Maya" is able to capture; Gabbert 2019). Annual commemorative events reinscribe the centrality of the conflict—or perhaps more importantly the anticolonial and pro-Maya autonomy it now represents for community members. At the national level, the Mexican Revolution, which is widely understood to have been a unifying event in the nation's history, often overshadows this conflict. However, the state of Quintana Roo began incorporating Caste War history into its own narratives about regional and national belonging in the 1990s. In fact, the once-localized commemorative celebration held in Tihosuco and its northern neighbor, Tepich, has become a stage for state politicians to lay claim to the Caste War's history as the foundation for a politically active and fully integrated regional polity. As Jose Esquivel Vargas, a local state representative who neither speaks Maya nor would be racialized as Maya, declared in a public speech in 2018 that celebrated the naming of Tihosuco as "Cultural Patrimony of the State of Quintana Roo":

> We all know *our* history. We have heard tell of the Maya Social War ... that the Maya decided to protect their lands and lifestyles ... rebels, they were called. ... Therefore, the protection of cultural patrimony is of utmost importance. It is *our* cultural heritage, we must maintain the uses and customs of our Maya ancestors.[1]

The result is a complicated milieu of competing narratives about the Caste War that walk a line between what becomes authorized public memory or heritage discourse and what does not (Delle 2008; Smith 2006). Among many residents of Tihosuco (and other towns throughout Quintana Roo), though, there remains an undercurrent that continues to challenge and subvert these authorized narratives through localized and community-based memory and heritage-making practices. The heritage assemblages encountered in Tihosuco may serve as media for mending the disconnect between present-day Maya, their pasts, and the state's (frequently extractive) heritage interests—including economic development through cultural tourism.

Two Heritage Assemblages

In his contribution to the edited volume *Reclaiming Archaeology*, Rodney Harrison (2013) proposes that archaeologists should be reimagining what archaeology offers to the present and the future—what archaeology is and what it does. His argument rests on understanding archaeology as the study of enmeshed and overlapping surface assemblages. Assemblage is a foundational archaeological concept that typically refers to a collection of materials related through contextual proximity (Joyce and Pollard 2010, 292; Hamilakis and Jones 2017). Surface assemblages are often undervalued in archaeology because they are seen as merely indicative of potentially more significant depositional assemblages that could be recovered through excavation. Although Harrison is not alone in his emphasis on assemblage, he departs from this conventional understanding and valuation of assemblages in a useful way. Without decreasing the importance of excavation, he suggests that even it is a process of exposing surfaces in the here and now. In contrast to the widely reinforced idea that all archaeology is destruction (Wheeler 1954), Harrison (2013) advances the position that archaeology is best suited to exposing obscured surfaces, to drawing out and actively assembling the fragments of the past that remain in the present:

> To think of archaeology as the study of surface assemblages emphasizes it not only as a creative act in the present—a process of assembling and reassembling—but as a discipline which is concerned explicitly with the present itself. This present is not fixed or inevitable, but is still in the process of becoming; it is active and ripe with potential. . . . Archaeology [that turns its attention toward the future] would abandon its focus on particular periods to work more fluidly across time and space, with a focus on the production of an intimate present and future, rather than a distant unknowable past. In doing so, we would work towards the development of an archaeology in and of the present, for the future. (51)

We agree with Harrison's reconfiguration of the concept of assemblage. In a research environment where we continuously seesaw back and forth between historical questions about the eighteenth and nineteenth centuries and today's ethnographic and social concerns, situating our aim as one that looks deeply at the ways each of these spatiotemporal surfaces interface is far more effective than attempting to draw arbitrary boundaries between past and present. Taking Harrison's lead, then, we offer two assemblages to demonstrate how amplifying localized heritage practices can provide a platform for supporting local communities now and into the future. Archaeologists and heritage practitioners must recognize that the communities they work in are likely organizing; they already have social, political, and economic agendas. Becoming allies in these spaces allows for more substantive heritage practices that upset the cycles of appropriation and disenfranchisement in neocolonial contexts such as those created by the tourism regime in Quintana Roo.

Assemblage One: In Kaj Jo'otsuko'e', or Tihosuco's Historic Core

There is perhaps no more clear evidence of the blurring between past, present, and future than what is represented by the extant prewar era structures, or *casas coloniales,* that many of Tihosuco's families live in. Most of these houses are in the center of the town near the central plaza, forming what we have come to refer to as the historic core of Tihosuco. The houses show use over time, adaptation to modern conveniences, and historical fabric, often all on the same wall (Figure 5.2).

Most casas coloniales were built in the eighteenth and nineteenth centuries, before the Caste War. Of the over sixty structures that we have identified, including walls, wells, and smaller elliptical-style houses, thirty-three are large masonry buildings that were previously identified for inclusion in the Catálogo Nacional de Monumentos Históricos (National Catalog of Historical Monuments), a register maintained by INAH. Today, the houses exist as an important piece of heritage for those who live in Tihosuco because of their use during resettlement in the early 1930s. The most iconic of the structures is the Templo del Santo Niño Jesus, a large church and former convent that was built in several stages beginning in the sixteenth century. Today, the church stands in partial ruin because Caste War insurrectionists bombed it in 1867.

Recent intentional destruction of the material remains of the past as an act of war (Al Quntar et al. 2015), and the use of historical symbols in divisive political agendas (Morgan 2018; Brundage 2018) makes the study of heritage as a tool in negotiating identities an urgent endeavor (Meskell 2002). Acts such as the bombing of the Temple Bel at Palmyra and the long-standing debate over Confederate monuments in the United States highlight questions about who controls heritage, who creates or destroys it, and who benefits from it. These questions about the use of heritage over time and the nature of power dynamics surrounding the control of heritage are a central concern of the Tihosuco Project. To contextualize these larger debates regarding heritage, we move beyond traditional archaeological practice by including community collaboration, ethnography, and historic preservation in order to understand how heritage assemblages, such as the casas coloniales, are being used and valued today.

Figure 5.2. Photo of a block of prewar homes in Tihosuco. Photo by Kasey Diserens Morgan.

In fact, who owns the casas coloniales is a contentious subject in Tihosuco. Each one houses one or more families that have signed a deed of agreement with the ejido to occupy them, but the ejido retains the rights to their land as part of the communal holdings. In addition, the inclusion of the houses on the national register adds a layer of protection and a perception that INAH owns these properties under federal law. That means that they require a permit for any construction or alteration to a property on the list. Moreover, because Tihosuco was abandoned during the war and reoccupied in the early 1930s, there are lingering fears among current residents that descendants of some of the original owners might come back and request the return of their houses. Many owners, when asked what living in a casa colonial means to them, speak of heredity: the idea that these houses have stood the test of time and can be passed down to their descendants. When pressed, many also recognize the benefits they would stand to gain from future tourism or for resources coming in for restoration, as has been the case in nearby cities such as Valladolid, Yucatan.

The idea for an official project to document and preserve the history of the casas coloniales came from within the community. Tihosuqueños wanted to clarify issues of ownership and value that some of the houses

recognized on the national register—and the increased interest from regional politicians in using that recognition as a stepping-stone to tourism
development —raised. Mariano Chan Pech, who was mayor when we began this subproject, formed a committee dedicated to helping local house
owners understand the laws associated with owning a colonial structure
and to working in tandem with INAH on permits and other regulatory
issues. Kasey and the sub-project's co-lead, Socorro Poot Dzib, regularly
report to this committee on their progress documenting the houses and
organize town-wide meetings to set the priorities for their work.

Kasey and Socorro have worked together for the last six years. The previous mayor connected Socorro with the project because she and her family
had recently moved back to Tihosuco from the Riviera Maya and she was
looking for work. The initial stages of the study involved entering houses
and speaking with their owners. Being a team of two women had its advantages. As men are often away from the house during the day, having Kasey
work with a local woman who could provide introductions to other local
women proved advantageous and reassuring for casas coloniales owners.
Now, in her capacity as the treasurer for the mayor's office, Socorro keeps
members of the project tuned into local politics and introduces the team to
regional politicians as they visit Tihosuco. Her position also enables her to
present the priorities of the casas coloniales committee to these politicians.

From the outset, Kasey and Socorro recognized that the scope of the
subproject had to be much more than documentation because of the various time periods that are represented and the different stakeholders who
are involved. They want to tell the histories of these houses in a way that
effectively bridges past, present, and future. They combine physical documentation, such as measured drawings and photographs, with oral histories and ethnographic interviews. They have fully drawn and documented
over thirty structures and have photographed and georeferenced another
thirty. On the practical side, their work needs to be useful to the owners
and the community at large. They are working to produce maps and a register of the houses most at risk for deterioration. Such a register can serve
as the basis for requesting restoration funds, tourism plans, and guided
tours or for future preservation plans. They also carefully observe and involve themselves in meetings with government actors such as INAH and
other officials interested in bringing tourism to town. Kasey walks the line
between her academic interests in how heritage preservation practices become localized and socially embedded and being an advocate for a heritage

preservation agenda that considers and benefits both the houses and the families who occupy them.

Recent interest on the part of the government further highlights the need for input and participation at the local level. Government actors such as INAH, state legislators, and the Secretary of Tourism began repairing and repainting the facades of ten houses in 2018. Much of that work was done without any real input from the owners. A few meetings were hastily thrown together where each owner had to sign the application for a work permit or was given a copy of a permit that had already been approved. No one was given a choice about paint color or was told when the work would start. Socorro and Kasey spent time with the owners, documenting concerns and bringing them to the appropriate authorities where possible. The work remains fraught with complications because of the differing levels of control over the project each of the actors has. The funding for the project came from the State Congress of Quintana Roo, who dispensed it through an entity called Sistemas Integrales para el Transporte (SINTRA; Ministry of Infrastructure) and the Secretaría de Turismo del Estado de Quintana Roo (the Secretary of Tourism). They, in turn, subcontracted the restorations to a private agency with only one available contractor. The hierarchy of actors involved in the project caused miscommunications, work stoppages, and a general discontent with the quality of the work within the Tihosuco community. This recent development has greatly impacted how Kasey approaches her role and further highlights the need for greater town involvement in the government's initiatives. What the restoration project needed was a strong group of advocates who could give permissions, guide the work, and speak up if things were not advancing appropriately. Kasey and Socorro hope that through this subproject they are providing tools and a platform from which they, the casas coloniales owners, and the attendant committee can advocate for more transparency and more government funding for future work.

As researchers from outside Mexico, Kasey and Tiffany (co-author) must work within these structures. We apply to INAH for permits, and we work within the protections in place at these sites. At the same time, we are helping to produce knowledge that strengthens the history of a multivocal counternarrative that continually negotiates what it means to be Maya in southern Yucatan. We want to work alongside Tihosuqueños to preserve the tangible and intangible remains of that story for the future, but we understand that government restrictions and controls (and, at times, affordances)[2] have very real and palpable impacts on the lives of those who live in and around Tihosuco's historic structures. We must take all of these perspectives into account as we continue our work.

Assemblage Two: In the Name of the Ejido

Similar to the work that Kasey and Socorro have been doing with the casas coloniales, Tiffany and several members of the ejido are working to bridge the gap between what is known about the period that led up to the war and what happened during and after the war, including the region's re-population (which happened around 1930). As Harrison (2013) notes, there are limits to the usefulness of periodization when what is at stake is how people engage with, understand, and make use of particular histories in the present and how they will do so in the future. The second assemblage we offer grapples with how to approach the many historic places within the 60,000 hectares of the ejido. Through the work we have undertaken together, members of the Tihosuco Project are challenging ideas about conventional archaeological practices, traditional approaches to dividing and categorizing time, and who has the power to contribute to and construct the narrative of the history of the region.

Over forty historic properties that date to the sixteenth through the nineteenth centuries, including depopulated towns, haciendas (plantation estates), and ranches, are scattered across ejido lands (Figure 5.3). Members of the archaeological subproject have so far encountered a limited amount of archival information pertaining to these places but they continue to investigate. Many official documents are rumored to have been destroyed during the Caste War; what does exist in regional archives is limited. Tihosuco appears frequently in secondary accounts, but these typically prioritize the history of Tihosuco as a key war zone following the uprising in 1847. This temporal bias obscures what we can know about the other historic places on the ejido, which would have belonged to the parish of Tihosuco before the outbreak of the war. After over seven decades of severe regional depopulation, Tihosuco was among the towns in the region that were reoccupied. Many other prewar settlements, including those we describe below, were not. But, as Kasey and Socorro's work makes clear, Tihosuqueños today continue to engage with these places through renewed dwelling practices. Many sites that were once ranches or haciendas (plantation estates) have been repurposed for similar locally controlled economic and/or social endeavors. They have become places for community festivals and family

Figure 5.3. Hacienda estate of insurrectionist leader and patron of Tihosuco, Don Jacinto Pat. Ejido de Tihozuco. Photo by Tiffany C. Fryer.

gatherings, making milpa (a kind of swidden agriculture) and cultivating traditional foods, keeping bees, raising cattle, hunting, and gathering medicinal plants. Some people even recall how their families set out in search of specific places that family members who had fled the region long ago told them to look for during the 1920s and 1930s, when Mexico's agrarian reforms began to make space for a new wave of communal landholding organizations.

One of these places, an unoccupied town, has been central to our archaeological work under the auspices of the Tihosuco Project. In the eighteenth and nineteenth centuries, Tihosuco had two associated subject towns that were administered by the colonial and then the republican government, together with the Catholic Church. (Some additional towns were under the purview of the Tihosuco parish before this period.) Although we do not fully understand why, Tihosuco and its northern subject settlement, Tepich, retained their prewar names when the region was repopulated in the twentieth century. The second of Tihosuco's subject towns, known then as Tela', did not. Although it is clearly recorded on the historic maps and census records that survived the war and even played a significant role in the peninsula's history of piracy, Tela' was largely forgotten. Today, Tihosuqueños refer to it as Lal Kaj, meaning "old settlement," or, in a word play achieved through the lengthening of vowels that is common among Yukatek Maya speakers, "place of thistles," referring to the overgrowth of jungle thistle, *láal*, found at the site today. Even INAH published a brief article on this place under the name Lal Kaj (Martos López 2006).

After Richard Leventhal (co-director of the Tihosuco Project and director of the Penn Cultural Heritage Center) had visited the region for several years, a group of Tihosuqueños invited him to help set up a collaborative project focused on documenting the remains of these pre–Caste War sites located on the ejido. He was also tasked with helping to envision a plan for a locally controlled niche tourism endeavor that drew on the resources identified in Tihosuco and its surrounding lands. Tihosuqueños were far more guarded about the Caste War sites, especially Tela', than they were about the prospect of allowing a foreign archaeologist to exploit the precolonial remains of the ejido (Leventhal et al. 2014, 217–218). Tihosuqueños identified these historic places as more salient to their own experiences, their collective identity, and their notion of local heritage. They routinely diverted the attention of outsiders as a form of preservation. But given the recent boom of the heritage industry on the peninsula and the absence of employment opportunities in town, ejido members are seeking new uses for their rich historical sites. In 2013, Leventhal invited Tiffany, then a graduate student, to join the project with the cautionary note that this would be a trial period: she would have to be invited back by the Tihosuqueño co-directors of the project. Her priority for the first season was to map and document Lal Kaj alongside Tihosuco's ejido members and work with them to imagine a much wider scope for the research.

Using a high-accuracy GPS unit, Tiffany, Secundino Cahum Balam, Alfredo Pat Pool, Elias Chi Poot, and a rotating group of other ejido members spent fourteen weeks over the course of two seasons mapping the three-square-kilometer town, which is characterized by densely interwoven limestone stone walls. During this time, many of the project members shared personal histories with Tiffany about how they and their families were connected to this place and about how they interpreted the connection between the town and the war. They told her that while they had long known Lal Kaj, that knowledge had centered on the sacred areas of the central plaza, the cenote, and the church. Our collaborative investigations opened up new possibilities for understanding the extent of this place, such as what daily life might have been like for people living here during the nineteenth century, the town's potential influence on the region, and how the war uprooted that influence. It also generated opportunities to use excavation and archival research to augment oral histories about the region. Now, the reference points for explaining the town's history have become anchored to its name: instead of speaking of the nineteenth and twentieth centuries, people speak of the time before it was Lal Kaj and the time after its historic name was reclaimed and it became Lal Kaj-Tela'.

Over time, project contributors became more excited to share the other places on the ejido that they and their families represent. For many, the most treasured of these are the former haciendas. As our survey of Lal Kaj-Tela' ended and the ejido's administrations changed with local elections, Tiffany and a new lead partner, Bartolome Poot Moo, expanded investigations to other historic properties based on an interactional snowball method (Noy 2007). To date, they have mapped ten hacienda sites and sixteen ranches. Like Lal Kaj-Tela', though, the knowledge of the original names of all but one of these properties has long faded. We refer to them by the names their current representatives gave them. The exception, xCulumpich, retained its name through oral histories. xCulumpich was the hacienda of Jacinto Pat, one of the initial organizers of the Caste War.

The ejido's growing register of historic sites includes two additional towns (with areas of about one square kilometer each), an extensive road system, and hundreds of defensive field fortifications erected during wartime. INAH did preliminary documentation at some of these places (and even listed the church at Lal Kaj-Tela' and the house at xCulumpich in its register). But our work is motivated by more than an interest in recovering presumably lost vestiges: members of the project team worked together to adjoin the many knowledges that members of the ejido and their families had already cultivated on smaller scales. One ejido member, Jose María Uc Cahun, even presented Tiffany with what turned out to be photocopies of transcribed vital statistics from the prewar parish records. Although he had guarded them for years in his personal library, he did not have the citation. Using the typeface as a guide, Tiffany was able to track them down in the university library (Arrigunaga Peón 1982), setting in motion her own archival research journey.

Many of the ejido members who contribute to the Tihosuco Project's archaeology program have worked with other archaeologists along the coast of the Yucatan Peninsula. Their experiences with these other projects have followed a conventional international model in archaeology (Berggren and

Hodder 2003; Pollock 2010). Archaeologists bring local residents in as laborers (who haul buckets of material, scout out sites, outline transects, and wash and sort artifacts) and then send them home or to small, temporary working settlements away from the archaeologists who employ them (Pollock 2010). Most of them will have names only on payday and will never be recognized for the products of their labor. Many archaeologists mistakenly assume that the historical and archaeological knowledge of their labor force is rudimentary at best (see Leighton 2016). Regrettably, this remains the unsavory state of most archaeological practice globally—although, thankfully, this ethos is slowly shifting. Putting labor organization into the hands of the ejido and making small shifts in the language used to characterize the collaborative nature of the project—such as emphasizing the unity of our team instead of segregating ourselves into archaeologists and workmen—engenders a vital difference in how labor is articulated and experienced on this project.

As a final note, every July during the Caste War Anniversary Festival held in Tihosuco, we create temporary installations in the central park and in the museum as a means of showcasing our collaborative work for the wider community. In 2017, we worked together to install a permanent exhibit in the ejido's administrative office. Part of the exhibit involved enlarging the enabling act of the ejido so that its members would be able to view it more easily. Until then, only a handful of paper copies were floating around the ejido's small office, making it difficult for even the ejido's members to access information about their rights as *ejidatarios*. The current administration sought ways to demonstrate the benefits of ejido membership that go beyond access to (occasional) financial aid and the right to land use. The exhibit enabled us to highlight many historic properties that residents had near-exclusive entitlements to through the act (with, of course, the caveat that INAH also has a legal claim to them). While these displays may someday be of interest to visitors, they are aimed at Tihosuqueños.

Focusing the benefits of this work inward, toward the Tihosuqueño community—ejido members, other town residents, and youths—means that negotiated control over how and why the research is done and the narrative that emerges from that research may provide a small respite from the ongoing disappointments Tihosuqueños receive from a sociopolitical and economic system that consistently undermines their power of self-representation and their capacity to invest in their own community.

Summary

In our discussion of these complementary heritage assemblages, we have tried to outline the ways members of the Tihosuco community negotiate and embrace their ever-present past. Tihosuco's colonial houses represent both the ambitions of late colonial Spanish creole society and the future that Maya residents who have reoccupied the dilapidated structures envision. The historic properties that pockmark Tihosuco's lands open an opportunity to join together dispersed community knowledge and mobilize a previously guarded assemblage in a way that may benefit the town. State-level interest in positioning Tihosuco's heritage as a key component of state-authorized heritage discourse and state-controlled heritage to be marketed is rising. Government interest need not be understood as an imminent threat, but the community's history of disenfranchisement at the hands of both governmental and private institutions makes residents uneasy and suspicious about whether the state will eventually seize control of this heritage. Organizing around these two assemblages to assert and maintain community autonomy reaffirms a heritage that nonlocals previously undervalued. These heritage opportunities also have the potential to improve social and economic prospects for the Tihosuco community. Our commitment to socially relevant heritage work and our belief in reciprocity and solidarity through action has cultivated a collaborative and dynamic effort to address contemporary problems in Tihosuco. Before concluding, we offer some takeaways from our work that have shaped the activist agendas and advocacy efforts of our team members.

Heritage Activism

Collaborative frameworks prioritize the redistribution of power in order to create equal footing between contributors. Negotiating the roles that each project member or group will fill is crucial to the success of the program (Shackel 2004; Cipolla and Quinn 2016). This is not a new notion, but we highlight it here because it greatly impacts the outcomes of our work. Juggling multiple initiatives—any of which could constitute whole projects on their own—requires constant discussion and reflection. Moreover, open conversation and diligent reflexivity facilitate flexibility in our work. As a team, we adapt to shifts in social and political agendas, economic needs, and academic responsibilities. Those of us associated with the Penn Cultural Heritage Center will serve the project for as long as we continue to be invited. However, that invitation rests precariously on our disciplinary constraints, academic schedules, funding cycles, and ambitions. Even though we have established a mission statement, created a research design, and received formalized approval from Penn's Institutional Review Board, we frequently need to make changes to that plan on the ground to accommodate the structures of life in Tihosuco. For instance, the number of ejidatarios means that the archaeological program involves a wide range of participants. It also means that we have to accept built-in participant turnover in order to fulfill local notions of access and fairness. Paid participants must rotate in order to provide as many families with a work opportunity as possible, all the while pursuing our jointly established research goals. The three-year election cycles for the ejido's administration and the mayor's office also complicate our ability to establish long-term working relationships with specific people. Nonetheless, we find strength in the constant hand-off of responsibility. Fresh ideas and an increase in the number of project advocates in the Tihosuco community are just two of the benefits. The heterogeneity of communities that collaborate in activist archaeology need not be understood as a problem or a potential root of failure; rather, it is a marker of opportunity.

Our own positionalities as nonlocal researchers also play an important role (Fryer 2020). On more than one occasion, colleagues have told us that we are somehow relinquishing earned status, "giving up" our expert cards, and effectively wasting the time and money that has gone into our educations to be just one more voice in the conversation. Various professionals have cautioned us against too heavy a focus on "peripheral concerns" or told us to stop focusing on the broader impacts of our work, to focus on the data and science of understanding the past and the history of the Caste War instead of "that heritage stuff." People have made these kinds of comments even as academic departments and university policies have started talking more about how much they value engaged scholarship.

We fundamentally reject such positions and we implore established scholars to provide their students with the support necessary to cultivate research that is intellectually rigorous precisely because it focuses on the broader consequences of the work. As Tilley (1989, 106) argued three decades ago, "people, and not inanimate machines, write and create the past. Archaeology is a process, a system of social relationships in the present within which the production of meanings take place." The Tihosuco Project has taught us that a commitment to community research involves an implicit understanding that the past has power over the future. Those who work in a bubble and only focus on "the past" are misleading themselves and others.

Giving lip service to engagement and advocacy does little more than reinforce the histories of disenfranchising indigenous and otherwise marginalized communities that our disciplines carry. Heritage practitioners, including archaeologists, public historians, museum specialists, and so forth, have no right to shift the burden of historical revisionism onto such communities under the guise of collaborative research. We are obliged to and should feel privileged to participate in the rebalancing of power engendered by removing disciplinary gatekeepers and by recognizing local communities as keepers and producers of valuable historical knowledge that can be mobilized to effect change in a world that continues its attempts to keep certain kinds of people down. We can, as Hernández Castillo and Hutchings (2019, 16) argued, destabilize "knowledge hierarchies through epistemic dialogues that recognize other ways of 'being in the world,' while we use our anthropological knowledge as 'expert knowledge' in the struggles for rights."

We recognize that if people do not care about a project or do not see it as a way to sustain their livelihoods, they will not fight for how it is run, who it involves, or what it stands for. It simply does not matter enough to them; why should it? There is nothing at stake. In Tihosuco, some people view the precolonial past (which more readily gains the attention of heritage practitioners and tourism agencies) as distinctly important. But the overwhelming sentiment we have encountered over our several years of working with Tihosuqueños is that while the precolonial past is something that other Maya folks might rightfully find important, it just does not resonate in the same way here. In fact, one local family that is known for having an affinity for the precolonial past managed to get in with a regional politician who wanted to make a showing of support for Tihosuco in hopes of earning votes. Under advisement from this family, the politician erected a statue along the main highway that depicted a Maya ball game player bunting a ball from his hip. When the politician unveiled the statue during the opening ceremony of the annual Caste War Anniversary Festival, the murmurs from the crowd ranged from unimpressed to indignant. We heard people whisper, "That's not our history" and "What does that have to do with Tihosuco?" These feelings may be a simple function of the fact that Tihosuqueños express little affinity with precolonial history. It is not denied by any means, but the distancing that McAnany and Parks (2012) addressed had real impacts here. For the moment, there is little to compel a rekindling of that relationship to the precolonial past in order to legitimately and authentically embody and represent Mayaness. Perhaps this will change as Mayan language use diminishes and customs transform. For the moment, however, war, abandonment, and repopulation are what figure most prominently in local narratives about what it is to be Maya and Tihosuqueño.

What is at stake for Tihosuqueños is not only control over the representation of their past but also the prospect that that past might contribute to how people make their livelihoods, today and in the future. Is there a chance that collaborating on a heritage project could provide any jobs in town? Could doing so keep people from having to leave for jobs in the Riviera Maya? Could heritage projects encourage people to return to their homeplaces? Could supporting a heritage project help get street lights and clean water systems installed or roofs on houses? Too many archaeologists believe that their influence ends at the sites they chose to study or with the reports and articles they write. But our efforts have clear impacts on the local communities where we work. It is incumbent upon us to recognize when there may be more pressing needs in the community than "doing archaeology." We need to be working toward an umbrella heritage practice for which collaboration is the baseline.

While substantive collaboration has been a pillar of the Tihosuco Project, it is not without its challenges. We continue to grapple with how to restructure the notion of "field seasons" so that work toward the various goals is not halted simply because the Penn portion of the team cannot be there. The traditional archaeological field season is impractical for this sort of grassroots work, but constraints imposed by the academic cycle interfere with our long-term goals and hopes for sustainability and practical action. Trying to sell to a granting agency that you need six or seven month-long trips spread out over a few years is daunting (Pyburn and Wilk 2000, 82–83). Yet as we reflect upon the project, this model makes the most sense. With the casas coloniales project, for example, while the data collection on the houses can be done rapidly, it is the conversations and events that take place after documentation that contribute to more meaningful ideas about heritage and the future. Moreover, there are still clear structural barriers that manifest, for instance, in the ability of someone who has not been professionally trained as an archaeologist to lead archaeological investigations. We don't mean to suggest that just anyone should be able to get a permit. Rather, we mean to underscore the fact that lack of access to education for people from places such as Tihosuco means that there are very few opportunities for potential collaborators (such as ourselves) to create on-the-ground partnerships that can function legally without their presence. Thus, we hope that the future will bring more educational opportunities for local students interested in archaeology and other heritage-related fields (in addition to tourism, which currently dominates postsecondary educational trajectories in the region for the reasons we outlined above).

Conclusion

In this chapter, we have argued for the utility of an umbrella heritage model for activism-oriented heritage work. By situating the Tihosuco Heritage Preservation and Community Development Project in the context of a globalized, multibillion-dollar tourism industry that exploits tropes of Maya identity for private and state gain, we demonstrate small acts of resistance that localized heritage initiatives can engender. Among these acts, we emphasize self-representation and community-controlled economic growth. We believe that our umbrella heritage model responds to various (and often well-founded) critiques about community archaeology by taking seriously how people in Tihosuco are themselves defining the different communities and subject areas within the project. We are reminded that humility, dignity, and epistemic deference are the greatest tempers for the hierarchies embedded in the expertise acquired through access to formal/higher education and are the greatest offsets to unequally distributed power. For our team, the Tihosuco Project is about positioning the community to claim heritage as a social, political, and economic tool that will begin to reframe the structures of inequality.

Both of us have come to realize that, in contrast to what the disciplines of archaeology and historic preservation have suggested we elevate as key values and roles, we do not practice heritage for the protection or preservation of the past as embodied by buildings, sites, and artifacts. Rather, we take people's histories seriously and acknowledge that such a disposition fundamentally alters the questions we are inclined to ask about the past because, ultimately, the interest lies in the future. We work where silencing the legacies of violence and dispossession has been rampant. Our hope is that this collaborative initiative has created a space where it is safe—albeit contentious and filled with dissent—to truly talk about this past and develop new, subversive ways of unsettling it that might promote growth, a sense of justice, and increased community cohesion.

Notes

1. Authors' transcription and translation of a speech recorded in Felipe Carrillo Puerto on March 24, 2018, during fieldwork.

2. Here we are invoking affordance in the way that materialism scholars in archaeology have used it to underscore the material realities of the conditions structures engender—in this case, structural inequities. That means recognizing that there may be positive potential (affordances) to some of these restrictive policies at the same time that they risk negatively impacting the very people they are put in place to uplift.

References Cited

Agbe-Davies, Anna. 2010. "Concepts of Community in Pursuit of an Inclusive Archaeology." *International Journal of Heritage Studies* 16 (6): 373–389.

Al Quntar, Salam, Katharyn Hanson, Brian I. Daniels, and Corine Wegener. 2015. "Responding to a Cultural Heritage Crisis: The Example of the Safeguarding the Heritage of Syria and Iraq Project." *Near Eastern Archaeology* 78 (3): 154–160.

Ardren, Traci. 2002. "Conversations about the Production of Archaeological Knowledge and Community Museums at Chunchucmil and Kochol, Yucatán, México." *World Archaeology* 34 (2): 379–400.

———. 2004. "Where Are the Maya in Ancient Maya Archaeological Tourism? Advertising and the Appropriation of Culture." In *Marketing Heritage: Archaeology and the Consumption of the Past,* edited by Yorke M. Rowan and Uzi Baram, 103–116. Walnut Creek, CA: Rowman and Littlefield.

Armstrong-Fumero, Fernando. 2009. "A Heritage of Ambiguity: The Historical Substrate of Vernacular Multiculturalism in Yucatan, Mexico." *American Ethnologist* 36 (2): 300–316.

Arrigunaga Peón, Joaquín de. 1982. *Demography and Parish Affairs in Yucatan, 1797–1897: Documents from the Archivo De La Mitra Emeritense.* With the assistance of Carol S. Dumond and Don E. Dumond. Eugene: Department of Anthropology, University of Oregon.

Atalay, Sonya, Lee Rains Clauss, Randall H. McGuire, and John R. Welch, eds. 2014. *Transforming Archaeology: Activist Practices and Prospects.* New York: Routledge.

Berggren, Åsa, and Ian Hodder. 2003. "Social Practice, Method, and Some Problems of Field Archaeology." *American Antiquity* 68 (3): 421–434.

Berry, Maya J., Claudia Chávez Argüelles, Shanya Cordis, Sarah Ihmoud, and Elizabeth Velásquez Estrada. 2017. "Toward a Fugitive Anthropology: Gender, Race, and Violence in the Field." *Cultural Anthropology* 32 (4): 537–65.

Breglia, Lisa. 2006. *Monumental Ambivalence: The Politics of Heritage.* Austin: University of Texas Press.

Bricker, Victoria Reifler. 1984. *The Indian Christ, the Indian King: The Historical Substrate of Maya Myth and Ritual.* Austin: University of Texas Press.

Brundage, W. Fitzhugh. 2018. "Exclusion, Inclusion, and the Politics of Confederate Commemoration in the American South." *Politics, Groups, and Identities* 6 (2): 324–330.

Bueno, Christina. 2016. *The Pursuit of Ruins: Archaeology, History, and the Making of Modern Mexico.* Albuquerque: University of New Mexico Press.

Castañeda, Quetzil E. 1996. *In the Museum of Maya Culture: Touring Chichen Itza.* Minnesota: University of Minnesota Press.

———. 2004. "'We are not indigenous!'": An Introduction to the Maya Identity of Yucatán." *Journal of Latin American and Caribbean Anthropology* 9 (1): 36–63.

———. 2009. "Heritage and Indigeneity: Transformations in the Politics of Tourism." In *Cultural Tourism in Latin America: The Politics of Space and Imaginary,* edited by Michiel Baud and Johana Louisa Ipeij, 263–298. Boston: Brill.

Castellanos, María Bianet. 2010. *A Return to Servitude: Maya Migration and the Tourist Trade in Cancún.* Minneapolis: University of Minnesota Press.

Cipolla, Craig N., and James Quinn. 2016. "Field School Archaeology the Mohegan Way: Reflections on Twenty Years of Community-Based Research and Teaching." *Journal of Community Archaeology & Heritage* 3 (2): 118–134.

Cojti Ren, Avexnim. 2006. "Maya Archaeology and the Political and Cultural Identity of Contemporary Maya in Guatemala." *Archaeologies* 2 (1): 8–19.

Clark, Dylan J., and David S. Anderson. 2015. "Past Is Present: The Production and Consumption of Archaeological Legacies in Mexico." *Archeological Papers of the American Anthropological Association* 25 (1): 1–18.

Crooke, Elizabeth. 2010. "The Politics of Community Heritage: Motivations, Authority and Control." *International Journal of Heritage Studies* 16 (1–2): 16–29.

Delle, James A. 2008. "A Tale of Two Tunnels: Memory, Archaeology, and the Underground Railroad." *Journal of Social Archaeology* 8 (1): 63–93.

Diserens Morgan, Kasey, and Richard Leventhal. 2020. "Maya of the Past, Present, and Future: Heritage, Anthropological Archaeology, and the Study of the Caste War of Yucatan." *Heritage* 3: 511–527.

Ely, Paula A. 2013. "Selling Mexico: Marketing and Tourism Values." *Tourism Management Perspectives* 8: 80–89.

Fryer, Tiffany C. 2020. "Reflecting on Positionality: Archaeological Heritage Praxis in Quintana Roo, Mexico." In "Engendering Heritage: Contemporary Feminist Approaches to Archaeological Heritage Practice," edited by Tiffany C. Fryer and Teresa P. Raczek. Special issue, *Archaeological Papers of the American Anthropological Association,* 31: 26–40.

Gabbert, Wolfgang. 2019. *Violence and the Caste War of Yucatán.* Cambridge, UK: Cambridge University Press.

Hale, Charles R. 2007. *Engaging Contradictions: Theory, Politics, and Methods of Activist Scholarship.* Berkeley: University of California Press.

Hamilakis, Yannis, and Andrew Meirion Jones. 2017. "Archaeology and Assemblage." *Cambridge Archaeological Journal* 27 (1): 77–84.

Harrison, Rodney. 2013. "Scratching the Surface: Reassembling an Archaeology *in* and *of* the Present." In *Reclaiming Archaeology: Beyond the Tropes of Identity,* edited by Alfredo González Ruibal, 44–55. New York: Routledge.

Hawn, Heather, and Jennifer Tison. 2015. "Tourism and Political Choices of Indigenous Populations in Yucatán." *Latin American Perspectives* 42 (5): 234–247.

Hernández Castillo, Aída, and Suzi Hutchings. 2019. "Introduction." In *Transcontinental*

Dialogues: Activist Alliances with Indigenous Peoples of Canada, Mexico, and Australia, edited by R. Aída Hernández Castillo, Suzi Hutchings, and Brian Noble, 3–33. Tucson: University of Arizona Press.

Hutson, Scott R., Galvin Can Herrera, and Gabriel Adrian Chi. 2014. "Maya Heritage: Entangled and Transformed." *International Journal of Heritage Studies* 20 (4): 1–17.

Instituto Nacional de Estadística y Geografía. 2010. Censo de Población y Vivienda Tulum. http://www.beta.inegi.org.mx/app/areasgeograficas/?ag=23009.

Joyce, Rosemary A., and Joshua Pollard. 2010. "Archaeological Assemblages and Practices of Deposition." In *The Oxford Handbook of Material Culture*, edited by Dan Hicks and Mary C. Beaudry, 291–309. Oxford: Oxford University Press.

Juárez, Ana M. 2002. "Ecological Degradation, Global Tourism, and Inequality: Maya Interpretations of the Changing Environment in Quintana Roo, Mexico." *Human Organization* 61 (2): 113–124.

Leighton, Mary. 2016. "Indigenous Archaeological Field Technicians at Tiwanaku, Bolivia: A Hybrid Form of Scientific Labor." *American Anthropologist* 118 (4): 742–754.

Leventhal, Richard M., Carlos Chan Espinosa, Eladio Moo Pat, and Demetrio Poot Cahun. 2014. "The Community Heritage Project in Tihosuco, Quintana Roo, Mexico." *Public Archaeology* 13 (1–3): 213–225.

Little, Walter E. 2004. *Mayas in the Marketplace: Tourism, Globalization, and Cultural Identity*. Austin: University of Texas Press.

Llanes-Ortiz, Genner. 2019. "Maya Knowledges, Intercultural Dialogues, and Being a *Chan Laak'* in the Yucatán Peninsula." In *Transcontinental Dialogues: Activist Alliances with Indigenous Peoples of Canada, Mexico, and Australia*, edited by R. Aída Hernández Castillo, Suzi Hutchings, and Brian Noble, 166–189. Tucson: University of Arizona Press.

Magnoni, Aline, Traci Ardren, and Scott Hutson. 2007. "Tourism in the Mundo Maya: Inventions and (Mis)Representations of Maya Identities and Heritage." *Archaeologies* 3 (3): 353–383.

Martos López, Luis Alberto. 2006. "Lalcah, un Pueblo Olvidado en la Selva de Quintana Roo." *Boletín de Monumentos Históricos* 3 (7): 2–20.

McAnany, Patricia A. 2016. *Maya Cultural Heritage: How Archaeologists and Indigenous Communities Engage the Past*. Lanham, MD: Rowman and Littlefield.

McAnany, Patricia A., and Shoshaunna Parks. 2012. "Casualties of Heritage Distancing." *Current Anthropology* 53 (1): 80–107.

McKercher, Bob, and Hilary du Cros. 2002. *Cultural Tourism: The Partnership Between Tourism and Cultural Heritage Management*. New York: Routledge.

Meskell, Lynn. 2002. "Negative Heritage and Past Mastering in Archaeology." *Anthropological Quarterly* 75 (3): 557–574.

Morgan, David. 2018. "Soldier Statues and Empty Pedestals: Public Memory in the Wake of the Confederacy." *Material Religion* 14 (1): 153–157.

Noy, Chaim. 2007. "Sampling Knowledge: The Hermeneutics of Snowball Sampling in Qualitative Research." *International Journal of Social Research Methodology* 11 (4): 327–344.

Pollock, Susan. 2010. "Decolonizing Archaeology: Political Economy and Archaeological Practice in the Middle East." In *Controlling the Past, Owning the Future: The Politi-*

cal Uses of Archaeology in the Middle East, edited by Ran Boytner; Lynn Swartz Dodd, and Bradley J Parker, 196–216. Tucson: University of Arizona Press.

Pyburn, K. Anne, and Richard R. Wilk. 2000. "Responsible Archaeology Is Applied Anthropology." In *Ethics in American Archaeology: Challenges for the 1990s*, edited by Mark J. Lynott and Alison Wylie. Washington, DC: Society for American Archaeology.

Re Cruz, Alicia. 1996. *The Two Milpas of Chan Kom: Scenarios of a Maya Village Life*. Albany: State University of New York Press.

Saldaña-Portillo, María Josefina. 2016. *Indian Given: Racial Geographies across Mexico and the United States*. Durham, NC: Duke University Press.

Scher, Phillip W. 2011. "Heritage Tourism in the Caribbean: The Politics of Culture after Neoliberalism." *Bulletin of Latin American Research* 30 (1):7–20.

Secretaría de Turismo del Estado de Quintana Roo. 2017. "Perfil y Comportamiento del Turista Tulum, Julio–Septiembre 2017." http://sedeturqroo.gob.mx/ARCHIVOS/TURISTA%20TULUM%20%20JUL-SEP%202017.pdf.

Shackel, Paul. 2004. "Introduction, Working with Communities: Heritage Development and Applied Archaeology." In *Places in Mind: Public Archaeology as Applied Anthropology*, edited by Paul Shackel and Erve Chambers, 1–18. New York: Routledge.

Smith, Laurajane. 2006. *Uses of Heritage*. London: Routledge.

Stump, Daryl. 2013. "On Applied Archaeology, Indigenous Knowledge, and the Usable Past." *Current Anthropology* 54 (3): 268–298.

Taylor, Analisa. 2009. *Indigeneity in the Mexican Cultural Imagination: Thresholds of Belonging*. Tucson: University of Arizona Press.

Taylor, Sarah R. 2018. *On Being Maya and Getting By: Heritage Politics and Community Development in Yucatán*. Boulder: University Press of Colorado.

Tilley, Christopher. 1989. "Archaeology as Socio-Political Action in the Present." In *Critical Traditions in Contemporary Archaeology*, edited by Valerie Pinsky and Alison Wylie, 104–116. Cambridge, UK: Cambridge University Press.

Torres, Rebecca Maria, and Janet D. Momsen. 2005. Gringolandia: The Construction of a New Tourist Space in Mexico. *Annals of the Association of American Geographers* 95 (2): 314–335.

Vázquez León, Luis. 2003. *El Leviatán arqueológico: Antropología de una tradición científica en México*. 2nd ed. México, DF: CIESAS.

Visit México. 2018. "Turistic [*sic*] Destinations." https://www.visitmexico.com/en/where-to-go/cultural-destinations. Accessed May 30, 2018.

Watanabe, John M. 1995. "Unimagining the Maya: Anthropologists, Others, and the Inescapable Hubris of Authorship." *Bulletin of Latin American Research* 14 (1): 25–45.

Watkins, Joe. 2005. "Through Wary Eyes: Indigenous Perspectives on Archaeology." *Annual Review of Anthropology* 34: 429–449.

Wheeler, Robert Eric Mortimer. 1954. *Archaeology from the Earth*. Oxford: Clarendon Press.

Wynne, Lauren A. 2015. "'I Hate It': Tortilla-Making, Class, and Women's Tastes in Rural Yucatán, Mexico." *Food, Culture, and Society* 18 (3): 379–397.

6

Ireland's Heritage and the Production of Knowledge in Historical Archaeology

STEPHEN A. BRIGHTON AND ANDREW J. WEBSTER

The aim of this chapter is to use the research program Archaeology of Modern Ireland in Skibbereen, County Cork, Ireland, to illustrate the importance of archaeological knowledge to issues of social justice and heritage production in the twenty-first century. Two questions structure this chapter: What is archaeology good for? and Who benefits from the knowledge produced through excavation and the interpretation of recovered materials? These are powerful questions. In the Republic of Ireland, prehistoric archaeological monuments from the island's "Gaelic" past have been used to shape a national identity since at least the 1880s (Cooney 1996; Hutchinson 2001). Until recently, there was silence both in academic circles and in public discourse about the violent events of the recent past, such as the Great Hunger, the Irish War of Independence, and the Irish Civil War (Laurence 2010, 102). Similarly, archaeological treatments of the postmedieval period on the island of Ireland were rare until the 1990s (Brighton 2009; Donnelly and Horning 2002). Since then, postmedieval archaeology in Ireland has largely focused on the sixteenth- and seventeenth-century plantation period in Northern Ireland, although some studies have focused on the eighteenth, nineteenth, and twentieth centuries.

The Archaeology of Modern Ireland research program is an attempt to use archaeology to address the silences in the historical and the archaeological record in Ireland. Drawing on Trouillot's concept of the "dialectics of mentions and silences," it uses artifacts to contest accepted national narratives of the past (Trouillot 1997, 53, 57–59). Moving away from an archaeology of the elite, We focus on the everyday people who shaped modern Irish history and culture and whose descendants form the communities we collaborate with today. Engaging in the archaeology of the recent Irish past in partnership with community stakeholders has the potential to create a more holistic and inclusive past for everyone. The archaeology of everyday people in Ireland's recent past illuminates historical injustices and connects them to modern issues of politics, identity, and inequality.

Historical Archaeology in the Twenty-First Century

Knowledge generated by archaeology is relevant to present-day social, economic, and political issues. In the twenty-first century, archaeology has become focused on constructing a meaningful connection between the past and the present in order to create a vehicle for change in contemporary communities (Brighton 2011, 348–350; Colwell-Chanthaphonh and Ferguson 2008, 9–10; Hamilakis 2007, 18–21; Leone 2008, 133; McDavid 2007, 67–68; Nicholas, Welch, and Yellowhorn 2008, 262; Shanks and McGuire 1996, 86). By emphasizing the interconnections between the past, the present, and the future, historical archaeology can challenge notions of the past that minimize the importance of marginalized populations and promote a more inclusive history and heritage.

Applied archaeology aims to benefit the public. This goal is based on the idea that knowledge is power (Ollman 2003, 20). The applied approach is based the concept of praxis, which McGuire defines as "theoretically informed action" (McGuire 2008, 4). Effective praxis requires genuine collaboration with communities who can use archaeology for positive social change (Little 2007; McGuire 2008). Applied archaeology's call for social action forces archaeologists to recognize that our interpretations have importance in the world and not just within the discipline. Because of this, archaeologists must be vigilant about how the knowledge we produce is perceived and used (Chambers 2004, 194; Shackel 2011, 91.)

Those of us who collaborate with communities outside academia attempt to create fairness within archaeology by creating benefits for community stakeholders as well as researchers. When multiple communities and stakeholders are involved, the web of relationships among them can become quite complex. Direct community collaboration leads to a more complex and layered view of the relationship between the past and present. This viewpoint can promote action for social change (Colwell-Chanthaphonh and Ferguson 2008; Stottman 2010). True collaboration establishes an environment for dialogue that includes differing perspectives and works to improve the well-being of disenfranchised people (Chambers 1987, 320,

[handwritten annotation at top: "Most citations are from texts that are almost 15 years old."]

325). Most scholars who engage in community collaboration strongly believe that our work has an important impact on living societies (Colwell-Chanthaphonh and Ferguson 2008; Little 2007; McGuire 2008; Shackel and Little 2007; Zimmerman 2008; Stottman 2010; Atalay et al. 2014).

Knowledge produced archaeologically has the potential to be used in present-day relations of power, and thus it is important to remember that it is not produced for its own sake and is not detached from the needs and interests of contemporary communities (Shanks and McGuire 1996, 86). *[handwritten annotation in left margin: "30 years"]* Most people understand society and the world through their localized surroundings—that is, through what they can see, hear, and feel (Ollman 2003, 13). What we perhaps sometimes fail to realize is that people are also part of a larger structure with others who may often understand history differently from them or have memories that conflict with theirs. This is what Bertell Ollman (2003, 3) refers to as an "interlocking nature of past, present, and future." Experiences and memories develop collectively over time as part of a larger system of social interaction and daily life where each experience can have an effect upon each of the component parts. This framework is useful for thinking about archaeological knowledge can be applied: it can used when certain memories or experiences speak over or mask those of others in the community. It is important for archaeologists to not only point to the origins of something but also to give voice to experiences and memories that have been silenced by local and national narratives of heritage. The aim of this is to denaturalize existing narratives and their ideologies in order to produce relevant knowledge in the present and to shape the discourse about the future. Thus, a deep connection exists between knowledge production and action (Ollman 2003, 20). We cannot change the past. However, when we disseminate knowledge about what something means, show where it originated, and show what its impact has been on past and present cultures, communities gain the knowledge to perhaps change the future.

Our project in Ireland takes the questions of who benefits from our work and what the impact of our work will be on local communities very seriously. We draw upon Paul Shackel and Erve Chambers's (2004, 146) perspective that applied research and knowledge production is always on the "public stage." This principle is a cornerstone for our direction of the Archaeology of Modern Ireland research program. We are working to demonstrate that historical archaeological knowledge is relevant in Ireland, especially the archaeology related to the formation of modern Ireland. Unlike historical archeology in the United States, the archaeology of the nineteenth and early twentieth centuries in Ireland is not often considered a worthy pursuit for archaeologists.

The Relevance of Modern World Archaeology in Ireland

In order to understand the history and politics that have shaped modern Irish notions of history and heritage, a simple overview of modern Irish history and geopolitics is necessary. In the sixteenth century, the indigenous population of Ireland was Catholic and was politically organized into several groups with Gaelic leaders, many of whom opposed Protestant British influence on the island. In the late sixteenth and seventeenth centuries, the British Crown enacted a plantation scheme in Ireland that was designed to "plant" or settle Protestants from Britain in Ireland as an attempt to gain political power and loyalty there by changing the island's demographics (Donnelly 2007). The two main plantations were in Munster (the southwest of Ireland) and Ulster (the north of Ireland). Ulster was the more extensive and long lived. In response to a series of uprisings and political maneuvers, the British settlers confiscated the lands of several Gaelic leaders, especially in Ulster. The new Protestant ruling class aimed to create model English settlements and convert the Catholic and pastoral Irish to Protestant rent-paying tenants (Mitchell and Ryan 1997, 317). This attempt failed to completely achieve its goals, especially in Munster, where a series of revolts eliminated the plantation scheme. However, in Ulster, while many native Irish remained Catholic and some still resided on their old lands, demographic change occurred on a large scale. The influx of Protestant settlers loyal to the English Crown left a legacy in the North of Ireland and can ultimately be seen as a major contributing factor to the division of Ireland into the Republic and the North.

In the late seventeenth and eighteenth centuries, during what is known as the Protestant Ascendancy in Ireland, the British Crown instituted the Penal Laws, restrictive policies that discriminated against the Catholic Irish. During this time, British soldiers removed thousands of native Irish Catholics from the most productive agricultural regions of the island and forced them to settle in the west of Ireland (Cronin 2001). In addition, laws barred native Catholics from voting or holding political office, from publicly practicing their faith, and from owning weapons. Other laws subjected Catholics to debilitating land policies that drove them into smaller and more marginal pieces of land (Donnelly 2004; Brighton 2009).

By the early nineteenth century, Ireland's population was heavily rural.

Under the system of agricultural capitalism, the rural poor labored on small parcels of land in order to make just enough to pay rent. They essentially lived at a subsistence level with no route to profit, advancement, or escape. When a series of potato crops failed in the period 1845 to 1852, the rural poor lost a major dietary staple. As a result, approximately one million Irish perished and two million emigrated during what is known in Ireland as An Ghorta Mór, the Great Hunger (Miller 1985). Throughout the nineteenth century but especially after the Famine, resistance to the British occupation of Ireland continued to grow through revolts and political movements, both in Ireland and in its far-reaching diaspora.

In the early twentieth century, the political momentum for rebellion in Ireland, which was backed in part by political movements in the diaspora, came to a head. The Easter Rising of 1916 was a week-long rebellion in Dublin that paved the way for the Irish War of Independence in 1919, which ended with the Anglo-Irish Treaty in 1921. The treaty split the island into the Irish Free State (today the Republic of Ireland) and Northern Ireland, which remains part of the United Kingdom. This did not put an end to the violence, however, as it was followed by a civil war until 1923 over the terms of the treaty—whether the new state should be part of the British Empire or a fully independent republic. The social and political tensions caused by partition have led to conflict in more recent times.

From the late 1960s until the 1990s, a violent conflict known as the Troubles transpired in Northern Ireland. The Troubles developed from a deep-seated divide between the mostly Protestant unionists, who wanted Northern Ireland to remain under British control, and the mostly Catholic nationalists, who sought a united Irish republic. Many Catholics also protested the discrimination of the Catholic minority by the Protestant majority in government and police contexts. What started as peaceful protests eventually turned to violence, leading to the rise of armed campaigns by paramilitary groups on both sides of the conflict, such as the Irish Republican Army (IRA) and the Ulster Volunteer Force. These groups, among other rival factions, committed targeted political shootings, car bombings, pub bombings, and attacks on civilian protesters. In response, British security forces fought back, at times resorting to the internment, or imprisonment without trial, of suspected members of the IRA, many of whom were innocent (McAtackney 2014). Thirty years of terrorism and targeted killings left over 40,000 people injured and more than 3,000 dead, half of whom were civilians (Mulholland 2002). The Good Friday Agreement of

1998 eventually led to a sustained period of uneasy cease-fire and peace building. Today, while the violence is mostly gone, the tension remains.

The history of modern Ireland has shaped the current political, social, and economic conditions on the island, but this history is not seen as the major component in Ireland's archaeological heritage. Instead, megalithic monuments, such as cairns and standing stones, provide the foundation for Ireland's heritage. Such monuments have been the inspiration and back-drop for cultural understanding and explanation of Ireland's extensive history and origins (Brighton 2009, 6–7). Ireland's prehistoric and medieval periods are the foci of contemporary Irish heritage and history, and the archaeological study of modern Ireland (the mid-nineteenth century to the first few decades of the twentieth) has largely been ignored.

At present, historical, or postmedieval, archaeology in Ireland is located on the margins of the discipline. Although the field is growing, a quick survey of Irish archaeology programs shows that the field tends to gravitate toward the prehistoric and medieval periods. The study of Ireland's historic period did not truly begin until the 1970s and 1980s (Donnelly and Horning 2002; Breen 2009). In 1999, the Irish Post-Medieval Archaeology Group (IPMAG) was formed to promote the study of postmedieval archaeology in Ireland (Donnelly and Horning 2002). IPMAG hosted its first conference in 2001 and the first major edited volume in Irish postmedieval archaeology was published in 2007 (Horning et al. 2007). While interest in the archaeological study of Ireland's postmedieval period grew in the 1990s and 2000s, most Irish postmedieval archaeology has focused on the early history of modern Ireland, the period before to the nineteenth century.

Neither archaeologists nor legislation define postmedieval archaeology in Ireland clearly or consistently. The majority of archaeologists agree that the most relevant of Ireland's postmedieval studies cover the period 1550 to 1700. This falls in line with legislation that does not cover sites that date to the nineteenth century or later, except for sites or monuments that are defined as having national significance (Donnelly and Horning 2002).

While a good deal of archaeology concerning the seventeenth century has been done in Ireland, knowledge produced by an archaeology of the formation, transformation, and resilience of the people of modern Ireland remains on the edges of the discipline. The reason archaeologists avoid the period from the nineteenth century into more recent times is that what we interpret as the memory of violence, conflict, death, and struggle forms a part of the discourse of Ireland's political economic and cultural present.

Although this is not generally discussed openly in Irish archaeology, Irish historians argue that the study of the recent past can have a profound impact on contemporary social and political issues (Kennedy and Johnson 1996, 34; O'Day 1996, 197). Brendan Bradshaw (1989) argued against the revisionist views of some Irish historians and developed theoretical insights for understanding the academic and political mindset in Ireland that disguised or avoided contentious events and actions in the past such as Protestant Ascendancy and the Great Hunger. Bradshaw notes that historians' interpretations of the history of modern Ireland have evaded, neglected, or normalized how and why events happened that culminated from longstanding violence and repression, such as the Great Hunger (Bradshaw 1989, 338–339).

Bradshaw's concept of neglect (1989, 339–340) is most relevant to the archaeological study of Ireland modern period. He defines neglect as the tendency to downplay the importance of the Great Famine because it looms so large in Irish consciousness both as a historical event and as a touchstone of national identity. The first academic study of the Famine did not appear until the 1950s (Edwards and Williams 1956), and after that, historians stopped focusing on the Famine for three decades. In the 1980s and 1990s, Irish scholars such as Mary E. Daly (1986), Joel Mokyr (1983), and Cormac Ó Gráda (1988, 1995) revisited the Famine with renewed interest in understanding the economic, social, and political causes and impacts of the Famine across the nation. Such scholars attempted to balance their interpretations between popular and revisionist history (Bradshaw 1989, 337). Today, researchers tend to favor and interpretation that apportions blame between the rural poor of Ireland and the shifting economic system brought on by the Industrial Revolution (e.g., Ó Gráda 1988, 1995).

This scholarship and its silences have established firm roots in Irish consciousness and heritage production in Ireland. It has certainly pervaded Irish archaeology, as can be seen in how the nation's heritage is promoted through its National Museum of Archaeology. The museum exhibits define Ireland's history from the Mesolithic to the end of the medieval period, giving visitors a glimpse of the deep roots of Ireland's cultural and material history. However, the museum exhibit ends before Ireland's early modern or postmedieval period, giving the visitors an impression that archaeology's contribution ends with the dawning of the modern world.

Mairéad Carew (2009) echoes Bradshaw's sentiments about the neglect of Ireland's modern history. She argues that politicians who structured heritage laws and policies in the 1920s and 1930s did so with the clear intention of promoting Ireland's ancient monuments and neglecting all potentially contentious or political monuments such as those associated with colonialism, the Great Hunger, or military activity (Carew 2009, 129). This intention can be seen in the original wording of the National Monuments Act and its amendments, which include subjective language that allow value (and therefore protection) to be assigned based on the political interest of the state.

The original definition of a national monument in the National Monuments Act of 1930 is "any artificial or partly artificial building, structure, or erection whether above or below the surface of the ground . . . the preservation of which *is a matter of national importance* by reason of the historical, architectural, traditional, artistic, or archaeological interest attaching thereto" (Oireachtas 1930, Part I, Section 2, emphasis added). The most recent definition comes from the 1987 amendment to the act, which states that a site or structure is protected by law if it is "prehistoric" or is "associated with the commercial, cultural, economic, industrial, military, religious or social history of the place where it is situated in existence before 1700 AD or such later date as the Minister may appoint by regulations" (Oireachtas 1987, Section 1). This definition explicitly gives preservation value to all prehistoric monuments and to historic monuments erected before 1700 but does not give protection to monuments from post-1700 except on a case-by-case basis.

This wording reinforces the perception that prehistoric archaeology is more valuable than historic or postmedieval archaeology. More worrisome is that it puts postmedieval sites at risk by leaving their protection to the political will of officials in the Department of Culture, Heritage and the Gaeltacht, who determine whether or not a site is of "national importance." The department's support for the protection of postmedieval sites has varied depending on the current administration. For example, in 1999, the Department of Arts, Heritage, Gaeltacht and the Islands published "Framework and Principles for the Protection of the Archaeological Heritage," which clearly supported the protection of postmedieval sites. It stated that "the scope of the National Monuments Acts is not restricted to pre-1700 AD monuments and the Acts can be applied to monuments of architectural and historical interest as well as to ones of archaeological interest" (Department of Arts, Heritage, Gaeltacht and the Islands 1999, 49). However, as recently as 2011, a different administration proposed delisting structures dating after 1700 from Ireland's Record of Monuments and Places, which would rescind their legal protection.[1] There was a strong response from archaeologists and historians and the proposal did not advance, but this attempt underscores the politics of preservation and the perception of some that postmedieval sites are not important.

However, within archaeology there is a growing and developing interest in the nineteenth century (e.g., Brighton 2005, 2009; Clutterbuck 2006; Forsythe 2013; Kuijt et al. 2015; MacDomhnaill 2015; Orser 1996, Skeffington, Scott, and Gosling 2013; Tierney and Toscano 2011a, 2011b; Whelan and O'Keeffe 2014) and the first few decades of the twentieth century (Myles 2016, 13–16). Nevertheless, little, if any of that work has linked the impact of traumatic events and oppressive social, political, and economic relations and power structures to causes of cultural crisis and resilience (but see McAtackney 2014). In essence, in the archaeology of the modern world, we have not really addressed how cultural groups respond to events that shake their very foundations.

On the surface, it appears that time is what determines what is important in Irish heritage. Coincidently or not, the more distant archaeology is from the origins of contemporary or modern Ireland, the more relevant it is perceived to be. This is exemplified by the temporal and disciplinary divide between the National Museum of Archaeology and the National Museum of Country Life. In the former, the exhibits span the Mesolithic to the medieval. In contrast, the Museum of Country Life details everything associated with the everyday lives and experiences of rural Irish families leading up to uprising and war during the period of the 1890s to 1930. What is strange is the absence of archaeological examples from this period.

 As archaeologists, it is our responsibility to produce knowledge relating to the origins of social and political economic conflict and inequity. Extreme events, challenges, and social or cultural stressors test the structure of a culture. This is what happened in the decades following Ireland's Great Hunger. The archaeology of modern Ireland, especially of the nineteenth and early twentieth centuries, studies the struggles in the formation of a post-Famine national identity that shaped contemporary Irish politics. It is important to position the archaeology of Ireland's modern history at the forefront of narratives of heritage and history because it creates a knowledge set for understanding and interpreting dramatic societal upheavals and transformations over time and space. Furthermore, the archaeology of this period demonstrates how such changes have impacted the everyday lives of all classes in Ireland. This focus brings marginalized groups and the silenced past into the conversation through archaeological remains and community memory. In what follows, we present our ongoing research on

Ireland's cultural resilience in the context of the Great Hunger, the Irish War of Independence, and the Irish Civil War. The focus is on how our archaeological research in Skibbereen, County Cork, illustrates how these events shaped modern Irish history, identity, and culture. In addition, we argue that when the archaeology of Ireland's past is done in the context of these events, it creates a more holistic and inclusive past for communities in the present.

Knowledge Production and the Archaeology of Modern Ireland Research Program

I founded The Archaeology of Modern Ireland, a long-term collaborative historical archaeology project, in 2014. Each field season is part of a larger research project that delves into the material history and heritage of Ireland before and after the Great Hunger. Through recovered material culture, primary historical sources, and memories of the communities in and around Skibbereen, the program seeks to track and interpret cultural change and resilience in Ireland from the period after the Great Hunger until the first decades of the twentieth century. Its aim is 1) to establish an extensive material and historical database that will help us better understand the dynamics of Ireland's material world in the period 1750 to 1930; 2) to understand the impact of material culture on the lived experiences of marginalized people in the past; and 3) to contribute to ongoing community discussions of the relevance of Ireland's recent past for modern-day issues of heritage, politics, and social justice.

Skibbereen, a town in the west of County Cork, is located 51 miles (82 kilometers) southwest of Cork City. The town originated in the seventeenth century and rose to prominence as an early industrial town. It is best known, however, as the infamous metaphor for the impacts of and the horrific sufferings caused by the Great Starvation (Donnelly 1975; Geary 2010; Miller 1985).

Skibbereen was deliberately chosen as a research site for the Archaeology of Modern Ireland research project not only because it was a location for one of the most influential events in Irish history, but also because the community was already confronting this difficult past through the Skibbereen Heritage Centre. The research program has been successful thus far because of our close relationship with the centre, a local museum that serves as the cultural and social center for regional history and heritage, especially surrounding the Great Hunger. The production of archaeological and historical knowledge has been a collaborative effort between the archaeologists and Skibbereen Heritage Centre staff, who have helped us form productive working relationships with the community; helped us identify archaeological sites of interest to local stakeholders; provided key insights into local, regional, and national history; and provided the space and time for educational and outreach efforts that bring archaeologists and the local community together.

Public outreach in conjunction with the centre has included site tours for town residents, tourists, and school groups and interviews and updates in print, radio, and social media. We have also collaborated with community groups who are interested in preserving and revitalizing the area where we conducted excavations as a public park. This research program, like all archaeological projects, is a work in progress. One of the main aims is to push collaboration further toward more direct and diverse community involvement, ultimately leading to education, commemoration, and perhaps healing. To that end, upcoming field seasons include plans to host public meetings and talks designed to initiate critical discussions about heritage, history, and archaeology. When collaborating with local communities, listening is often far more important than talking. We hope this will give a voice to more members of the diverse community in Skibbereen so we can learn what they would like to see done with the project and the material culture we are recovering. We are also adding an ethnographic component to the upcoming field season. This aspect of the project is designed to do more than simply extract information about the past to aid in the archaeology; we want to learn how the community views modern Irish history and the importance and relevance of postmedieval archaeology. This information will contribute to our efforts to use the project for the good of the public.

In order to illuminate the silences of the past, create a more holistic history, and contribute to discussions of modern Irish heritage, we use a holistic approach to time and space. The study does not fixate on a single event or period in history; instead, it brings together the dynamic and layered periods of modern Irish history. The study establishes a deep connection between microlevel or site-specific data and the larger national and international stages so we can understand sociocultural transformations, expressions of collective identities, and shifting world views (Brighton 2009, 2011; Brighton and Orser 2006; Leone 1999; Mullins 1999; Orser 1996; Walker 2008).

This holistic approach to research is also a multidisciplinary practice that integrates archaeological data with social history and social identity studies from anthropology and sociology as a means of exploring the materiality of Irish identities over time and space. The reflection of diverse identities in Ireland's material culture is multifaceted, and yet those identities are structured on a foundation of shared cultural codes and collective experience that can be identified through material remains (Brah 1996; Hall 1990). These identities, both past and present, have been shaped by the events of modern Irish history. The study of the material culture of modern Ireland is a discourse in the processes of how Irish collectivities negotiated their place in a complex history (De Nie and Farrell 2010; Donnelly 2001; Errington 2007; Kinealy 1995; Miller 1985). Their material world is the reflection of their cultural senses of identity, home, and family. This is something that cannot be interpreted from documents alone.

Witness to Time: History, Windmill Hill, and the Great Hunger in Skibbereen

A natural shale outcropping named Windmill Hill (also known as The Rock) overlooks Skibbereen's market and industrial center. This was the location of the first field season of the Archaeology of Modern Ireland research project. The name Windmill Hill appears on late-eighteenth-century maps, as does Windmill Lane, which leads from the center of town to the hill. These names indicate the likely past presence of a windmill on the site. Besides the name of the hill and the lane leading up to it from town, there is no concrete archival or archaeological evidence at the moment that indicates a windmill's existence. However, it would not be uncommon or rare for a windmill to be in this part of Ireland, as Anglo-Normans introduced them in the thirteenth century. From that time to the early nineteenth century, windmills were primarily used for harnessing wind power to process grain (Rynne 2006, 37). As the centuries progressed, the number of windmills increased; by the end of the 1830s, 250 windmills were recorded in Ireland. In the nineteenth century, the number of small, single-room cabins that housed a growing and impoverished population increased along the lanes and alleyways leading from Skibbereen's center toward Windmill Hill.

Today, the ruins of six rock-cut cabins remain atop Windmill Hill. These cabins were the focus of the first season of the Archaeology of Modern Ireland project (Figure 6.1). Archival research shows that families lived in

Figure 6.1. Remains of rock-cut cabins atop Windmill Hill. Photograph by Stephen A. Brighton.

these structures from the mid-nineteenth century, but their earlier occupation history and relationship to the possible windmill are unclear. Excavations within and around three of these structures in the summer of 2015 revealed various architectural elements such as postholes, drains, and hearths. The investigations also revealed the trash middens associated with the row homes that were constructed in front of the older cabins in the late nineteenth-century. These row homes were demolished in the 1960s.

Archival resources, such as Griffith's Valuation (1848–1864), suggest that by the 1840s the structures were occupied by six families leading up to, during, and decades after the Great Hunger.[2] Family surnames include Driscoll, McCarthy, Sullivan, and Burke.[3] The valuation provides some information about class or status in Skibbereen society. First, the inhabitants paid rent on the rock-cut structures, not on any parcel of surrounding land. Thus, it appears that the families were part of the landless tenant class. Second, the various sizes of the single-room cabins provides material evidence that landless tenants were at the bottom end of the socioeconomic structure. Finally, the location of the cabins is significant. Although Windmill Hill is located above the town's center, it has the feeling of being detached from Skibbereen and daily life. The residents atop the hill would likely have been alienated from Skibbereen society.

A series of row homes known as Johnson's Terrace was constructed in front of the rock-cut structures in 1890. By 1901, eight working-class families were living on Windmill Hill, six families in the new housing and two in the rock-cut structures. For the next decade there were few demographics changes on Windmill Hill. While the names of the families living on the hill changed in the period 1901 to 1911, the social and economic statistics did not. The new families were all part of Ireland's working class, and while they did not live in utter poverty, they were part of the poorer classes in Skibbereen. Census records of 1901 and 1911 record the occupations of residents as peddler and laborer for men and charwoman, domestic, and egg merchants for women. Moreover, most families had boarders living with them.

Archaeology of Post-Famine Skibbereen and Daily Life on Windmill Hill

The excavations conducted in the summer of 2015 exposed anomalous features within the rock-cut structures and artifacts that detailed life on the hill throughout the first half of the twentieth century. The excavations have revealed a dynamic period in modern Irish history, including evidence of post-Famine recovery and the reformation and transformation of complex social relations affected by revolution, civil war, and a world war.

The recovered artifacts revealed daily life decades after the Great Hunger. The objects include the materials men, women, and children used, cherished, and discarded from the 1850s to the 1930s (Figure 6.2). A total of 1,350 artifacts, mostly ceramic and glass vessels, were recovered from the six-week excavation. Whiteware and white granite represent the bulk of the ceramic collection. The forms represented are mainly vessels associated with drinking tea and dining. Tableware and teaware sets included plates, serving plates and platters, dishes, tureens, teacups, teapots, and slop jars, to name just a few. White granite vessels not related to food consumption were associated with sanitary functions such as washbasins and chamber pots. The ceramic assemblage also highlights economic connections between the market town of Skibbereen and larger markets in Ireland and abroad. The ceramics from Windmill show a wide range of origins, providing evidence of Skibbereen's connections to worldwide trade networks. Most of the glass objects are beer and whiskey bottles, although we recovered personal items such as a single glass marble and three small beads. The latter most likely belong to a strand of glass beads associated with a rosary.

Figure 6.2. English and Scottish refined earthenware plate, teacup, and jam jar sherds recovered just outside the walls of the rock-cut structures. Photo by Stephen A. Brighton.

As with the ceramic assemblage, the glass assemblage can be used to understand how Skibbereen was connected with global trade networks in the early twentieth century. The bottles in the glass assemblage from Windmill Hill were manufactured in Ireland, England, and Scotland. They included several clear glass mineral water bottles with "Beamish Bandon" embossed on their exteriors. Beamish and Crawford was an Irish manufacturer of beer and soda. While the company was primarily based in Cork City, they operated a bottling plant in Bandon from 1913 to 1967 (Ó Drisceoil and Ó Drisceoil 2015, 239). Other embossments and company names paint a trail through the market towns of County Cork to Irish and English cities. These include Clonakilty, Cork, Dublin, Ireland, Glasgow, England, and Great Britain. These places of origin can be used to reconstruct the networks of trade that the rural Irish of West Cork were a part of.

Our research has begun to interpret changes in the material record that reflect the impact of famine, drastic population decline due to death and emigration, the collapse of cultural and economic systems, social and political uprisings, and civil war on the lives of Irish people. The artifacts reflect social networks, closeness of family life, and spirituality on the hill, in Skibbereen, and throughout Ireland.

It is not the intention of this chapter to explore the material record in its entirety but rather to illustrate cultural complexity and diversity in social

Figure 6.3. English penny dated 1906. Photo by Stephen A. Brighton.

identity and identity politics that point toward a complex socioeconomic and political landscape. While many of the artifacts are everyday objects such as plates, cups, and bowls, a small subgroup reveals something more. A class of small finds that includes coins and buttons tentatively reflect an alternative, and perhaps more complicated, narrative in the decades of world war, the waning years of the British Empire's rule in Ireland, and civil war. These objects relate to modern concepts of Irish heritage and heritage production. Contemporary heritage production in the area promotes the narrative that the population in its entirety was pro-independence, Catholic, and anti-British. Much of this heritage production gives the impression of an uncomplicated monolithic cultural identity. County Cork, especially Skibbereen, was and is known as rebel country (Casey 2018, 5; Ó Súilleabháin 2013, 308–311). Famous historic and legendary rebel figures associated with West Cork include people such as O'Donovan Rossa and Michael Collins.

Six objects are associated with the British Empire, including two English pennies that date to 1906 and 1918 (Figure 6.3). The coins represent a time when the empire was embroiled in an ever-increasing global crisis. The latter coin is of interest as it is associated with the years leading up to and including the end of World War I and with the start of the rebellion that ultimately led to Ireland's independence.

Figure 6.4. Copper alloy button with a Celtic harp. Photograph by Stephen A. Brighton.

Three British military buttons were located in the same matrix as the coins. Two of the buttons were decorated with the lion and unicorn on either side of a shield and crown; these were standard on British military uniforms. The third button, a simple brass button with a large anchor on its face, is associated with the Royal Navy. Census data reveals that at least one resident, Cornelius Collins, was enlisted in and eventually discharged from the navy; in the census he is listed as discharged as an invalid resulting from service.[4] The presence of the buttons and coins points to the impact and influence of the British Empire on Irish lives during the first decades of the twentieth century.

Objects related Irish resistance were recovered from the same stratigraphic sequence as that of the British materials, including a copper-alloy button adorned with a Celtic harp (Figure 6.4). The button is believed to be associated with the uniform of the Irish Volunteers, a group that began as a defensive military organization in 1913 and served as a military unit of citizen soldiers throughout World War I and was instrumental in the Easter Rising of 1916. In the 1920s, the military organization formed an important wing of the guerilla-style attacks on members of the Royal Irish Constabulary stationed in large towns. What lends to the power of the button is the death of Patrick McCarthy. Roughly 200 feet from the site is a monument that commemorates where a British sniper shot and killed Patrick McCarthy. McCarthy, who was not a resident of Windmill Hill but was stationed there, was part of the Irish Volunteers. The *Southern Star* reports that on July 3, 1922, he was a sniper who was harassing the local police and military barracks downhill.[5] Local oral history corroborates the newspaper's report that while he was positioned behind one of the rock-cut cabins on Windmill Hill, he lit a cigarette. That action revealed his position and he was shot dead. It is unknown if he knew people living on the hill or how or if the Irish Volunteer button is related to his activities on the hill. The button is part of the complex and diverse narrative of identity in post-Famine Ireland. It takes its place alongside British coins and military buttons and serves as a metaphor for the nuances of Irish heritage.

The materials illustrate the contradictions of modern Irish society in terms of identity formation and social beliefs. Neighbors and community members had to negotiate these potentially contentious identities every day. They included leanings toward Empire and leanings toward rebellion. The late nineteenth and early twentieth centuries were decades of violence and struggle that changed the sociopolitical landscape of Ireland. These conflicts were enacted in everyday life through social interactions that contributed to shifts in cultural values. Collectivities were transformed and reformed based on changing conceptions of personal and group identities. While we may never know what the residents on Windmill Hill were thinking when they acquired, wore, and discarded items such buttons, we can see the importance of these objects as reflections of larger issues and transformations that were happening in Ireland. Although this is a preliminary look into such topics, our analysis of the material culture we have excavated and our collaborative efforts with the Skibbereen Heritage Centre are efforts to move away from a static description of Irish culture and society in the nineteenth and early twentieth centuries and toward an explanation of the complexities and dynamic nature of Ireland's social and political landscape, both past and present.

Conclusion

The chapter began by asking What is archaeology good for? and Who benefits from the production of knowledge? I hope that the research I have presented here will serve as a gateway for discussing the meaning and importance of the archaeology of modern Ireland in terms of social justice and heritage production. My colleagues and I intend to use the work in Skibbereen for the public good by confronting difficult pasts. Skibbereen was chosen as a research site not only because it was a location for one of the most influential events in Irish history but also because the Skibbereen Heritage Centre uses its platform to confront Ireland's contentious heritage. Today, the centre has in-depth historical exhibits about the Famine, and it recently released a book and a walking-tour app for mobile phones (Kearney and O'Regan 2015). These products allow visitors to explore Skibbereen's Famine heritage at their own pace while experiencing the relevant sites in person.

The intellectual merit of this direction of research has two parts. First, a holistic approach to time and space structures this research. The study does not fixate on a single event or period in history but brings together the multiple dynamic and layered periods of modern Irish history. The study relies on the theoretical and practical development of a synchronic and diachronic approach that creates a deep connection between microlevel or site-specific data and the larger national and international stages in order to better understand sociocultural transformations, expressions of collective identities, and shifting world views in Ireland. Second, the project's integration of archaeological data with social history and applied anthropology allows us to explore the complexities of social and political identities over time. The material culture we have excavated reflects the diversity of identities in Ireland in material culture.

This is rather uncharted territory in the archaeology of modern Ireland. Ultimately, this is a study of the past in the memory of the present. To understand modern Ireland is to understand how the memory impacts the history of life before and after the Famine. I do not think that individuals who came through the Great Hunger and the generations who followed them can be considered the same people as those who lived before that event. They may be similar, but those who look for a pristine ethnic or cultural identity are asking the wrong questions. Our intention is to produce knowledge that is both accessible and relevant in the present and to understand the politics of identities, however marginalized they might be, and how those identities were expressed, received, and confronted.

The work presented here is a work in progress, an initial effort into making the archaeology of the contemporary relevant in Ireland. More collaborative projects about the archaeology of modern Ireland need to be conducted, and we hope that over time other archaeologists in Ireland will come to understand the importance of such pursuits.

Notes

1. Frank McDonald, "Archaeologists Warn against Delisting of Post-1700 Historical Structures," *The Irish Times*, September 16, 2011.

2. Griffith's Valuation, http://www.askaboutireland.ie/griffith-valuation/.

3. Census of Ireland, 1901, manuscript Form A for selected residents of Windmill Hill, National Archives of Ireland, genealogy search page, http://www.census.nationalarchives.ie/search/.

4. Census of Ireland, 1901, manuscript form A for "Residents of a house 2 in Windmill Hill (Skibbereen Urban, Cork)," National Archives of Ireland, http://www.census.nationalarchives.ie/pages/1901/Cork/Skibbereen_Urban/Windmill_Hill/1155548/.

5. "Death of Volunteer P. McCarthy," *Southern Star*, July 8, 1922.

References Cited

Atalay, Sonya, Lee Rains Clauss, Randall H. McGuire, and John R. Welch. 2014. "Transforming Archaeology." In *Transforming Archaeology: Activist Practices and Prospects*, edited by Sonya Atalay, Lee Rains Clauss, Randall H. McGuire, and John R. Welch, 7–28. Walnut Creek, CA: Left Coast Press.

Bradshaw, Brendan. 1989. "Nationalism and Historical Scholarship in Modern Ireland." *Irish Historical Studies* 26 (104): 329–351.

Brah, A. 1996. *Cartographies of Diaspora: Contesting Identities*. London: Routledge.

Breen, Colin. 2009. "Twenty Years A'Growing: University-Based Teaching and Research of Historical Archaeology on the Island of Ireland." In *Crossing Paths or Sharing Tracks? Future Directions in the Archaeological Study of Post-1550 Britain and Ireland*, edited by Audrey Horning and Marilyn Palmer, 55–64. Woodbridge, UK: Boydell & Brewer Ltd.

Brighton, Stephen A. 2009. *Historical Archaeology of the Irish Diaspora*. Knoxville: University of Tennessee Press.

———. 2011. "Applied Archaeology and Community Collaboration: Uncovering the Past and Empowering the Present." *Human Organization* 70 (4): 344–354.

Brighton, Stephen, and Charles E. Orser Jr. 2006. "Irish Images on English Goods in the American Market: The Materialization of a Modern Irish Heritage." In *Images, Representations, and Heritage: Moving Beyond Modern Approaches to Archaeology*, edited by Ian Russell, 61–88. New York: Springer.

Carew, Mairéad. 2009. "Politics and the Definition of National Monuments: The 'Big House Problem.'" *The Journal of Irish Archaeology* 18: 129–139.

Casey, William. 2018. *The Cradle of Fenianism: Skibbereen and the Early Fenian Movement, 1850–67*. Cork: William Casey.

Chambers, Erve. 1987. "Ambiguities and Ironies: Applied Anthropology in the Post-Vietnam Era." *Annual Review of Anthropology* 16: 309–337.

———. 2004. "Epilogue: Archaeology, Heritage, and Public Endeavor." In *Places in Mind: Public Archaeology as Applied Anthropology*, edited by Paul A. Shackel and Erve Chambers, 193–208. New York: Routledge.

Clutterbuck, Richard. 2006. "Wretched beyond Description: The Excavation of a Cot-
tier's Cabin in Cookstown, Co. Meath." *Seanda* 1: 46–47.

Colwell-Chanthaphonh, Chip, and T. J. Ferguson. 2008. "Introduction: The Collaborative Continuum." In *Collaboration in Archaeological Practice: Engaging Descendant
Communities,* edited by Chip Colwell-Chanthaphonh and T. J. Ferguson, 1–32. Lanham, MD: AltaMira Press.

Cooney, Gabriel. 1996. "Building the Future on the Past: Archaeology and the Construction of National Identity in Ireland." In *Nationalism and Archaeology in Europe,*
edited by Margarita Diaz-Andreu and Timothy Champion, 146–163. Boulder, CO:
Westview Press.

Cronin, Mike. 2001. *A History of Ireland.* New York: Palgrave.

Daly, Mary E. 1986. *The Famine in Ireland.* Dublin: Dundalgan Press.

De Nie, M. and S. Farrell, eds. 2010. *Power and Popular Culture in Modern Ireland: Essays
in Honour of James S. Donnelly, Jr.* Dublin: Irish Academic Press.

Department of Arts, Heritage, Gaeltacht and the Islands. 1999. *Framework and Principles
for the Protection of the Archaeological Heritage.* Dublin: The Stationery Office.

Donnelly, Colm J. 2004. "Masshouses and Meetinghouses: The Archaeology of the Penal
Laws in Early Modern Ireland." *International Journal of Historical Archaeology* 8 (2):
119–132.

———. 2007. "The Archaeology of the Ulster Plantation." In *The Post-Medieval Archaeology of Ireland 1550–1850,* edited by Audrey Horning, Ruari O Baoill, Colm Donnelly,
and Paul Logue, 37–50. Dublin: Wordwell.

Donnelly, Colm J., and Audrey J. Horning. 2002. "Post-Medieval and Industrial Archaeology in Ireland: An Overview." *Antiquity* 76: 557–561.

Donnelly, James S. 1975. *The Land and the People of Nineteenth-Century Cork: The Rural
Economy and the Land Question.* Boston: Routledge and Kegan Paul.

———. 2001. *The Great Irish Potato Famine.* Stroud, UK: Sutton Publishing.

Edwards, R. D., and T. Desmond Williams, eds. 1956. *The Great Famine.* Dublin: Brown
and Nolan.

Errington, E. J. 2007. *Emigrant Worlds and Transatlantic Communities: Migration to Upper Canada in the First Half of the Nineteenth Century.* Montreal: McGill-Queen's
University Press.

Forsythe, Wes. 2013. "The Measure and Materiality of Improvement in Ireland." *International Journal of Historical Archaeology* 17: 72–93.

Geary, Lawrence H. 2010. "The Great Famine in County Cork: A Socio-Medical Analysis." In *Power and Popular Culture in Modern Ireland: Essays in Honour of James S.
Donnelly, Jr.,* edited by Michael De Nie and Sean Farrell, 31–49. Dublin: Irish Academic Press.

Hall, Stuart. 1990. "Culture Identity and Diaspora." In *Identity, Community, and Culture
Difference,* edited by Jonathan Rutherford, 222–237. London: Lawrence and Wishart.

Hamilakis, Yannis. 2007. "From Ethics to Politics." In *Archaeology and Capitalism: From
Ethics to Politics,* edited by Yannis Hamilakis and Philip Duke, 15–40. Walnut Creek,
CA: Left Coast Press.

Horning, Audrey, Ruari O Baoill, Colm Donnelly, and Paul Logue. 2007. "Forward: Post-
Medieval Archaeology in and of Ireland." In *The Post-Medieval Archaeology of Ire-*

land 1550–1850, edited by Audrey Horning, Ruari O Baoill, Colm Donnelly, and Paul Logue, xviii–xx. Dublin: Wordwell.

Hutchinson, Josh. 2001. "Archaeology and the Irish Rediscovery of the Celtic Past." *Nations and Nationalism* 7 (4): 505–519.

Kearney, Terri, and Philip O'Regan. 2015. *Skibbereen: The Famine Story.* Skibbereen: Macalla Publishing.

Kennedy, Liam, and David S. Johnson. 1996. "The Union of Ireland and Britain, 1801–1921." In *The Making of Modern Irish History: Revisionism and the Revisionist Controversy,* edited by D. George Boyce and Alan O'Day, 34–70. New York: Routledge.

Kinealy, Christine. 1995. *This Great Calamity: The Irish Famine, 1845–52.* Boulder, CO: Roberts Rinehart.

Kuijt, Ian, Meagan Conway, Katie Shakour, Casey McNeill, and Claire Brown. 2015. "Vectors of Improvement: The Material Footprint of Nineteenth- through Twentieth-Century Irish National Policy, Inishark, County Galway, Ireland." *International Journal of Historical Archaeology* 19: 122–158.

Laurence, Anne. 2010. "Heritage as a Tool of Government." In *Understanding the Politics of Heritage,* edited by Rodney Harrison, 81–114. Manchester: Manchester University Press.

Leone, Mark P. 1999. "Ceramics from Annapolis, Maryland: A Measure of Time Routines and Work Discipline." In *Historical Archaeologies of Capitalism,* edited by Mark P. Leone and Parker B. Potter, 195–216. New York: Kluwer Academic/Plenum Press.

———. 2008. "The Foundations of Archaeology." In *Ethnographic Archaeologies: Reflections on Stakeholders and Archaeological Practices,* edited by Quetzil E. Castañeda and Christopher N. Matthews, 119–138. New York: AltaMira Press.

Little, Barbara. 2007. "Archaeology and Civic Engagement." In *Archaeology as a Tool of Civic Engagement,* edited by Barbara J. Little and Paul A. Shackel, 1–22. Lanham, MD: AltaMira Press

MacDomhnaill, Brian. 2015. "Post-Medieval and Early Modern Settlement." In *Through the Lands of the Auteri and St. Jarlath: The Archaeology of the M17 Galway to Tuam and N17 Bypass Schemes,* edited by Teresa Bolger, Martin Jones, Brian MacDomhnaill, Ross MacLeod, Colm Moloney, and Scott Timpany, 77–105. Dublin: Wordwell.

McAtackney, Laura. 2014. *An Archaeology of the Troubles: The Dark Heritage of Long Kesh/Maze Prison.* Oxford: Oxford University Press.

McDavid, Carol. 2007. "Beyond Strategy and Good Intentions: Archaeology, Race, and White Privilege." In *Archaeology as a Tool of Civic Engagement,* edited by Barbara J. Little and Paul A. Shackel, 67–88. New York: AltaMira Press.

McGuire, Randall H. 2008. *Archaeology as Political Action.* Berkeley: University of California Press.

Miller, Kerby A. 1985. *Emigrants and Exiles: Ireland and the Irish Exodus to North America.* New York: Oxford University Press.

Mitchell, Frank, and Michael Ryan. 1997. *Reading the Irish Landscape.* Dublin: Town House.

Mokyr, Joel. 1983. *Why Ireland Starved: A Quantitative and Analytical History of the Irish Economy, 1800–1850.* London: Allen and Unwin.

Mulholland, Marc. 2002. *The Longest War: Northern Ireland's Troubled History.* Oxford: Oxford University Press.

Mullins, P. R. 1999. *Race and Affluence: An Archaeology of African-America and Consumer Culture.* New York: Kluwer Academic/Plenum Press.

Myles, Franc. 2016. "The Archaeology of 1916." *Archaeology Ireland* 30 (3): 13–16.

Nicholas, George P., John R. Welch, and Eldon C. Yellowhorn. 2008. "Collaborative Encounters." In *Collaboration in Archaeological Practice: Engaging Descendant Communities,* edited by Chip Colwell-Chanthaphonh and T. J. Ferguson, 273–298, New York: AltaMira Press.

O'Day, Alan. 1996. "Revising the Diaspora." In *The Making of Modern Irish History: Revisionism and the Revisionist Controversy,* edited by D. George Boyce and Alan O'Day, 163–187. New York: Routledge.

Ó Drisceoil, Donal, and Diarmuid Ó Drisceoil. 2015. *Beamish & Crawford: The History of an Irish Brewery.* Cork: Collins Press.

Ó Gráda, Cormac. 1988. *Ireland Before and After the Famine: Explorations in Economic History, 1800–1930.* Manchester: Manchester University Press.

———. 1995. *The Great Irish Famine.* Dublin: Macmillan.

Oireachtas. 1930. National Monuments Act 1930. In *Acts of the Oireachtas 1930.* Dublin: The Stationery Office.

———. 1987. National Monuments (Amendment) Act 1987. In *Acts of the Oireachtas 1987.* Dublin: The Stationery Office.

Ollman, Bertell. 2003. *Dance of the Dialectic: Steps in Marx's Method.* Champaign: University of Illinois Press.

Orser, Charles E., Jr. 1996. *A Historical Archaeology of the Modern World.* New York: Plenum Press.

Ó Súilleabháin, Micheál. 2013. *Where the Mountainy Men Have Sown: War and Peace in Rebel Cork in the Turbulent Years 1916–21.* Cork: Mercier Press.

Rynne, Colin. 2006. *Industrial Ireland, 1750–1930: An Archaeology.* Cork: Collins Press.

Shackel, Paul A. 2011. *New Philadelphia: An Archaeology of Race in the Heartland.* Berkeley: University of California Press.

Shackel, Paul A., and Erve Chambers, eds. 2004. *Places in Mind: Public Archaeology as Applied Anthropology.* New York: Routledge.

Shackel, Paul A., and Barbara J. Little, eds. 2007. *Archaeology as a Tool of Civic Engagement.* Lanham, MD: AltaMira Press.

Shanks, Michael, and Randall H. McGuire. 1996. "The Craft of Archaeology." *American Antiquity* 61 (1): 75–88.

Skeffington, M. Sheehy, N. E. Scott, and P. Gosling. 2013. "Numbered Seaweed Mearing Stones on Island Eddy and the Adjoining Mainland at Carrowmore Townland, Ballinacourty, Galway Bay." *Journal of Irish Archaeology* 22: 93–109.

Stottman, M. Jay. 2010. "Introduction: Archaeologists as Activists." In *Archaeologists as Activists: Can Archaeologists Change the World?* edited by M. Jay Stottman, 1–18. Tuscaloosa: University of Alabama Press.

Tierney, John, and Maurizio Toscano. 2011a. "Early Modern Sites." In *In the Lowlands of South Galway: Archaeological Excavations on the N18 Oranmore to Gort National Road Scheme,* edited by Delaney Finn and John Tierney, 160–180. Dublin: Wordwell.

———. 2011b. "Rural Settlement in the Early Modern Landscape." In *In the Lowlands of South Galway: Archaeological Excavations on the N18 Oranmore to Gort National Road Scheme,* edited by Delaney Finn and John Tierney, 59–70. Dublin: Wordwell.

Trouillot, Michel-Rolph. 1997. *Silencing the Past: Power and the Production of History.* Boston: Beacon Press.

Walker, Mark. 2003. "Aristocracies of Labor: Craft Unionism, Immigration, and Working-Class Households in West Oakland, California." *Historical Archaeology* 42 (1): 108–132.

Whelan, David A., and Tadhg O'Keeffe. 2014. "The House of Ussher: Histories and Heritages of Improvement, Conspicuous Consumption, and Eviction on an Early Nineteenth-Century Irish Estate." *International Journal of Historical Archaeology* 18 (4): 700–725.

Zimmerman, Larry J. 2008. "Unusual or 'Extreme' Beliefs about the Past, Community Identity, and Dealing with the Fringe." In *Collaboration in Archaeological Practice: Engaging Descendant Communities,* edited by Chip Colwell-Chanthaphonh and T. J. Ferguson, 55–86. Lanham, MD: AltaMira Press.

7

Race and Play

Toys and the Socialization of Children into Racial Ideologies

CHRISTOPHER P. BARTON

Individuals are socialized into structures through numerous media. In previous works (Barton and Somerville 2012, 2016), Kyle Somerville and I showed that the majority of racialized toys in the United States during the nineteenth and early twentieth centuries depict stereotypes of Black peoples, particularly African Americans. In this chapter, I explore how these toys altered how children saw themselves and each other as part of an everyday practice used to dehumanize and disenfranchise Black people. I discuss the psychological and social effects of racial identity on Black children as Kenneth and Mamie Clark researched and discussed in their doll experiment (Clark and Clark 1947). The Clarks' interpretations of race and racism reveal how children's material culture was one of many socializing media that formed their individual habitus and world views. Given that I am dedicated to using archaeology as a means of social activism, I go further to discuss contemporary forms of the Clark experiment conducted by the Cable News Network (CNN) and how race continues to influence how children see their self-worth.

First, I examine the use of children's toys, specifically dolls and mechanical banks from the mid-nineteenth to early twentieth centuries, to socialize children in the United States, with a particular focus on racist Black toys. I believe that these toys were used to recreate ideologies of white superiority and Black inferiority as innate categories to ensure that children would continue the practices of racialism and racism. These racialized objects were didactic media that socialized white children into a collective identity of whiteness through the dehumanization of Black people. By mobilizing racial stereotypes and racism, they taught white children perceived notions of how a Black person should look and act. This was meant as a binary contrast to the perceived ways that proper, middle-class white people should look and act. The actions and situations of toys like the dancing Alabama Coon Jigger or the Chicken Snatcher mechanical bank, which depicted a Black man with chicken in hand and a dog biting his behind, contrasted with the white Victorian ideals of beauty, restraint, and genteel behavior (Barton and Somerville 2016).

Additionally, many of these toys reinforced class and gender roles through play. Engendered objects such as dolls and mechanical banks socialized children into the behaviors and practices that white adults deemed appropriate for boys and girls in a racialized, engendered, and class-oriented landscape. Toys are not merely passive objects. They are powerful social agents that reflect and reconstruct identities and social practices. Every toy is a lesson and every child is a student.

Critical Theory, Ideology, and Toys

Critical theory in archaeology seeks to uncover the ideologies and social structures that have created inequality (Leone 2010). Building upon the class consciousness of traditional critical theory, archaeologists have used critical race theory to explain the origins of thought that regard race as a perceived natural state of humans. The central focus of each critical theory is that present-day social injustices, for example systematic racism or economic inequality, are legacies of socially constructed structures and ideologies. If such modern social issues are legacies, then their origins are rooted in history and thus can be uncovered by archaeologists. For example, today many people incorrectly view race as biological categories of humans that are based on physical traits such as skin color, hair, and eye shape. The concept of race emerged out of the Enlightenment as scholars sought to categorize their world and justify their ideologies of biological and social hierarchy. Our modern concept of race suggests that there are concrete differences between types of people that are inherently hierarchical as some groups are given opportunities and privileges at the expense of others.

Racial thinking is an ideology that shapes society. As an ideology, it masks the social realities that groups share and pits marginalized peoples against one another. Racialized thinking shapes the structure of society as it is internalized and reproduced through the practices of groups, institutions, and individuals. The modern results of racial thought extend far beyond individual acts of racism, like those seen at the 2017 Unite the Right white nationalist rally in Charlottesville, Virginia, where participants chanted "Jews will not replace us."[1] Modern racism is a structural reality that can be seen in mass incarceration rates, economic poverty, police brutality, and unequal access to healthcare among peoples of color. These systemic, structural injustices of racial thinking affect the everyday lives and futures of marginalized people. While race is not an innate or biological state of our species, racial though is very much a social reality and a lived experience for us all. Critical race theorists try to walk the tightrope of emphasizing that race is not a scientific, objective truth while also stressing that racial thought is a real social structure that gives opportunities to some groups while limiting them for others. It is not an easy act, especially for archaeologists who try to connect the archaeological record, the documented record, and the oral histories of localized sites to the vast contextual networks of the past. Those tasks become even more difficult when we understand that an individual or group's identity is not limited to a single point, like race, but contain myriad intersecting identities at any given time, in any given situation, and that those identities can vary depending on different relationships.

Understanding how identities intersect is paramount when discussing how adults use toys to socialize children into social structures and everyday practices. Society projects a host of identities onto children such as class, gender, and race through immaterial and material forms of culture. Rarely, if ever, does material culture like toys reflect and reconstruct a single identity. For example, Mattel's Barbie doll socializes young girls into gendered identities through the doll's physical appearance and perceived gender-specific actions that are deemed appropriate for women (Pearson and Mullins 1999). The original Barbie doll in 1959 was depicted as white with blonde hair and blue eyes. Mattel did not produce a Black doll until 1968, when it offered the Christie doll. Christie, like Barbie, had physical traits and was associated with stereotypes that racialized her identity, including skin color, hair color/style, and facial features.

Barbie dolls also convey messages about social status and economic class. Mattel does not make a poor Barbie or a working-class Barbie; rather, the doll is firmly upper middle class: her outfits, housing, automobiles, and jobs reinforce her affluent economic status. Adults purchase the Barbie product line because they have internalized these identities of capitalism and hope to pass them on to girls. Barbie thus becomes a focal point for the intersection of several identities that reflect long-standing social structures of class, gender, and race that are then reproduced when adults purchase the dolls and children play with them. Scholars have analyzed how Barbie socializes children in ideas about queerness (Rand 1995), gender (Thomas 2003), race (Rogers 1999), and class (Lord 2004). Although that literature extends beyond the scope of this chapter, the modern doll serves as a launching point for a discussion about historical racialized toys.

Topsy-Turvy

The topsy-turvy doll was one of the more popular racialized toys in the nineteenth and early twentieth centuries. This doll is traditionally made of cloth with the head, torso, and arms of a Black doll attached at the waist to the head, torso, and arms of a white doll. Although the doll can have different races, ages, and classes, the traditional topsy-turvy doll depicted a young, white middle- to upper-class girl with an older, enslaved or formerly enslaved Black "mammy" counterpart. The doll's most important component was a reversible skirt: when one half of the doll was being played with the other would be covered. Topsy-turvy dolls originated in the antebellum American South and were created by enslaved Black women to teach their children and their "master's" children the intersections of age, class, gender, and race (Battle-Baptiste 2011). The first part of name of the doll is likely drawn from Harriet Beecher Stowe's character Topsy, a young enslaved girl in the novel *Uncle Tom's Cabin* (Sánchez-Eppler 1997, 133) and the "turvy" portion refers to the action of turning or reversing the doll. It should be noted that the doll originated well before the publication of *Uncle Tom's Cabin* in 1852 (Bernstein 2011, 81–82), so the toy was likely renamed after the book's character in the mid-1850s. Due to the popularity of the book, doll manufacturers began producing topsy-turvy dolls that depicted both the Topsy character and Evangeline St. Clare (or Eva), a young white girl who is one of the protagonists in the novel. It is unlikely that there was any uniformly accepted name for the doll prior to the label topsy-turvy.

Karen Sánchez-Eppler (1997, 133–134) argues that enslaved Black women

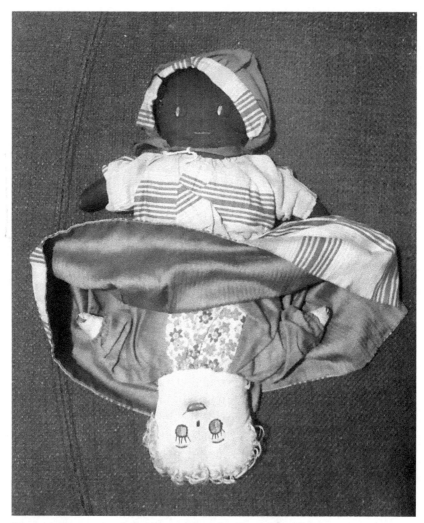

Figure 7.1. Topsy-turvy doll, ca. 1940s. Photo by Christopher P. Barton.

made the dolls for their daughters to teach them to resist rape from their white masters. She notes that no genitalia or even legs are exposed when the Black doll is topside; all that is under the doll's skirt is the white doll. Sánchez-Eppler interprets the white half of the doll as a stand-in for the master's daughter, arguing that when the master would go up the Black doll's skirt he would be reminded of his white daughter. There is no evidence to corroborate this interpretation of topsy-turvy as a medium for contesting sexual assault, but it is an interesting reading of the doll as a teaching tool.

Robin Bernstein (2011, 81–82) suggests that the dolls were used as teaching tools for both enslaved Black and free white girls. She contends that topsy-turvy dolls taught children the importance of race and gender roles. In her analysis, the racialized doll faces, which feature perceived phenotypic traits such as dark and light cloth to represent skin color, fine or coarse thread to depict hair, and varying presentations of noses, lips, and eye color, project ideologies and identities of race. These portrayals of how Black females should look as opposed to white females conveyed ideas about biological differences between the races to the child.

Although children of any gender could play with the toy, social structures and roles have historically limited ownership of dolls to females. Thus, racialized topsy-turvy dolls reinforced and reconstructed gender identities and ideologies on multiple levels. The physical forms of the dolls as females wearing dresses underscored concepts of femininity. The dolls also taught children about nurturing, caregiving, and responsibility; a child had to look after her doll so it did not get damaged or lost. Through the power of imagination shaped by social norms, dolls often become extensions of the child—they become the child's friend or their own child. Such explicit nurturing socialization through the media of dolls is rarely passed onto boys as they mature into men. The fear is that boys will develop traits of comfort and care, attributes that society has assigned to women and the domestic sphere. Dolls made for girls are purposely passive, meaning that everything happens to the doll through play or in the child's imagination. Conversely, today dolls for boys are called action figures. These dolls are active, moving social agents that do not need to be always operated by the boy. Boys thus interact with an already lively social agent. This is meant to socialize boys to the competitive, aggressive, and always moving public sphere. In contrast, the passive, static disposition of a doll for girls is meant to represent the perceived stasis of the domestic sphere, and to convey the message that that sphere is supposed to be a steady and comforting sanctuary from the chaos of the outside world.

This socialization into caregiving and nurturing as exclusively female traits is shown in the dialectic relationship between the Black mammy and the white girl of the topsy-turvy doll. Even though the two segregated halves could never be able to occupy the same space, and thus the mammy could never truly tend to the girl, the existence of the two halves of the doll reflected social ideologies of females as caregivers.

The doll also helped reconstruct the ideologies and practices of an engendered, racialized world. Bernstein (2011, 81–82) argues that enslaved Black women made topsy-turvy dolls to teach their daughters to understand what their responsibilities would be as adults, when they would have to take care of both their own and their master's children. While Bernstein's interpretation of the topsy-turvy doll as a medium for teaching gender ideologies and identities may provide an origin for the toy, it fails to explain the popularity of the doll with both Black and white children. Simply put, outside of Black rag dolls, the topsy-turvy dolls were the most popular handmade and mass-manufactured racialized dolls made for girls in the nineteenth and early twentieth centuries (Barton and Somerville 2016). The dolls taught children the importance of race, gender, and social and economic class in American society.

The topsy-turvy doll exhibited the racialized system of slavery, the diametrically opposed and conjoined relationships between the enslaved Black and freed white populations in the antebellum South. Although there were large populations of free Black peoples in the prewar United States, the foundation of the racialized slave system was a binary ideology that equated "Black" with enslavement and "white" with free (Barton 2012). The duality of the races defined them as complete opposites, and yet, they could not exist without each other. The American white race was created in opposition to the enslavement of Black peoples and the racialization of slavery (Epperson 1994). The topsy-turvy doll of the nineteenth century embodies the duality of the races on beliefs of inferiority versus superiority, enslaved versus free, and Black versus white. These dialectics did not disappear with the end of slavery, but they morphed in the transitioning social landscapes of the mid-nineteenth century. While the core message of the Black and white doll was no longer enslaved versus free, the message changed to underscore inferiority versus superiority through the racialized caste system that quickly developed in the American South. In the postbellum era, everyday forms of racism worked in concert with structural and institutional racism to continue the dehumanization of the Black race and to ensure that they were socially and economically repressed. The mammy portion of the doll was no longer enslaved, but she was still in a subservient position as a paid employee of the young white girl's parents. Although both the Black and the white halves were subservient to a patriarchal society because of their gender and were further restricted because of the Black woman's race and the white girl's age, eventually the white girl would grow up and achieve a higher social and economic position. These divisions manifested in the doll reflected the racial segregation of the postbellum South.

The fact that both halves represented so many different ideologies and identities that they physically could not be played with at the same time and yet were unable to exist without the other was a discourse on relations between Black and white people during the Jim Crow era. Jamie Brandon (2004, 197) states that the topsy-turvy doll was a

> horrific metaphor for racialization in America; the two are inextricably attached and cannot exist without the other, while simultaneously they are unarguably in two different worlds as they cannot be seen together, and this is perhaps a precursor to the "separate but equal" policies that would become a defining aspect of the modern South.

From the aftermath of the Civil War into the twentieth century, racialized toys such as the topsy-turvy doll were part of a complex network that sought to maintain the order of a racially, economically, and socially separated United States. Children's toys influenced how children saw each other and themselves, including their own self-worth.

The Clark Doll Experiment and Today

In the 1940s, Kenneth and Mamie Clark developed the doll test to understand the effects of segregation on Black children (Clark and Clark 1947). The experiment involved two identical plastic dolls, one Black and the other white. The experiment was conducted in segregated schools in Arkansas and Washington, DC, and in integrated schools in Massachusetts and New York. It involved 253 children ages three to seven. In one phase of the study, researchers simply asked the children to hand them either the Black or white doll. The results showed that 94 percent of the children could identify the white doll and 93 percent could identify the "colored" doll (170). This phase showed that nearly all of the 253 children in the experiment had been socialized into an understanding of racialism and its connection to the doll's race. The Clarks then said things like "Give me the doll that you like to play with," "Give me the doll that is a nice doll," "Give me the doll that looks bad," or "Give me the doll that looks like you" (169). The results of this and other experiments by the Clarks throughout the 1940s showed that two-thirds of Black children liked the white doll best or preferred to play with it over the Black doll.

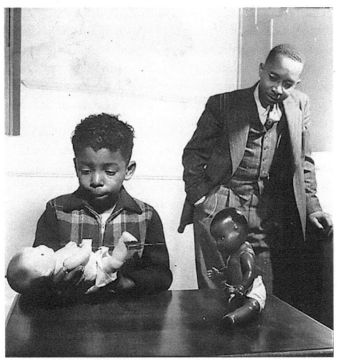

20th c. black scholarship

Figure 7.2. Dr. Kenneth Clark conducting the doll test with a young male child, 1947. Photograph by Gordon Parks, Prints and Photographs Division, Library of Congress.

Additionally, most of the children saw the white doll as "nicer"; 55 percent said that the "colored" doll looked bad and only 17 percent said that the "white" doll looked bad. The most disheartening aspects of the experiment were that most of the children attributed the negative characteristics of "ugly," "dirty," and "bad" to the Black doll (Clark and Clark 1947, 174). As the Clarks continued to conduct similar experiments in different locations throughout the North and South, they showed that racial segregation had a negative effect on Black children, including their self-worth.

When Kenneth Clark was called on as an expert witness in the United States Supreme Court case *Brown v. Board of Education* (1954), he used the Clarks' doll experiment as one of the key forms of evidence against racial segregation. The Clarks' work and testimony from several other experts in the fields of political science, economics, and others, proved that "segregation of children in public schools based solely on race deprives children of the minority group of equal educational opportunities, even though the physical facilities and other 'tangible' factors may be equal."[2]

The Clarks' work captivated the attention of the world, and their experiments were replicated in various forms for decades. One recent example was undertaken in 2010 by sociologist Margaret Beale Spencer in collaboration with CNN (CNN 2010). The study included 133 children (75 African American and 58 white) ages four to ten from four schools in New York and four schools in Georgia. Each child was shown a sign with five nearly identical depictions of a cartoon girl or boy. The only differences between the depictions were the hair and skin color, which ranged from the lightest to darkest. In response to the instruction, "Show me the dumb child," about 76 percent of the younger white children (four to five years old) selected the two darkest skin tones. Additionally, 66 percent of the younger white children selected the two darkest skin tones when asked to "Show me the mean child." Fifty-nine percent of the older white children (nine to ten years old) pointed to the two darkest skin tones after being asked to "Show me the bad child" (CNN 2010). The results demonstrated that, despite some race neutral responses, most white children had a bias against the two darkest skin tones.

Similarly, when younger Black children were asked to "Show me the ugly child," 57 percent of them pointed to the two darkest figures. When asked to "Show me the color that you think most children would think looks bad on a boy," more that 70 percent of the older Black children and 61 percent of the younger Black children also selected the two darkest skin tones. Finally, when the children were asked to "Show me the child that has your skin color," all of the white children pointed to the two lightest skin tones and all but four of the Black children selected the darkest. These findings were similar to those of the Clark experiment and demonstrated that children's perceptions about skin color and their understanding of race and self-worth had changed very little in sixty-three years (CNN 2010).

The CNN report exposed the predominance of negative emotional connections with darker skin among white children as a systemic issue of racial bias in society. Images in the media continually show villains as having darker skin tones and clothing, in contrast to the lighter tones associated with protagonists (Rockler 2004). An example of this is seen in Rockler's (2001) analysis of Disney's animated film *The Lion King*. Rockler discusses how everything from coloring to the casting of minority-voice actors in roles of villainous hyenas has racialized undertones in the film. Rockler argues that even the places where the protagonist Simba lives, the Pridelands, a lush, savannah environment where the lions rule the animal kingdom in perfect harmony, is contrasted with the home of the hyenas, a dark barren region that is ruled by the savage hyenas that is known as the Elephant Graveyard. After the leader of the lions is killed and the hyenas take over the Pridelands, the harmony of life is disrupted and the lands go to waste. Rockler argues that this interplay is a metaphor for racial segregation in which the Pridelands are seen as the white suburbs while the Elephant Graveyard is interpreted as the intercity ghetto that is inhabited by African Americans and Latinx hyenas. "They [the hyenas] represent the *concept* of the feared and hated outsider whom the mainstream culture fights to keep out. The order of the circle of life depends on the hyenas staying outside of the Pridelands" (Rockler 2001, 181). Rockler concludes that it is important to understand the context in which media such *The Lion King* teach people about race: "Members of a culture learn implicitly what the rules, norms, and power structure of their culture ought to be. They learn the *ideology* of their culture. Certainly, *The Lion King* does not turn children into racists. However, when members of a culture view many messages such as *The Lion King,* the ways in which we as a culture view ideological concepts such as race, segregation, and hierarchy are shaped" (183). Through this lens we can better understand the CNN report's interpretations that racial awareness in the media may help explain the differences in positive and negative responses between Black and white children. The study unequivocally showed, as Spencer concluded, that "we are still living in a society where dark things are devalued and white things are valued" (CNN 2010).

While toys were not explicitly discussed in the CNN report and dolls were only used as tools in the Clark experiment, both studies underscore the connections between children, material culture, and identity. Mattel's Barbie doll illustrates this. While a search for "African American" dolls in Mattel's Barbie Doll collection yielded forty-seven female dolls, only three had "natural" hair and only two had "dark" skin.[3] (While this quick search is by no means conclusive and Mattel does have more dolls with dark skin and natural hair, it can be quite difficult for a consumer of color to find a representative, Black doll.) This is important because Barbie is still one of the key mediums through which girls are socialized into intersecting identities and social structures. Parents of dark skinned, natural-hair children are left with the limited options of purchasing light-skinned, treated-hair dolls that continue to recreate the same type of color bias and decreased self-worth as the children in the CNN report exhibited. As various analyses of the topsy-turvy doll, the Clarks' doll experiment, and the recent CNN report show, the intersectionality of race, identity, and self-worth is conveyed through the material culture that adults give to children to play with, and children recreate those same structures through play.

Conclusion

Toys are powerful didactic tools that reflect and reconstruct intersecting identities and social practices. The topsy-turvy doll taught girls the ideologies and identities of race, gender, and class. The doll was popular from the antebellum period well in to the twentieth century, but the meanings of the doll did not stay static; the mammy character changed from being enslaved to being wage earner. In the Clark experiment, Black children assigned negative and positive attributes to racialized dolls, as they saw their own self-worth as a racialized "Other" reflected through the Black doll. Despite the success of the Clarks' experiment in the 1940s, the 2010 CNN report shows that children still assign positive and negative attributes based on skin color. These lasting ideologies of race are manifested through the lack of dark-skinned, natural-hair Mattel dolls. As critical theorists and archaeologists focused on using our craft as social activism, it is our goal to identify modern racist ideologies projected in toys and to uncover their historical origins. One fruitful avenue for this social activism has been my presentations and discussions of race with children. Over the past few years, I visited several schools in New Jersey and in Galway, Ireland, to talk with children ages five to thirteen about the ideologies of race and gender as manifested through toys. This continues to be a useful way to engage with audiences that rarely interact with archaeologists. What I have found in my limited experience in presentations and observations at primary schools is that children are becoming more understanding of race and gender as social constructions. Most can readily identify the characteristics of social constructs and rarely assign positive and/or negative attributes to stereotyped racial identifiers, such as skin color. Even though these interactions are by no means a rigorous experiment, they help me see that despite the shadows created by past ideologies of race and gender, our future could be better. This form of activism is basic, but sometimes the biggest movements start with the smallest steps.

Notes

1. Yari Rosenberg, "'Jews Will Not Replace Us': Why White Supremacists Go After Jews," *Washington Post,* August 14, 2017.
2. Brown v. Board of Education, 347 U.S. 483 (1954).
3. This analysis is based on my visit to https://barbie.mattel.com/shop on May 21, 2020.

References Cited

Barton, Christopher P. 2012. "Tacking between Black and White: Race Relations in Gilded Age Philadelphia." *International Journal of Historical Archaeology* 16 (4): 634–650.

Barton, Christopher P., and Kyle Somerville. 2012. "Play Things: Children's Racialized Mechanical Banks and Toys, 1880–1930." *International Journal of Historical Archaeology* 16 (1): 47–85.

———. 2016. *Historical Racialized Toys in the United States.* Walnut Creek, CA: Left Coast Press.

Battle-Baptiste, Whitney. 2011. *Black Feminist Archaeology.* Routledge, New York.

Bernstein, Robin. 2011. *Racial Innocence: Performing American Childhood from Slavery to Civil Rights.* New York: New York University Press.

Brandon, Jamie C. 2004. "Reconstructing Domesticity and Segregation Households: The Intersection of Gender and Race in the Postbellum South." In *Household Chores and Household Choices: Theorizing the Domestic Sphere in Historical Archaeology,* edited by Kerri S. Barile and Jamie C. Brandon. Tuscaloosa: University of Alabama Press.

Clark, Kenneth B., and Mamie P. Clark. 1947. "Racial Identification and Preference in Negro Children." In *Reading in Social Psychology,* edited by T. M. Newcomb and E. L. Hartley, 169–178. New York: Henry Holt and Company.

CNN. 2010. "Study: White and Black Children Biased toward Lighter Skin." *CNN,* May 14. http://www.cnn.com/2010/US/05/13/doll.study/index.html.

Epperson, Terrence W. 1994. "The Politics of Empiricism and the Construction of Race as an Analytical Category." In *Transforming Anthropology* 5 (1): 15–19.

✳ Leone, Mark. 2010. *Critical Historical Archaeology.* Walnut Creek, CA: Left Coast Press.

Lord, M. G. 2004. *Forever Barbie: The Unauthorized Biography of a Real Doll.* New York: Walker & Company.

Meskell, Lynn. 2002. "The Intersections of Identity and Politics in Archaeology." *Annual Review of Anthropology* 31: 279–301.

Pearson, Marlys, and Paul R. Mullins. 1999. "Domesticating Barbie: An Archaeology of Barbie Material Culture and Domestic Ideology." *International Journal of Historical Archaeology* 3 (4): 225–259.

Rand, Erica. 1995. *Barbie's Queer Accessories.* Durham, NC: Duke University Press.

Rockler, Naomi R. 2004. "Race, Hierarchy, and Hyenaphobia in the 'Lion King.'" In *Race/Gender/Media: Considering Diversity across Audiences, Content, and Producers,* edited by R. A. Lind, 177–191. Boston: Pearson.

Rosenberg, Yari. 2017. "'Jews Will Not Replace Us': Why White Supremacists Go After Jews." *Washington Post,* August 14.

Rogers, Mary F. 1999. *Barbie Culture.* London: Sage Publications.

Sánchez-Eppler, Karen. 1997. *Touching Liberty: Abolition, Feminism, and the Politics of the Body.* Berkeley: University of California Press.

Thomas, Jeannie B. 2003. *Naked Barbies, Warrior Joes, and the Other Forms of Visible Gender.* Chicago: University of Illinois Press.

8

Himalayan Heritage in Danger

How Digital Technology May Save the Cultural Heritage of Uttarakhand, India

BERNARD K. MEANS AND VINOD NAUTIYAL

Uttarakhand is one of India's newest states. It was formed on November 9, 2000, out of the northern part of the state of Uttar Pradesh. Located on the southern slope of the Himalayan mountain ranges, Uttarakhand shares borders with Tibet and Nepal. This Himalayan region is well known for four sacred Hindu temples and shrines that are important features of the landscape because they attract pilgrims from across the globe. Uttarakhand is colloquially known as Dev Bhoomi, a term that is translated as "God's Land," the "abode of the gods," or the "land of the gods." The region is important to worshippers of Brahma, Vishnu, and Siva, among other deities (Gupta 1995, 13; Nautiyal 1969). Several sacred rivers originate in Uttarakhand, notably the sacred Ganga (or Ganges) and Yamuna (Saklani and Nautiyal 2001, 314).

Unfortunately, the cultural heritage of Uttarakhand is imperiled by rapid growth; cyclical disasters that include landslides, earthquakes, and massive floods; and a general indifference and apathy toward heritage preservation among government agencies. Critical steps are needed to preserve heritage sites, including making politicians and the general public aware of what is known—and what can still be learned—about that state's past. The Department of History including Ancient Indian History, Culture and Archaeology at Hemwati Nandan Bahuguna (HNB) Garhwal University in Srinagar (Garhwal) has carried out extensive archaeological expeditions in Uttarakhand to highlight the antiquity of its cultural past and add new dimensions to Indian archaeology. This work has documented Uttarakhand's heritage and has raised local and international awareness of the state's rich cultural past. Highlights of this work are exhibited in the HNB Garhwal University Museum of Himalayan Archaeology and Ethnography (hereafter University Museum). However, these rich resources are available only to a small academic circle and have not reached far and wide to students and the general public. This situation is the result of the poor visibility of the University Museum and its inability to tap the technological opportunities available in India and elsewhere in the world. In order to open doors in this direction, HNB Garhwal University partnered with the Virtual Curation Laboratory at Virginia Commonwealth University (VCU) in Richmond, Virginia, to develop and implement strategies to digitally conserve artifacts and art pieces excavated from numerous archaeological sites of Uttarakhand, India, and adjacent areas in the Trans-Himalayan region. This partnership is also designed to raise awareness of Uttarakhand's rich cultural legacy and perhaps spur local efforts to protect this heritage, which is on the verge of deterioration and disappearance due to natural and manmade disasters.

A digital approach based on virtual curation through three-dimensional (3D) visualization and 3D printing offers a cost-effective way to raise awareness of and preserve the region's heritage. Such an approach will popularize the rich collection of the University Museum globally through the internet and will transport the museum's collection of art and archaeological objects virtually and make temporary exhibits possible through 3D printing. We can raise awareness of the heritage of this part of the world without disturbing the original artifacts. Scholars and students of all ages in India and across the planet can use these 3D digital resources to conduct cooperative research projects that highlight the cultural heritage of the Uttarakhand Himalayan region. Additionally, through this digital approach, the public can advocate for the importance of Uttarakhand's past to government officials who are directing construction projects that endanger cultural resources and are restricting funding for researchers who want to explore this past. Here, we briefly describe the collaboration between HNB Garhwal University and the Virtual Curation Laboratory at VCU and discuss the ways we use 3D visualization and 3D printing to highlight Uttarakhand's past.

Replicating Reality? Visualizing the Past through 3D Scanning and 3D Printing

Three-D scanning and 3D printing of cultural heritage objects are technologically sophisticated ways of creating copies of the material past. The techniques used at the Virtual Curation Laboratory and HNB Garhwal University—3D laser and structured light scans and photogrammetry—only capture the surface morphology of an object and its color attributes, although in some cases the color capture may be imperfect. Thus, the 3D scans generated during digital documentation of Himalayan heritage are copies that do not capture the full characteristics of an object. Replicas made through 3D printing are also imperfect copies. While it is possible to 3D print in a wide range of materials, including metals, glass, and clay, the 3D-printed replica of a real object will lack attributes of the object from which it was derived. For example, when a ceramic jar is 3D printed in clay, the 3D print will not completely reflect the manufacturing techniques used for the real object. The replica might look wheel thrown like the original, but it will actually be built up layer by layer in an accretional process. Because of cost considerations and the types of 3D printers that are readily available to consumers, 3D prints are frequently made from colorful plastics that represent every hue seen in the most vibrant rainbow and colors that are never seen in nature. In the Virtual Curation Laboratory, skilled technicians use readily available acrylic paints to provide 3D-printed plastic replicas that are as close as possible to the color of the original object (Figure 8.1).

Since Means founded the Virtual Curation Laboratory in August 2011, he has encountered a number of objections to 3D scanning and 3D printing, largely from museum curators and professional archaeologists. Objections fall into two major categories. The first derives from the fact that, whether in digital form or as a 3D-printed item, the 3D replica is missing some essential characteristic(s) of the original object. People emphasize that digital models are not tangible and that 3D-printed replicas lack the weight of the original item. Interestingly, some professional archaeologists have commented that they prefer black-and-white static illustrations to color 3D models that the viewer can freely manipulate. We will return to this issue shortly. The second major objection, which comes primarily from museum curators but also from a few professional archaeologists, is that 3D replication is unnecessary not only because it creates an imperfect copy but also because the curator or archaeologist has the real thing.

Ultimately, the two major categories of objections to 3D digitization of cultural heritage that Means encountered are rooted in concerns about making copies of real objects. Smith (2015, 23), who draws on art theory to consider the concept of copies, notes that copies are often seen as inauthentic, either "fakes" made to fool potential purchasers or "useless derivatives"

Figure 8.1. The NextEngine at HNB Garhwal University 3D scanning a devotional figurine dated ca. 200 BC to AD 200. Photo by Bernard K. Means.

that fail to emulate the real objects. In today's capitalist world order, copies of designs, forms, and styles—even of mass-produced items—are seen as unauthorized reproductions and are protected by international laws and treaties (23–24). However, Smith points out that duplication is not always inauthentic, especially if it serves the state and reinforces ideology, for example coins, stamps, and other items that reflect authority (24).

Historically, replicative manufacturing has demonstrated an acceptance and even an appreciation of copying (Smith 2015, 28). Technologies developed over the centuries to create reasonably accurate duplicates include molds, woodcuts, moveable type, and photography (26), to which we would add 3D scanning and 3D printing. Using an example from ancient India, Smith demonstrates how using molds helped spread shared religious iconography and architectural styles (30–32). Some of the objects we have 3D scanned at HNB Garhwal University represent copying in the past through molds to make devotional figures—and one mold to make ceramic figurines—that enabled people to share portable manifestations of their shared belief systems 2,000 years ago (Figure 8.2). The act of copying—whatever

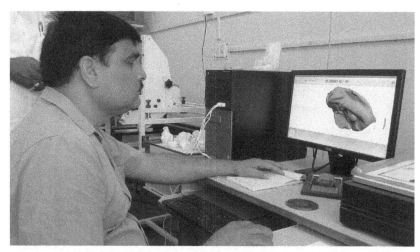

Figure 8.2. HNB Garhwal University archaeologist Mohan Naithani editing the 3D scan of a model created with the NextEngine. Photo by Bernard K. Means.

technique is used—can be reconciled with cultural practices even if the copies are imperfect.

What motivates museums to make and use copies besides a basic ethos of preservation? From their inception in the late nineteenth century, the Cast Courts of the Victoria and Albert Museum in London, England, have relied on the power of copies—some quite massive in scale—as an integral part of the museum's mission (Patterson and Trusted 2018; Trusted 2018). As Patterson and Trusted (2018, 17) state, "The Museum's mission was two-fold: to act as a school of art education for practitioners, and to enlighten the public." Directly analogous to the discussion above regarding 3D printed replicas, the casts were drawn from across Europe. Parts of the world under the dominion of the British Empire were seen as important in terms of their forms and decorative attributes, not in terms of their physical structures (ibid.). In an attempt to bring as much of the world, at least the European world, to the Victoria and Albert Museum and the local residents of its South Kensington neighborhood, the museum's first director, Henry Cole, led an effort in 1867 for a Convention for Promoting Universally Reproductions of Works of Art for the Benefit of Museums of All Countries. Fifteen European princes signed this convention (Trusted 2018, 30). An interest in creating copies that can be shared among museums and the public continues to be relevant. On the 150th anniversary of the 1867 convention, a new convention recognized that copying encompassed developments in digital technology, including 3D scanning and 3D printing. This new convention was entitled the Reproduction of Art and Cultural Heritage (ReACH). The idea behind ReACH was to link "heritage organizations around the world and encourag[e] them to record and protect archaeological sites at risk" (31).

The Cast Courts help preserve the past and meet the Victoria and Albert's missions of showcasing artistic and cultural diversity and bringing the world's (largely European) heritage to a local community. Preservation is one motivation for 3D scanning at HNB Garhwal University, but we emphasize using local heritage to reach out to a world that likely will never see the real Himalayan heritage and can only interact with 3D digital models or 3D-printed copies. However, we should recognize that even a visitor to the HNB Garhwal University Museum of Himalayan Archaeology and Ethnography would have a limited ability to interact with museum collections. Even sculptures, figurines, and vessels on exhibit are safely behind glass and can be seen but not touched. We thus should not be dismissive of individuals who only interact with 3D digital models or 3D-printed replicas of objects from the past. Digital models are a form of archaeological visualization that moves the tangible past into a virtual realm where individuals have more freedom to explore an object than is possible with the exhibited item itself or with more traditional static representations such as photographs. The past becomes more democratic and more accessible through 3D scanning, while the artifacts themselves are carefully preserved (Bowles 2014; McCuistion 2013; Means 2015, 2017a, 2017b; Means et al. 2013; Means, McCuistion, and Bowles 2013). *But where / by whom ?*

HNB Garhwal University and the Museum of Himalayan Archaeology and Ethnography

The HNB Garhwal University Museum of Himalayan Archaeology and Ethnography is located in the town of Srinagar (Garhwal) in Uttarakhand. The museum showcases a heritage that includes tools from the lower Paleolithic period, the pottery of habitation and burial sites, and ethnographic collections that highlight how people live today in the Himalayan foothills (Khanduri and Negi 2007; Nautiyal and Khanduri 1986, 1991; Nautiyal et al. 2014; Saklani and Nautiyal 2001).

Among the museum's holdings are spectacular Hindu, Buddhist, and Jain sculptures and hundreds of terra-cotta sculptures and figurines datable to the period 600 BC to AD 1400. Since its founding in 1976, HNB Garhwal University's Department of History including Ancient Indian History,

Culture and Archaeology has led research and preservation efforts related to the cultural heritage of Uttarakhand's central and western Himalayan regions. An earlier project used 3D visualization techniques and web-enabled applications in archaeology to create a database of Indian pottery (Nautiyal et al. 2000, 2007).

Because of their common interest in 3D visualization of archaeological artifacts, the authors developed a collaborative project that focused on objects recovered from excavated sites in Uttarakhand's central and western Himalayan regions initially using a NextEngine 3D Laser Scanner. The joint program also provided a unique opportunity for graduate students at HNB Garhwal University to be trained to use this 3D scanning technique as it applies to archaeology. The goal of the university's archaeological visualization laboratory is to promote and introduce computing and visualization tools in archaeological practice. But what is more important to emphasize here is that the 3D visualization techniques used in this joint study enable us to preserve the most precious heritage of Uttarakhand. This heritage was almost lost in a landslide that damaged the old museum building. Although the artifacts were saved, it was four years before they could be placed in a new museum, during which time they were inaccessible to scholars and the general public alike. If critical objects had been 3D scanned, they could have acted as virtual avatars until the actual objects became available or they could have become the sole representation of objects that had been destroyed. This incident shows that heritage objects are prone to damage and loss and that it is imperative that we find ways to preserve this precious past not only digitally but also as 3D replicas in case objects are damaged or lost forever. A tragic example that reverberated around the world was the loss of Brazil's rich cultural and natural heritage when its national museum was ravaged by a destructive fire. Many of its holdings are gone forever and do not even have a digital analog (Dreyfuss 2018). This event has added urgency to our efforts to digitize the artistic, historical, archaeological, and other museum objects HNB Garhwal University holds should such a tragedy occur here.

The Department of History including Ancient Indian History, Culture and Archaeology at HNB Garhwal University is one of the largest at the university. Archaeology faculty members and other technical staff specialize in Himalayan archaeology, environmental archaeology, and ethnoarchaeology. As part of his research interests, Dr. Vinod Nautiyal has long been involved with computer applications in archaeology. Recently, Dr. Nautiyal and his team have been excavating sites in the Trans-Himalayan

Figure 8.3. Mohan Naithani using a Structure Sensor attached to an iPad mini to 3D scan the priest at Ukhimath Temple. Photo by Bernard K. Means.

region of northern India, an area that has not been widely studied because of its rough terrain. Their investigations of Lippa and Kanam, two cist burial sites, show that this area was used earlier than had been thought and that there was greater cultural integration across northeastern India, Nepal, and western Tibet than was previously known (Nautiyal et al. 2014). Following the initial investigations of Lippa and Kanam, Dr. Nautiyal and his students began creating 3D digital models of selected items from their excavations and their museum's collections using a NextEngine 3D Laser Scanner. This specific piece of technology led HNB Garhwal University to reach out to the Virtual Curation Laboratory, which also uses this scanner.

Since August 2015, the archaeological visualization laboratory of the department has worked with the Virtual Curation Laboratory to 3D scan terra-cotta figurines and sculptures dating to AD 300–400 using the department's NextEngine 3D Laser Scanner (Figure 8.3). The resulting digital models were edited using software at the Virtual Curation Laboratory. The Virtual Curation Laboratory printed these 3D models from the museum and Means brought them on a subsequent visit to HNB Garhwal University. Nautiyal was then able to showcase the Himalayan heritage at conferences for the first time. Unlike the replicas, the original objects cannot be safely removed from the museum. This was the biggest success of this joint collaborative program between two departments located in India and the United States. The activities related to digital archaeology were further incorporated into educational and outreach activities for students, including teenage students from a school near HNB Garhwal University.

Virtual Curation Laboratory at Virginia Commonwealth University

Founded in August 2011, the Virtual Curation Laboratory has evolved into a steward of the tangible past—archaeologically recovered artifacts and historical items—by embracing technologies that make it possible to preserve rare and fragile finds from archaeological sites around the world. The Virtual Curation Laboratory was established in August 2011 with funding from the Legacy Resource Management Program of the Department of Defense (DoD). This initial project was designed to explore how 3D documentation with the NextEngine 3D Laser Scanner could help preserve and share cultural heritage resources recovered from DoD lands in the United States (Means et al. 2013). The NextEngine scanner uses lasers to capture the surface morphology of an object. In a manner akin to echolocation, lasers emit from the 3D scanner toward an object placed on a rotating platform. These lasers reflect back to the scanner, which records the distance to the object. This information creates a point cloud of distance readings, which the scanner interpolates to create a solid 3D digital model. The NextEngine scanner also photographs the object and maps the resulting image onto the 3D digital model.

The sharing of digital artifact models in the Virtual Curation Laboratory was not initially focused on the general public; instead, models were shared between land managers on DoD facilities and consulting archaeologists, who conducted archaeological investigations under various federal laws or regulations on resources threatened by military training activities or construction. The basic notion was that consulting archaeologists could save time and effort if researchers or collections repositories could make digital artifact models available. This action would lead to more accurate identification of materials recovered from archaeological sites and better determinations of whether the sites were significant according to federal or state criteria. Sites that were deemed significant would be subject to further archaeological investigations (Means et al. 2013).

Undergraduate VCU anthropology students were fully integrated into the Virtual Curation Laboratory at its founding. The initial DoD Legacy project was designed to have an experiential learning component for undergraduates. As they learned 3D scanning, the students documented the steps they followed, then developed protocols that nonspecialists could use should the DoD decide to expand this 3D scanning program across the United States (Means et al. 2013). Virtual artifact curation has become a tool for the professional development of undergraduate VCU students as they learn collections management, exhibit development, public engagement, research, writing, presentation, and publication skills. VCU undergraduates use the portable laser scanner to record artifact morphology, edit the resulting digital models, and 3D print plastic replicas that they often paint to resemble the original items. The digital models and printed replicas of artifacts from across time and space have been incorporated into a variety of educational and community outreach settings, providing students with the opportunity to engage people from all walks of life and apply what they are actively learning at VCU. Undergraduate students are able to more easily make the transition from knowledge obtained in traditional classroom settings to ways to use knowledge in real-world settings. These students also see how museums use 3D digital models and printed replicas to reach the public, both on site and at other venues, such as schools, in ways that are not possible or at least are very unwise with real artifacts.

To test how well the NextEngine scanner would work with archaeological findings, the Virtual Curation Laboratory, which has little in the way of an archaeological collection of its own, teamed with a wide range of cultural heritage institutions and museums, including Jamestown Rediscovery, Ferry Farm and Mount Vernon (properties of George Washington), Gunston Hall (George Mason), Montpelier (James Madison), Poplar Forest (Thomas Jefferson), the State Museum of Pennsylvania, the New York State Museum, and the Virginia Museum of Natural History (Means 2014; Means et al. 2013; Means, McCuistion, and Bowles 2013; Selden et al. 2014). These locations all have active programs designed to educate and engage the public about the past. It became clear within months of establishing the Virtual Curation Laboratory that the creation of 3D digital artifact models holds tremendous potential for actively engaging with the public in addition to meeting the research requirements of professional archaeologists, such as accurate identification of artifacts recovered from archaeological sites.

Most activities in the Virtual Curation Laboratory today are focused on working with museums and K–12 teachers on outreach and educational programs through 3D scanning objects and, especially, 3D printing of the accurately scaled digital models of the artifacts. The 3D-printed artifact replicas have the potential to reach a wider audience for museums than is possible with traditional exhibits, including people who are blind and visually impaired (Means 2014, 2015, 2017a,b; Means et al. 2016). Using 3D digital public archaeology through the Virtual Curation Laboratory or other similar organizations, museums can extend their reach beyond their brick-and-mortar facilities to a potentially global audience.

Toward a Virtual Global Classroom *— great idea*

Appropriately enough, the authors of this chapter and our respective institutions became linked through online social media. Nautiyal contacted Means via Facebook to discuss issues he and his team were having using the NextEngine scanner. After meeting in Washington, DC, in December 2014, the authors decided to develop a virtual global classroom that would link researchers and students at HNB Garhwal University with those at VCU and, by extension, the entire world. A pilot project was funded through the VCU Global Education Office. VCU undergraduate students were trained to preserve digital cultural heritage through the Virtual Curation Laboratory and to work with HNB Garhwal University to make important archaeological and ethnographic research conducted in the Trans-Himalayan region of northern India more widely available digitally. Students who enrolled in a museum anthropology course developed exhibit content centered on 3D printing replicas in Virginia based on 3D artifact scans from the Garhwal Himalayan region and a few other north Indian sites.

To facilitate this project, Means traveled to HNB Garhwal University in August 2015 and again in May 2016 to develop the best practices for using the NextEngine scanner on select objects from the collections at the University Museum of Himalayan Archaeology and Ethnography, including terra-cotta figurines and ceramic vessels on exhibit (Figure 8.4). These best practices include how to properly orient an object to maximize 3D scanning of its entire surface and how to edit the resulting digital model to create a version that can be shared online and even 3D printed. At the beginning of this project, the museum was still in a rebuilding phase because its original location had been destroyed by a landslide. The digital models created through 3D scanning gave researchers and the public access to significant parts of the collection while the museum itself was unavailable.

Infrastructure problems, especially intermittent power from a fragile electrical grid and a tornado in May 2016, revealed some significant

Figure 8.4. Bernard Means using an EinScan Pro 2X to 3D scan a sculpture of the goddess Mahishasuramardini in Ranihat Temple. Photo by Mohan Naithani.

unanticipated issues with implementing this project. It is challenging to 3D scan artifacts fully when the power might fail at any moment. A typical 3D scanning session with the NextEngine scanner is at least one hour long using our preferred settings. Objects are placed in at least two positions when they are being 3D scanned, usually a horizontal and vertical orientation, to ensure that the scanner's lasers completely cover them. Each orientation takes half an hour for 3D scanning. More complex objects might require three or more half-hour scanning sessions. An extensive battery system prevented data loss while 3D scanning for any given session but was not sufficient to power the NextEngine for multiple sessions. The NextEngine is also susceptible to high temperatures and the cooling system could not operate on battery power. This limited the number of artifacts from the museum's collections that could be 3D scanned.

Another aspect of this project was intended to create active lines of communication between students and researchers at HNB Garhwal University and VCU that went beyond simple sharing of digital artifact models generated from 3D scans. We anticipated that the 9.5-hour time difference between Srinagar and Richmond, Virginia, would pose scheduling issues. However, internet connectivity issues precluded extended conversations beyond text-based email. Sharing of digital artifact models—especially the large raw 3D scan files—over the internet was also challenging. In fact, it was simpler for Means to archive 3D-scanned data on portable digital storage devices and bring them back to Richmond than to try to share the models digitally. Digital models of Himalayan artifacts became important for VCU students as they designed virtual and physical exhibits. The latter rely on 3D-printed and painted replicas. Means (2015) has argued that a technological interface through a virtual museum can help a digitally connected population make their own meaning by interacting with 3D digital artifacts, especially through 3D printing. An individual user can easily download 3D digital models and 3D replicate them to create their own exhibits. A virtual extension of the University Museum of Himalayan Archaeology and Ethnography seemed an ideal way to deal with the challenges of gaining access to the real museum and an ideal way to enhance awareness of the museum's collections that people may never visit in their lifetime. The Virtual Curation Laboratory has archived numerous digital models generated through the cooperative project with HNG Garhwal University on the digital sharing platform Sketchfab.[1] At present, only temporary venues have been found at VCU for physical exhibits for the replicated artifacts from north India—and not in prominent campus locations with high foot traffic or high visibility.

Although the basic aims of the virtual global classroom initiative were not met, a digital humanities approach is still considered the best way to protect and possibly foster a preservation ethos for the archaeological and cultural heritage of the Himalayan region of north India. After all, while direct access to the University Museum of Himalayan Archaeology and Ethnography is challenging because of its location even for residents of Srinagar (Garhwal), digital access is not problematic for savvy users of smart phones and digital content, as most residents have smart phones.

In May 2017, supplemented by funding from a VCU Humanities Research Center Research Travel grant, Means returned to HNB Garhwal University to use 3D scanning to document the university's collection and make it more accessible to both citizens of northern India and people located across the globe. During one day of this May 2017 research visit, the project team made the long journey to Ukhimath Omkareshwar Temple, which is located about 1,311 meters above mean sea level. The trip was along a narrow, winding road that wove its way through the foothills of the Himalayas. Once we arrived, we asked the temple's priest for permission to digitally record elements of the temple. He gave permission to scan all minor icons except for those inside the two main shrines. We drew on the low-cost handheld digital 3D Structure Sensor to document both important sculptures at the temple and the temple's priest himself. Drawing on this experience, we realized that we could develop a systematic program using low-cost techniques to 3D digitally document temples across the state, making it possible for this important aspect of Uttarakhand's heritage to reach out to a wider world.

The VCU Humanities Research Center funded subsequent research trips in May 2018 and May 2019. While the May 2018 trip followed the parameters of the May 2017 research trip, the May 2019 excursion incorporated a recently acquired 3D scanner that uses structured light rather than lasers to capture an object's shape. The Einscan Pro 2X was integrated into the May 2019 joint scanning efforts of HNB Garhwal University and the Virtual Curation Laboratory at a nearby Hindu temple. The portability of this high-resolution scanner makes it quite suitable for scanning larger objects that are not scannable with the NextEngine, but it is still hampered by a need for a stable electrical grid. When we went to the Hindu temple at Ranihat to 3D scan the sculpture of the goddess Mahishasura Mardini, we planned to use the temple's electrical outlets. These were not functioning when we visited, but fortunately the owner of a nearby residence loaned us access to their power to enable us to 3D scan the goddess sculpture.

Crowdsourcing Cultural Heritage

The efforts of HNB Garhwal University and the Virtual Curation Laboratory to create digital analogs of Uttarakhand's tangible heritage of temples and archaeological artifacts is obviously important. These digital models of artifacts and sculptures can foster a dialogue between the people of north India and their past. Unlike a static image, passive video, or even an exhibited item, people can freely manipulate online digital models and choose how they wish to examine the object. Those with access to 3D printers can create their own replicas and recontextualize them as they choose, creating a truly participatory culture (Means 2015; Simon 2010). The pilgrims who are rushing to major shrines and the people in Uttarakhand in general can engage with aspects of their past without having to make their way to the University Museum of Himalayan Archaeology and Ethnography—although we hope that seeing the virtual models will encourage people to visit the museum at least once in their lifetime to see the real objects of Uttarakhand's cultural heritage. In essence, the museum experience could prove analogous to a pilgrimage to a Hindu holy shrine. Advocates of a co-creation approach in museum outreach and public archaeology argue that museums should no longer be viewed as passive purveyors of knowledge but rather as places that must embrace visitors who want to create and generate their own perspectives (Bollwerk, Connoly, and McDavid 2015). For the museum at HNB Garhwal University, this can be done through 3D visualization.

Yet we know that the efforts of HNB Garhwal University and the Virtual Curation Laboratory to digitally 3D document the Himalayan past can capture only a small fracture of the region's rich and diverse history. We need to target our 3D documentation to artifacts and sites that are endangered, whether from anthropogenic destruction or the ravages of nature and time. Means's annual treks for short periods of time to Srinagar (Garhwal) have helped address issues that have arisen since the first visit and have stimulated the development of new strategies for recording Uttarakhand's past, but they are not sustainable in the long run. We have to carefully target what we 3D scan and ensure that we are digitally documenting items that capture people's attention through the romance of the past and that make local denizens of Uttarakhand feel invested in their past.

What we really need to do is crowdsource the preservation and promotion of the past. The people who are so intrinsically connected to the environment and culture they live in in the Himalayas are equally the guardians of their past. The explosion of digital media has brought people even in remote locations in the Himalayas closer to virtual worlds that encompass their own heritage and the heritage of people across the glove. The smartphones that are seemingly inseparable from everyone's hands can be harnessed in a number of ways. People can be encouraged to document their past, share that past via social media, and bring important and threatened resources to the attention of archaeologists at HNB Garhwal University. We can foster a preservation ethos that draws on a citizen scientist approach (Smith 2014) and create a broader and more inclusive community dedicated to protecting the past for the future.

Conclusions

Technology is not the only solution to the challenges we face in preserving, protecting, and promoting Uttarakhand's heritage. However, technology can be part of a solution to these challenges using 3D digital tools that combine carefully targeted projects led by professional archaeologists and experts in 3D scanning technology. How successful such an approach might be in the long run is hard to say at this point. No matter how sophisticated the technology is, unless the citizens of Uttarakhand feel that protecting their tangible cultural heritage is worthwhile, that heritage will continue to be lost to the forces of development in this impoverished Indian state. If even at first only a few of the many people who live in Uttarakhand learn more about their heritage and become engaged with digitally documenting their past, their efforts may prompt others to join them.

Acknowledgments

The research presented here has been supported by grants from the Virginia Commonwealth University Global Education Office through a Virtual Global Classroom Initiative grant awarded in 2015 and Virginia Commonwealth University Humanities Research Center travel research grants awarded for travel in 2017, 2018, and 2019. HNB Garhwal University has always been a gracious host to the first author. This study would not have been possible without the work of Sudhir Nautiyal, laboratory assistant, and Mohan Naithani, technical assistant, both of HNB Garhwal University. Their help is duly acknowledged.

Note

1. Virtual Curation Lab, Richmond, Virginia, https://sketchfab.com/virtualcurationlab.

References Cited

Bollwerk, Elizabeth, Robert Connoly, and Carol McDavid. 2015. "Co-Creation and Public Archaeology." *Advances in Archaeological Practice* 3: 178–187.

Bowles, Courtney. 2014. "Moving between Reality as Virtual and Reality as Actual." *Pennsylvania Archaeologist* 84 (1): 4–8.

Dreyfuss, Emily. 2018. "Brazil's Museum Fire Proves Cultural Memory Needs a Digital Backup." *Wired*, September 7, 2018. Accessed September 11, 2018. https://www.wired.com/story/brazil-museum-fire-digital-archives/.

Gupta, S. S. 1995. "Uttarakhand: A Profile." In *Uttarakhand: Past, Present and Future*, edited by J. C. Aggarwal and S. P. Agrawal, 13–45. New Delhi: Concept Publishing Company.

Khanduri, B. M., and S. S. Negi. 2007. *Uttarakhand: A Historical Profile*. Srinagar (Garhwal): The Department of History including Ancient Indian History, Culture and Archaeology at Hemwati Nandan Bahuguna Garhwal University.

McCuistion, Ashley. 2013. "Promoting the Past: The Educational Applications of 3D Scanning Technology in Archaeology." *Journal of Middle Atlantic Archaeology* 29: 35–42.

Means, Bernard K. 2014. "Virtual Curation and Virtual Collaboration." In *Blogging Archaeology*, edited by Doug Rocks-Macqueen and Chris Webster, 121–144. Sheffield: Landward Research, Ltd. in association with Succinct Research and DIGTECH LLC.

———. 2015. "Promoting a More Interactive Public Archaeology: Archaeological Visualization and Reflexivity through Virtual Artifact Curation." *Advances in Archaeological Practice* 3(3): 235–248.

———. 2017a. "A Digital Passport to the Past: The 'Accidental' Public Archaeology of the Virtual Curation Laboratory." *Public Archaeology* 15: 1–9.

———. 2017b. "Printing the Past: 3D Printed Artifact Replicas Aid in Research, Education." *Research & Design Magazine* 59 (3): 20–23. Accessed October 14, 2017. https://www.rdworldonline.com/printing-the-past-3d-printed-artifact-replicas-aid-in-research-education/.

Means, Bernard K., Courtney Bowles, Ashley McCuistion, and Clinton King. 2013. "Virtual Artifact Curation: Three-Dimensional Digital Data Collection for Artifact Analysis and Interpretation." Prepared for the Department of Defense Legacy Resource Management Program, Legacy Project #11-334. Richmond: Virtual Curation Laboratory, Virginia Commonwealth University.

Means, Bernard K., Ashley McCuistion, and Courtney Bowles. 2013. "Virtual Artifact Curation of the Historic Past and the NextEngine Desktop 3D Scanner." *Technical Briefs in Historical Archaeology* 7: 1–12. http://www.sha.org/documents/VirtualArtifacts.pdf.

Means, Bernard K., Mariana Zechini, Ashley McCuistion, Terrie Simmons-Erhardt, Jeff Aronowitz, Elizabeth Moore, Laura Galke, Lauren Volkers, Vivian Hite, Liz Ale, Zoë Rahsman, and Allen Huber. 2016. "Virtual Mobility Archaeology Project with Further Applications of Three Dimensional Digital Scanning of Archaeological Objects." Prepared for the Department of Defense Legacy Resource Management Program, Legacy Project #13-334. Richmond: Virtual Curation Laboratory, Virginia Commonwealth University.

Nautiyal K. P. 1969. *The Archaeology of Kumaon (including Dehradun)*. Varanasi, India: Chawkhamba Sanskrit Series Office.

Nautiyal, K. P., and B. M. Khanduri. 1986. "New Cultural Dimension in the Central Himalayan Region of Uttarakhand: An Archaeological Assessment." *Stratton da Annali dell'Istituto Universitario Orientale* 6: 77–100.

———. 1991. *Emergence of Early Culture in Garhwal, Central Himalaya: A Study Based on Excavations at Thapli and Ranihat*. Srinagar-Garhwal: HNB Garhwal University Museum of Himalayan Archaeology and Ethnography.

Nautiyal, Vinod, Sudhir Nautiyal, and Mohan Naithani. 2000. "Optical Plotting and Autocad® for Drawing Pottery." *CAS Newsletter* 22 (3). https://www.csanet.org/newsletter/winter00/nlw0003.html.

Nautiyal, Vinod, R. C. Bhatt, Pradeep M. Saklani, Veena Mushrif Tripathy, C. M. Nautiyal, and Hari Chauhan. 2014. "Lippa and Kanam: Trans-Himalayan Cist Burial Culture and Pyrotechnology in Kinnaur, Himachal Pradesh, India." *Antiquity* 88 (339). http://antiquity.ac.uk/projgall/nautiyal339/.

Nautiyal, Vinod, Vandana Dixit Kaushik, Vinay Kumar Pathak, S. G. Dhande, Sudhir Nautiyal, Mohan Naithani, Sanjeev Juyal, Rahul Kumar Gupta, Ashish Kumar Vasisth, Krishna Kumar Verma, and Anand Singh. 2007. "Geometric Modeling of Indian Archaeological Pottery: A Preliminary Study." In *Digital Discovery: Exploring New Frontiers in Human Heritage,* edited by J. T. Clark. and E. M. Hagemeister, 493–501. Budapest : Archaeolingua.

Patterson, Angus, and Marjorie Trusted. 2018. "Introduction." In *The Cast Courts,* edited by Angus Patterson and Marjorie Trusted, 14–19. London: V&A Publishing.

Saklani, Pradeep, and Vinod Nautiyal. 2001. "Archaeology: A New Perspective." In *Garhwal Himalaya: Nature, Culture, and Society,* edited by O. P. Mandarin and O. P. Gusain, 309–328. Srinagar-Garhwal: TransMedia.

Selden, Robert Z., Jr., Bernard K. Means, Jon C. Lohse, Charles Koenig, and Stephen L. Black. 2014. "Beyond Documentation: 3D Data in Archaeology." *Texas Archaeology* 58 (4): 20–24. https://scholarworks.sfasu.edu/crhr/263.

Simon, Nina. 2010. *The Participatory Museum.* Creative Commons version. Accessed December 9, 2017. http://www.participatorymuseum.org/read/.

Smith, Monica. 2014. "Citizen Science in Archaeology." *American Antiquity* 79: 749–762.

———. 2015. "The Concept of Copies: An Archaeological View of the Terracotta Ornaments from Sisupalgarh, India." *West 86th* 22: 23–43.

Trusted, Marjorie. 2018. "The Cast Courts." In the *Cast Courts,* edited by Angus Patterson and Marjorie Trusted, 20–31. London: V&A Publishing.

9

Data Sharing and Database Management as Activism, or Solving the Curation Crisis One Small Project at a Time

STACEY L. CAMP

> Curation is the responsibility of the entire archaeological community. It can no longer be an afterthought or left to non-archaeologists to pursue. Curation is everybody's business and all of us, everywhere, need to contribute to the solution.
>
> Trimble and Marino 2003, 110

The database is one of the most fundamental elements of archaeological research and analysis. In its most idealized form, a database includes a basic description and the geospatial coordinates of each artifact and ecofact recovered or observed during archaeological survey and/or excavation. Databases are used to interpret archaeological collections, to develop conclusions regarding patterns in the data, and to give other researchers the opportunity to form their own assessments and reinterpretations of the data. The database is an essential component of what Hodder (1999) terms "the archaeological process" and of reflexive archaeology because it informs and helps construct the very foundation of an archaeological argument. For these reasons, database "sharing should be the 'default' for archaeological knowledge, especially when the majority of projects are funded directly or indirectly through public resources" (Morgan and Eve 2012, 531).

Yet despite their importance, databases are often perceived as a means to an end in archaeological research, as a way of compiling and organizing data in preparation for the "real" work: analysis and interpretation (Labrador 2012, 237). The preservation and curation of databases and archaeological data (e.g., cataloged artifacts, photographs, field notes) are frequently an afterthought in allocations of funding (Richards, Austin, and Hardman 2010, 25). Depending on the size of the archaeological collection, the process of database development and data entry can be tedious, expensive, and extraordinarily time consuming. In academic contexts, granting agencies often consider such work to be an unallowable expense, foisting the responsibility of this work on repositories and principal investigators.

While databases may seem like quotidian objects, they function as a doorway through which archaeologists can democratize and openly share their data and cataloging and recordation processes for the communities, descendant groups, and other scholars they serve. Although they are labor intensive, interactive, and accessible digital databases can expand the narrative about archaeological research and findings, transporting data out of antiquated Microsoft Access databases found only on a project director's or collection manager's hard drive and into the sphere of public discourse. The technological revolution offers new ways of visualizing, representing, managing, and sharing data. It has wrestled databases from licensed software, enabling users to create and share data in open-source software and/or public-facing content management systems (Gaffney and Exon 1999). This chapter explores the centrality of the database in generating archaeological knowledge and the challenges involved in managing data and preserving databases. It also reframes the database as a space of productive public engagement, discussion, and social activism.

Archaeological Collections Management in the United States

Databases have been ignored because archaeologists face other pressing data management challenges, of which the "curation crisis" is the direst. The curation crisis refers to the lack of storage space for archaeological collections in the United States and the lack of space that complies with National Park Service legislation 36 CFR 79 (1991), which regulates the conditions for federal collections and associated documentation. 36 CFR Part 79 was an "unfunded mandate" that "authorized archaeologists to build costs for curation directly into their contracts with the agency sponsoring the investigation" (Trimble and Marino 2003, 101). Snow has remarked that "the curation problem is at crisis proportions," and Majewski of Statistical Research Incorporated has described the curation crisis as marking "the end of the days of endless archaeology" (quoted in Bawaya 2007, 1025). In the United States, state-run archaeological repositories are predominantly responsible for managing, curating, and storing archaeological collections

and their associated data, though a number of nonstate, nonfederal repositories are also contracted to store collections (Childs 1995). The United
States lacks a centralized data storage facility for all archaeological data
(Kintigh and Altschul 2010, 264), leaving it up to states, the federal government, cultural resource management firms, county museums, historical societies, independent archaeologists, academics, and tribes to fund
and support the curation of collections. Additionally, 36 CFR 79 does not
contain any "deadlines for compliance" and did not include enforcement
policies, which means that collections can be abandoned without any legal
repercussions.[1] Furthermore, collection deaccessioning policies vary from
agency to agency, if they even exist at all, which means that archaeological
collections are often not culled after excavation.

The lack of funding to support the curation and analysis of archaeological collections has been well documented since the early 1970s (Lipe 1974;
Marquardt, Montet-White, and Scholtz 1982) and is not a uniquely American conundrum (Jeffrey 2012, 554; Jones et al. 2003). The curation crisis has
been compounded by multiple factors, including the growth of cultural
resource management as a profession; the pressure placed upon academic
archaeologists to excavate as part of undergraduate and graduate student
training and in order to achieve academic placement, tenure, and promotion; and the requirements and expectations placed on doctoral candidates
pursuing a PhD. In addition, granting agencies prefer to fund excavation
rather than long-term archaeological laboratory work and curation (Kersel 2015, 44). The U.S. Army Corps of Engineers, a federal agency tasked
with the development and management of a wide range of public projects,
has generated "millions of artifacts occupying nearly 50,000 cubic feet of
space that could fill a dozen tractor-trailers" (Bawaya 2007, 1025). In a 2000
report, the U.S. Army Corps of Engineers observed "that in about 75% of
cases, artifacts had been stored in improper conditions and were quietly
disintegrating" due to lack of funding (ibid.). That report also stated that rehabilitating and properly curating the collections "would cost an estimated
$20 million" (ibid.). The advent and aftermath of the 2008 recession in the
United States has exacerbated the curation crisis (Majewski 2010, 268), and
today cultural resource management firms are struggling to survive the
effects of the financial drought. Consequently, agencies have been "forced
by contracting officers to accept low bids" that sometimes fail to include
curation costs (ibid.).

Curation requires not only physical storage space but also a long-term,
ongoing commitment to maintaining proper curatorial environments and

properly managing collections. Most repositories charge a per-box fee to store collections in order to recover some of the associated costs, while some charge an annual fee for storage costs in addition to a per-box fee. In their report of a 2006–2007 survey of 221 archaeological repositories, Childs, Kinsey, and Kagan (2010, 192–193) observed that 58 percent of repositories charged a per-box storage fee that ranged from $72.50 to $1,200 per box (ibid., 195). More recently, repositories have begun charging a third fee that covers "maintenance or rehabilitation when additional care and/ or conservation of objects or associated records are needed on a periodic basis" (ibid., 194). Cultural resource management firms struggle to estimate the approximate amount of material culture they will recover from a site because of the many unknowns of archaeological research. This can result in limited to no curatorial funding for an entire excavated assemblage (Majewski 2010, 174). Additionally, both professional and academic contracts do not permit unknown variables, such as unforeseen issues of curation, to be resolved at the end of the project; this is especially true for contracts with federal or state agencies (ibid., 174–175). As a result, differential curation strategies are enacted. The absence of a national fund to support curation has resulted in the disrepair and endangerment of collections. For example, Chaco Culture National Historic Park used an abandoned car wash to temporarily store collections. Unfortunately, the car wash lost its roof during a storm, leaving collections exposed to the elements (Milanich 2005, 57). In times of state-level economic crises, data has been rendered inaccessible in state-run museums and repositories. Despite a long-standing curation fee structure, Arizona State Museum was unable to accept archaeological collections for an entire year due to a lack of storage space. As a result, cultural resource management firms were forced to retain collections until space could be found for them (Lyons and Vokes 2010, 217). In another example, Illinois State Museum, which houses over 8 million artifacts, shuttered its doors for nine months due to a budget impasse (Cosier 2015; Reynolds 2016).

The challenge of finding physical storage space for archaeological collections will not be easily resolved, especially in the context of the anti-regulatory climate in the United States. Nonetheless, archaeologists can take steps to make their data accessible and available amid the curation crisis. If even a small chance exists that they will be unable to preserve or access their archaeological collections in the future, archaeologists need to consider how data can be made accessible by other means. The online database is a good starting point for addressing the curation crisis and data access issues.

If they are done well and adequately funded, online databases make data immediately accessible even when the data is physically inaccessible.

The Internet and Archaeology

Archaeologists have historically used the internet as a place of creativity, play, and experimentation for communicating archaeological findings. For many scholars, putting archaeological data online "has been seen as a move away from a hierarchal structure of interpretation to a more networked or multivocal approach" (Boast and Biehl 2011, 126). Archaeologists began to use the internet as a space to share and disseminate data in the mid-1990s. Early online projects took a top-down approach to determining what content to share and who to share it with (Hoopes 1997, 88). While the power of representation lies in the hands of the interpreter, the data-entry technician, or the curator behind the website, taking the object out of the repository or museum and putting it into the space of the internet gives others the opportunity to provide more contextual information about the object. Joyce and Tringham were early adopters of technology to communicate archaeological science; they saw it as a novel way of intertwining feminist theory with archaeological praxis (Tringham 2010, 83). They used digital media to disrupt and undermine the authoritative voice of academic archaeologists and to create spaces where multiple voices could interpret the past (Joyce and Tringham 2007). One of Tringham's earliest experiments with digital archaeology was the Chimera Web, a CD-ROM that featured photographs, audio, and texts associated with a Neolithic village in Yugoslavia as a way of sharing the process of archaeological interpretation with the public. Joyce, Guyer, and Joyce's (2000) Sister Stories, a collaborative venture that featured multiple feminist scholars interpreting primary texts about the Aztec city of Tenochtitlan, was also an early foray into putting archaeological information online. In historical archaeology, McDavid (1999) was among the first to adopt and promote the use of websites to share data and elicit discussions from the public and from stakeholder groups associated with her research. McDavid created her website (www.webarchaeology.com) to "decenter the archaeologist as the authoritative source of The Truth" about the Levi Jordan Plantation in Brazoria, Texas, a nineteenth-century sugar plantation (2004, 49). McDavid emphasizes the importance of incorporating "situated knowledge," or knowledge that derives from community members and descendants, in interpretations of archaeological data (Haraway 1988). McDavid's website features oral history transcriptions from white descendants of the plantation owners and descendants of the African American tenant farmers; a diary composed by a granddaughter of Levi Jordan's owners; historical documentation associated with the site; and archaeological data excavated from the Levi Jordan Plantation.

More recently, archaeologists have begun experimenting with new ways of democratizing digital media, including developing virtual reality representations of archaeological sites and artifacts. Archaeologists are also providing archaeological data, such as field notes and multiple fieldworkers' interpretations of excavation units and stratigraphy to the public in real time as a site is being excavated (Morgan and Eve 2012, 527). LP Archaeology, a consulting firm in the United Kingdom, has offered digitized data as excavations were taking place at the Prescot Street excavation, offering "a radical transparency rarely found on commercial excavations" (524). This practice gives researchers and the public immediate access to the project's raw data, which is available for reinterpretation, extra-site analysis, and "remixing of the meaning" (528). Releasing raw data into the vastness of the World Wide Web also aided in the process of artifact identification, which could be crowdsourced on social media platforms such as Twitter and Facebook (531). Second Life, an online virtual world that is free to anyone with a computer and an internet connection, has also been used to recreate and reinterpret archaeological sites and engage interested members of the public with archaeology. As some scholars have argued, the website has its own heritage and archaeological sites (Morgan 2009; Harrison 2009). Archaeologists working at Çatalhöyük in Turkey virtually recreated a Neolithic site on a Second Life island that they named OKAPI, which stands for the Open Knowledge and the Public Interest Research Group. There they facilitated "virtual events," such as public archaeology days and "digital collaborations in the form of mash-ups" (Morgan 2009, 474), where users could modify, build upon, or erase aspects of Çatalhöyük's reconstruction.

The internet can also be a place of loss, structural inequality, and displacement, which means that digital data require long-term curation. As Morgan and Eve observe, "an untended digital garden will quickly wilt and rot away" (2012, 534). The virtual reconstruction of Çatalhöyük on OKAPI island, for instance, became "archaeological" in 2012 when project managers could no longer afford the cost of renting space for Second Life (Tringham 2013, 190). The premises of public archaeology and multivocality were likewise tested when "virtual squatters . . . set up a parking lot high in the sky over OKAPI island" and "left crushed hulks of virtual cars, half-built weapons and, oddly enough, empty soda bottles around the site" (Morgan

2009, 478). As a result of such mischief, the archaeologists who managed OKAPI island were put in a position where they had to "enforce certain restrictions regarding the interpretation of the site," something they "were hereto unprepared to do" (ibid.).

In addition, while internet access nearly spans the globe, many barriers still prevent people from going online, an issue known as the "digital divide" (Norris 2001). Such limitations include limited or no internet service in rural, impoverished, or remote areas; inability to pay for internet service; and unfamiliarity with using the internet (McDavid 2004, 44; Richardson 2013, 5). As newspapers, magazines, books, and nearly all forms of communication migrate to digital platforms, the digital divide widens. Norris (2001, 235) asserts that narrowing this divide is critical to increasing "cyber-democracy" and civic participation across the globe. Law and Morgan (2014) document another form of inaccessibility, one that concerns the loss of websites created to share archaeological data with the public. They trace the downfall of the hosting of GeoCities, which resulted in the loss of eighty-eight archaeologically oriented websites that included personal websites authored by academics and archaeological heritage societies. Internet hosting companies can go under water at any moment and content can disappear in the blink of an eye. As one of Law and Morgan's article reviewers observed, developing online archaeological content "is akin to building critical infrastructure on a fault line; there should be some degree of earthquake preparedness for a lasting digital presence" (2014, 5). Given the temporal and unpredictable nature of web-based content, Law and Morgan recommend "diversifying" online archaeological content by placing content on multiple digital media platforms (e.g., Twitter, Facebook, Reddit, Wikipedia) rather than with one web-hosting company (6). They also recommend taking screenshots of content and saving it on external storage servers and hard drives in case data are deleted when a web-hosting company or social media platform fails. This is a practice I have followed with my own digital projects, such as a blog I created in 2005 about my archaeological research on a Mexican American railroad workers' settlement in Los Angeles, California.

Kintigh and Altschul (2010) also voice concern about digital data preservation, especially "born-digital" and digitized archaeological data that lacks paper recordation. They argue that this represents a "second curation crisis that receives much less attention, but whose importance is growing daily" (264; see also Richards et al. 2010, 255). Archaeological projects create a diverse array of data that require different file formats generated by "hundreds of types of devices, hundreds of software packages, and the whole gamut of archaeological techniques" (Jeffrey 2012, 557). There is a need to manage digital data due to issues such as "data corruption, hardware redundancy, changes in file formats, software migration, and insufficient documentation" (Richards et al. 2010, 255). Failure to manage this data properly can result in complete loss of project data, rendering an archaeological collection useless. A consideration of who physically owns and manages born-digital data is likewise essential to its long-term preservation. Projects are often anchored to an institutional or company server, which means that websites and data can be deleted if a project manager leaves unless a plan is in place to ensure data transfer from one institution to another. Some workplaces perceive websites or data created and placed online to be proprietary knowledge since the employer funded their creation. However, the closure of a firm can result in the loss of data if no one can pay its storage and maintenance fees.

Several online archaeological data repositories have emerged in response to the threat of digital data loss. In recent years, data management software has been developed to organize archaeological notes and the multimedia generated as part of research. Some online archaeological data warehouses charge a fee, which is presumably built into the fabric of grant proposals or contract negotiations before archaeological fieldwork. The Integrated Archaeological Database (www.iadb.co.uk) provides open-source software for organizing archaeological data (Morgan 2012, 526), although it does not offer data storage services. The Archaeological Data Service has been providing free digital data storage and curation to academic archaeologists in the United Kingdom (Richards et al. 2010, 256). In the United States, The Digital Archaeological Record (tDAR) (http://tdar.org) and Open Context (https://opencontext.org/) have been proposed as solutions for open-access, long-term digital data migration and curation (Kintigh and Altschul 2010; Kansa and Kansa 2014). Archaeologists who want to use tDAR and Open Context are required to pay a fee to cover staff salaries, data storage fees, and the "long-term anticipated costs for such things as migration of data as digital formats and media change and the future costs of computer storage" (Kintigh and Altschul 2010, 265). These digital warehouses provide a solution for projects that are adequately funded in the private or public sector, but they do not offer a feasible solution for collections that are perceived as less than desirable, such as assemblages that lack provenience or that funding agencies do not want to finance. Thus, while tDAR is a viable solution for future archaeological projects, its fee structure limits the ability of underfunded repositories and museums to deposit data from existing assemblages and legacy collections. As a result, many archaeologists have "gone rogue" and have started their own digital projects.

Bringing Data Out of the Archives

While this chapter does not promise to solve the digital data and curation crises, it presents alternatives for attending to our ethical obligation to make collections accessible and disseminate archaeological data in a timely manner. As funds dwindle for even marketable cultural heritage in the United States, repository managers, academics, and students can be stewards of databases by giving the public access to data. Archaeologists in the academic sector can make a dent in the curation crisis by working on one small project at a time. Projects can be embedded into college and university classes, research projects, and/or can involve work-study student employees who want training in archaeology. Labrador (2012, 244) encourages archaeologists to "imagine and experiment with more such projects whereby the archaeological database becomes a platform for forming participatory learning environments with associated communities and beyond."

A good example of putting old data to work as an online database is the Colonial Encounters project (http://colonialencounters.org/index.aspx), which has put forgotten legacy collections—assemblages that institutions have inherited—into the digital realm to facilitate comparative work. The legacy collections were excavated as early as the 1930s and 1940s by a variety of institutions, including universities, museums, cultural resource management firms, and volunteer groups (King 2016, 8). The project's goal is to explore different permutations of colonialism across the lower Potomac River from 1500 to 1720 CE (7–8). Data from the collection has been standardized and digitized, including "2.4 million items recovered from 9,000 contexts" (8). Collaborators on the project digitized thirty-four discrete archaeological collections housed in nine separate facilities in Maryland, Michigan, North Carolina, and Virginia in order to compare and contrast the experiences of colonizers and the colonized.

This laborious work has resulted in new understandings of colonial interaction. For example, comparing data across the entire Potomac has demonstrated that European colonization was a much more nuanced and complex intercultural process than was previously thought. Comparative research across these sites revealed trade routes in the Potomac Valley

(King 2016, 9). Mapping these sites "along with the types and distributions of artifacts recovered from them . . . revealed that English and Native settlements were located in much closer proximity in the Potomac Valley," a discovery that was not visible in the historical records (10). This project has also directly influenced and shaped new archaeological fieldwork in the region, including standardizing the size of excavation units and screens in order to conduct statistical analyses of archaeological finds and using consistent descriptive language and standardized vocabularies for artifacts (9). It has helped archaeologists prioritize collection-based projects, formulate better-informed research designs when archaeological fieldwork is proposed, and limit unnecessary or redundant fieldwork. As King argues, "By looking not just at the scholarly findings of collections-based research but the methods that resulted in the creation of those collections, archaeologists can resolve to dig smarter. Dig less, catalog more. Create collections that will be usable and that will be comparable, now and in the future" (15).

Internment Archaeology Website and Database

In 2015 and 2016, with $2,000 from the Idaho Humanities Council and matching funding in salary expenditures from the University of Idaho, I oversaw and managed the creation of the website Internment Archaeology (www.internmentarchaeology.org), which is dedicated to the archaeology of World War II internment and incarceration camps in the United States. The project's goals include creating a publicly accessible online data warehouse, giving researchers a place to deposit cataloged data free of cost, and providing information about the sites for stakeholders and the public. The project was born out of frustration with trying to locate, access, and interpret archaeological datasets associated with Japanese migrants and Japanese Americans, which are often confined to the gray literature of unpublished or difficult-to-locate site reports. The Internment Archaeology project sought to break down the barriers that are often involved in accessing data from an archaeological project. It specifically emphasized getting the "raw" cataloged data online before it was analyzed and interpreted. The long-term goal of the project is to bring other archaeological datasets into the online database so that comparative work can be performed. When archaeological data from other incarceration camps are added to the database, scholars will be able to explore many topics, including how prisoner experiences varied across incarceration camps and the differential circulation of goods at incarceration camps in the United States. Some scholars may critique this approach for being too open with a dataset before publishing analysis of the data. However, this fear is unwarranted, given the amount of backlogged, unanalyzed data sitting in repositories and storage facilities and archaeologists' tendencies to ignore data once it is in the lab.

The project started off small, focusing on inputting data from one internment camp, the Kooskia Internment Camp in Idaho. The University of Idaho's Northwest Knowledge Network (https://www.northwestknowledge.net/home) developed the website on a Drupal-based platform with funding from the Idaho Humanities Council and the website went live in February 2017. In the three years it has been online, the website has been viewed 1,553 times by 854 unique visitors. Visitors have spent an average of twenty minutes on the website, looked at an average of nine pages of data per unique session, and visited a total of 14,194 pages on the website. The majority of visitors are from the United States (88 percent). Visitors from Brazil (4 percent), Canada (3 percent), Australia (1 percent), the United Kingdom (1 percent), Japan (1 percent), Germany (0.5 percent), and China (0.3 percent) constitute the remainder of the statistically significant visitors.

The cataloging and database entry workflow for Internment Archaeology was designed to generate opportunities for conversation and critique. After all of the artifacts from the Kooskia Internment Camp had been cleaned, students, volunteers, and employees trained in archaeological laboratory methodologies cataloged them. The cataloged information was written down on a paper catalog sheet, which was then placed in a binder that was labeled with the range of artifact accession numbers it contained. Then a data-entry technician checked the paper catalog sheet for errors and missing information and transcribed the paper catalog sheet into the Internment Archaeology online database. If any errors were found (such as a misidentified artifact or a missing artifact weight count), the physical artifact(s) were located and used to rectify the error(s) on the paper catalog sheet. Once the errors were fixed, the paper catalog sheets were entered into the Internment Archaeology database. Any diagnostic information that could help date an artifact, such as a sketch of a maker's mark or artifact illustration, was uploaded to the digital catalog form. Next, diagnostic artifacts—the ones that feature maker's marks, are datable, and/or are special or unique finds (such as gaming pieces)—were singled out to be photographed. These photographs were added to the digital catalog form. Finally, I reviewed the digital catalog form to ensure the accuracy of the data and consistency in recordation. Thus, at least three to four different sets of eyes are involved in checking the digital catalog record.

The interactive, recursive nature of Internment Archaeology has generated discussion regarding cataloging and typologizing archaeological data among my laboratory team and has helped me, as a principal investigator, identify data-entry issues. It has also made me realize that our typologies often fail us and that artifacts can sometimes escape typologization no matter how hard we attempt to shove them into two or three categories. When a new employee joins the project, they often expose presumed knowledge about the database, cataloging procedures, and the Kooskia Internment Camp's archaeological data. Staff may ask how we have defined a "container" versus a "bottle" or made a distinction between "olive glass" and "green glass." These discussions forced me to clarify how we make such decisions and refine how I train my laboratory employees. They also demonstrate that we have been cataloging the same types of artifacts differently. This process is critical, as it forces me to update the definitions of terms and procedures for cataloging in the data-entry manual and edit the part of Internment Archaeology's website that explains how data was cataloged. My staff and I hope that this clarification process will ensure that future repository employees and scholars working with Internment Archaeology's dataset will be able to interpret and understand our cataloging procedures and artifact provenance. We want them to avoid the present-day struggles of repositories that inherit orphaned collections or maintain legacy collections to reconstruct how decisions were made in the cataloging process in the absence of documentation (MacFarland and Vokes 2016, 162).

The public-facing portion of the Internment Archaeology website features information from the websites of many other archaeological projects, including links to publications associated with World War II incarceration sites, blog postings about our work, and a "special finds" page that highlights artifacts that may interest the public and scholars. The nonpublic component of the website has also been a site of productive discussion. There, employees and volunteers are assigned a unique username and their data-entry work is tracked. The administrator or principal investigator of the project can track how long each employee takes to enter an individual catalog entry, employee cataloging errors, and overall employee activity minute by minute. This data can be used to help estimate time to data-entry completion for the purpose of writing grant proposals and for consulting projects associated with future Internment Archaeology cataloging work. This data can also help quickly identify and rectify repeated data-entry errors and identify the individual responsible for generating such errors. For example, while most entries are made using a drop-down menu of terms, in a few cases those who enter the data are responsible for typing in a category from a paper manual. This increases the likelihood of spelling errors and has resulted in the generation of redundant categories. These mistakes were easily rectified on a Drupal-based platform that displays errors visually.

Internment Archaeology also provides a wide range of flexible, user-friendly search options, including permitting visitors to use their own search terms, by catalog number, and by cataloging typologies, which include artifact category (e.g., ammunition, cosmetic, clothing), artifact type (e.g., closure, tableware, jewelry), artifact description (e.g., baking dish, bead, basket), and artifact group (e.g., activities, domestic, industrial). Because each artifact or set of artifacts is associated with multiple descriptors, user searches generally produce the desired results. For example, an improved whiteware bowl is cataloged with the following terms: domestic, tableware, bowl, food prep/consumption, white improved earthenware, rim, body, base, foot ring, and Bailey-Walker China Company.

A press release to media outlets publicized the launch of Internment Archaeology. We also sought to establish a social media presence for Internment Archaeology as a way of drawing users to the database and the story of the Kooskia Internment Camp. Establishing a social media presence and gaining followers is time consuming and the results can be fleeting. In order to have conversations with the public at large and other scholars, you must establish a Twitter profile (or other related social media profile) and find interested users and scholars who will follow your profile and tweets. Curating content of interest to your followers takes time and attention to their posts. And while Twitter has been a great venue for connecting with scholars and the public at large, that and other social media platforms are not designed to last the test of time. The downside of using social media platforms such as Twitter to share data with the public is that if Twitter were to shut down, all posts would be lost unless the poster backed up their own content.

To maintain interest in Internment Archaeology, I have used Twitter to post about diagnostic artifacts that have been added to the database. Tweeting about the database and using hashtags related to the artifacts' histories and associations circulates the information to many potential visitors to the site. Twitter provides analytical data that can be used to determine public interest in certain types of archaeological finds, which can then be used to inform future Twitter tweets. Twitter can also be used to identify artifacts. In one example, we posted an image of a possible Japanese export stoneware vessel that has yet to be found in reference and collector books. We used multiple hashtags (e.g., #Japanese, #stoneware, #ww2) so that Twitter users searching for those same terms could locate this object. Two other Twitter users retweeted the image and three other Twitter users liked it, which expanded its social media reach beyond my personal Twitter page. Tweeting archaeological finds became part of the cataloging process. It was a way to both reach audiences and gauge public interest in a particular artifact type.

Twitter also helped us connect with corporations that manufactured some of the artifacts found at the Kooskia Internment Camp, such as W. F. Young, Inc., which manufactures Absorbine Jr., a pain relief medication for both humans and horses. Getting in touch with companies through social media can help archaeologists obtain information about a product's history, date of manufacture, price, date of circulation and production, stylistic changes in the maker's mark (which are sometimes associated with particular date ranges), and place of manufacture.

Regularly tweeting special finds as they were cataloged helped me find artifacts after a move from the University of Idaho to Michigan State University in 2017. Because many of our paper catalog forms still need to be entered into the digital database, I would have had to search through hundreds of catalog forms to locate some of our special finds. However, since I had tweeted about them as they were cataloged using the paper forms, I was able to search my Twitter feed from previous years of cataloging by artifact name or manufacturer (e.g., Absorbine or Colgate) and locate the original tweet. Our practice of tweeting about artifacts included providing a photograph that features the artifact next to its paper catalog form and accession number. Thus, when I found a tweet about a special find, I also found the artifact's accession or catalog number, which enabled me to physically locate it in a storage box labeled sequentially by accession number.

Every digital project presents its own unique challenges, as does the social media outlets used to advertise the project and its data. I chose Drupal (www.drupal.org) to manage Internment Archaeology's data because the members of my previous institution's data management unit (Northwest Knowledge Network) were well versed in Drupal and provided user support for it. In addition, the Drupal-based platform enabled me to download data in commonly used file formats, such as csv. Because of this format, the database can be opened in software such as Microsoft Access or open-access software programs that mirror the functionality of Access. The advantage of using Drupal is that users affiliated with a project do not need to buy expensive software (e.g., Microsoft products) to enter data into the database. They only need access to the web and a unique log-in ID that I assign. This made the transfer of data somewhat manageable when I moved from the University of Idaho to Michigan State University in the summer of 2017. To take my data with me to my current institution, I had to ensure that a new data management team (Michigan State University's MATRIX) would be willing to host and support it. Luckily, MATRIX (https://msus-tatewide.msu.edu/Programs/Details/1219) was willing to support it, but it is not a content management system the university regularly uses or troubleshoots for. Even if my current institution did not support Drupal, the database could have still been downloaded into a standardized csv format that is transferable to any database format on Macs or PCs.

One of the common frustrations of an archaeologist is differential cataloging of artifacts from the same time period and geographical region, a situation that hinders comparative research. Internment Archaeology was designed to help encourage archaeologists working on the same type of sites to use a uniform language for cataloging data. In the United States, data recordation standards and the vocabularies and typologies used to describe and order artifacts can vary widely across federal, tribal, and state agencies and among academic archaeologists. This diversity in cataloging archaeological data is, in some cases, attributable to the temporal and historical contexts in which archaeologists worked. Spanish colonial ceramics, for instance, look very different than mass-manufactured whitewares or "ironstones" found in the twentieth-century United States. In addition, despite the fact that a number of goods began circulating globally with the emergence of capitalism in the late 1400s (Orser 1996), the rate of adoption of such goods varied by nation and region (Purser 1999). Archaeologists who want to capture how people used objects might want to use local vernacular and words that do not appear in internationally established standardized vocabularies (Singleton and Bograd 2000). Labrador (2012, 242) notes that international vocabularies "set limits" by "recognizing certain features while excluding others."

Despite the difficulties involved in standardizing data, a uniform vocabulary for data description facilitates comparative work and aids in "identifying analogies, constructing inferences, and addressing questions of social and cultural difference" (King 2016, 6). To permit cross-site interpretations, Internment Archaeology employs a controlled vocabulary that is commonly in American historical archaeology. It draws upon the language used in the Sonoma State Historic Artifact Research Database

(SHARD). SHARD was created to "provide a consistent and (mostly) idiot-proof system to catalog artifacts from mid-19th to early 20th-century archaeological sites."[2] Sonoma State University's Anthropological Studies Center developed and provided the database and a user manual for free after the database had been "circulating on the archaeological underground of several years." SHARD was invented in the spirit of collaboration. Sharing digital databases embodies this ethos of openness. It represents a new era of archaeological activism in which archaeological interpretation and analysis is made accessible and it is no longer necessary to visit a physical place to access an archaeological collection.

Discussion

Reframed as activist work and public outreach, digital databases and their associated curatorial work are spaces where research and curation can intersect in fruitful, productive, and activist-oriented ways. In an era when data science has the potential to alter politics, the protection, dissemination, and sharing of our data can be perceived as a subversive yet important act. One strategy that cultural resource management firms, repository directors, academics, and collections managers can use is prioritizing the digitization of data that may contribute to policy issues. Jeffrey (2012, 563), for instance, cites the example of how "nineteenth-century whaling records" are "being used in modern climatology research" (cf. de la Mare 2009). To facilitate these types of socially useful analyses, data must be shared in accessible, open-source formats and must be publicized via email, media, and social media platforms.

Why is database management and the creation of digital databases social activism? At this time, resources are limited (and are dwindling under the current U.S. administration), museums and repositories are being shuttered and staff is being slashed, and universities—which have historically been centers of research and scholarship—are being reshaped by neoliberalism and arguments about the demands of the external market (Berg and Seeber 2016). Choosing to do work that may not produce short-term gains, what Berg and Seeber have termed the "slow professor" movement in academia and what Caraher (2019) has called an "archaeology of care," is a way of resisting a world that emphasizes expediency, efficiency, and deliverables. It means pushing back against "increasing workloads" (Berg and Seeber 2016, 25); saying no to service overloads, new assessments, and strategic planning that only benefits a university's administration; making space for one's academic writing and creativity; and valuing and cultivating a meaningful personal life beyond academia. Although digital archaeology evangelists have been prone to touting technology as a solution for efficient and expedient data collection (Kersel 2016, 478), collections-based digital archaeologists should be wary of adopting any platform that promises to speed up our work, an ideological remnant of the industrial revolution (Caraher 2019, 2). Instead, we should leverage the tools of digital archaeology to preserve, disseminate, and dust off artifacts that have been stored in boxes for decades thanks to the "fast" archaeology of the 1950s, 1960s, 1970s, and 1980s.

However, not every collection needs to be digitized. Digital archaeology databases must be created in consultation with the communities that are associated with such data and with attention to the language we choose to standardize. Digitizing data must also be done with the consent and support of the communities we serve. For instance, in certain circumstances, tribes or community groups would prefer that their heritage, landscapes, and artifacts remain out of the public eye. With the exception of those situations, online data sharing should be a foundation of archaeological praxis and should be addressed in every project proposal, much like permitting agreements. The worry-about-it-tomorrow mentality, where archaeologists assume that their collections are "safe" in repositories and museums and will be analyzed by another archaeologist in the future, is no longer ethical or realistic (Barker 2003, 80). We must record our collections in an accessible format, otherwise we run the risk of a future where huge numbers of collections are inaccessible and, worse, potentially deaccessioned due to limited storage space. Archaeologists have yet to seriously heed the call to our ethical responsibilities to collections (Collins, Lipe, and Curewitz 2010).

Conducting ethical archaeological work means resisting the pressure to run more field schools and it means reconfiguring archaeological practice to truly value laboratory work, indoor work that has been historically relegated to women due to their second-class status in archaeology (Gero 1985). We must be careful not to leave this data digitization work to one particular group, as digital archaeology has been critiqued as a boys' club (Kersel 2016, 485). Working with databases can also generate conversations that reconsider methods of fieldwork (MacFarland and Vokes 2016, 173). A cultural heritage field school where students catalog, interpret, digitize, and build pop-up museums for interested stakeholder groups is one potential solution to the collections backlog. Students and employees who work to reconstruct provenance and excavation procedures through data entry often begin to realize how seemingly discreet but critical practices, such as good handwriting on catalog and field forms, can make or break the long-term preservation of the archaeological record. Careful attention to legacy and orphaned collections and their often-unclear paperwork is a worthy effort that can improve how archaeologists practice fieldwork. How a site was excavated, where the site was located (if there are no maps), and what data was analyzed may be clear to the archaeologist who performed the work, but it may be completely mindboggling to an archaeologist trying to reconstruct what happened thirty years after the project was completed. Examining other archaeologists' yellowed, earmarked field notes and coffee-stained maps has forced me to think about what another archaeologist might glean from my field notes, site reports, and artifact catalog thirty years from now. The reflexive process I use is also comforting to me; the archaeological process and knowledge about the past is in the hands of archaeologists working in the present. We now have the digital tools to record, in great detail if desired, our fieldwork practices, our field notes, and our cataloging methods. There is no excuse for avoiding this work. Rather, it is imperative we make our data transparent and accessible if we wish to preserve the past for future generations and continue to make a case for the relevance of archaeology in a world that continues to devalue the social sciences, arts, and humanities. Working with previously excavated data reminds us of our role as professional stewards of it for future generations and makes for conscientious field archaeologists in the present.

Funding Details

This work was supported by the Idaho Humanities Council under the National Endowment for Humanities Program CFDA Number 45.129, Grant #2015043.

Notes

1. "Managing Archaeological Collections: Curation of Federally Owned and Administered Archaeological Collections (36 CFR 79)," National Park Service, https://www.nps.gov/archeology/collections/laws_04.htm.

2. Anthropological Studies Center, Sonoma State University, "SHARD: Sonoma Historic Artifact Research Database: The How-To Manual," 2, https://sha.org/documents/research/SHARD_how_to_manual.pdf.

References Cited

Barker, Alex W. 2003. "Archaeological Ethics: Museums and Collections." *Ethical Issues in Archaeology,* edited by Larry J. Zimmerman, Karen D. Vitelli, and Julie Hollowell-Zimmer, 71–83. AltaMira Press, Walnut Creek.

Bawaya, Michael. 2007. "Archaeology: Curation in Crisis." *Science* 317: 1025–26.

Berg, Maggie, and Barbara K. Seeber. 2016. *The Slow Professor: Changing the Culture of Speed in the Academy.* Toronto: University of Toronto Press.

Boast, Robin, and Peter F. Biehl. 2011. "Archaeological Knowledge Production and Dissemination in the Digital Age." In *Archaeology 2.0: New Approaches to Communication & Collaboration,* edited by Eric C. Kansa, Sarah Whitcher Kansa, and Ethan Watrall, 119–155. Cotsen Digital Archaeological Series 1. Los Angeles: Cotsen Institute of Archaeology Press.

Caraher, William. 2019. "Slow Archaeology, Punk Archaeology, and the 'Archaeology of Care.'" *European Journal of Archaeology* 22 (Special issue 3): 1–14.

Childs, S. Terry. 1995. "The Curation Crisis." *Common Ground: Archaeology and Ethnography in the Public Interest* 7 (4). Accessed September 12, 2017. https://www.nps.gov/archeology/cg/fd_vol7_num4/crisis.htm.

Childs, S. Terry, Karolyn Kinsey, and Seth Kagan. 2010. "Repository Fees for Archaeological Collections." *Heritage Management* 3 (2): 189–212.

Collins, Mary B., William D. Lipe, and Diane C. Curewitz. 2010. "Curating Research Careers." *Heritage Management* 3 (2): 233–254.

Cosier, Susan. 2015. "Amid Budget Fight, Illinois State Museum Prepares to Close." *Science,* September 30.

De la Mare, W. K. 2009. "Changes in Antarctic Sea-Ice Extent from Direct Historical Observations and Whaling Records." *Climate Change* 92: 461–493.

Gaffney, Vince, and Sally Exon. 1999. "From Order to Chaos: Publication, Synthesis and the Dissemination of Data in the Information Age." *Internet Archaeology* 6. https://intarch.ac.uk/journal/issue6/index.html.

Gero, Joan M. 1985. "Socio-Politics and the Woman-at-Home Ideology." *American Antiquity* 50: 342–350.

Haraway, Donna. 1988. "Situated Knowledges: The Science Question in Feminism and the Privilege of Partial Perspective." *Feminist Studies* 14 (3): 575–599.

Harrison, Rodney. 2009. "Excavating Second Life: Cyber-Archaeologies, Heritage and Virtual Communities." *Journal of Material Culture* 14 (1): 75–106.

Hodder, Ian. 1999. *The Archaeological Process: An Introduction.* Oxford: Blackwell.

Hoopes, John W. 1997. "The Future of the Past: Archaeology and Anthropology on the World Wide Web." *Archives and Museum Informatics* 11: 87–105.

Jeffrey, Stuart. 2012. "A New Digital Dark Age? Collaborative Web Tools, Social Media, and Long-Term Preservation." *World Archaeology* 44 (4): 553–570.

Jones, M., S. Bullick, M. Crump, N. Merriman, H. Swain, and E. William. 2003. "Too Much Stuff: Disposal from Museums." National Museums Directors Conference Report. Accessed September 1, 2018. http://www.nationalmuseums.org.uk/media/documents/publications/too_much_stuff.pdf.

Joyce, Rosemary A., and Ruth E. Tringham. 2007. "Feminist Adventures in Hypertext." *Journal of Archaeological Method & Theory* 14 (3): 328–358.

Joyce, Rosemary A., Carolyn Guyer, and Michael Joyce. 2000. *Sister Stories*. New York: New York University Press.

Kansa, Eric C., and Sarah Whitcher Kansa. 2014. "Publishing and Pushing: Mixing Models for Communicating Research Data in Archaeology." *International Journal of Digital Curation* 9 (1): 57–70.

Kersel, Morag M. 2015. "Storage Wars: Solving the Archaeological Curation Crisis?" *Journal of Eastern Mediterranean Archaeology and Heritage Studies* 3 (1): 42–54.

———. 2016. "Response: Living a Semi-Digital Kinda Life." In *Mobilizing the Past for a Digital Future: The Potential of Digital Archaeology*, edited by Erin Walcek Averett, Jody Michael Gordon, and Derek B. Counts, 475–492. Grand Forks: Digital Press at the University of North Dakota.

King, Julia A. 2016. "Comparative Colonialism and Collections-Based Archaeological Research: Dig Less, Catalog More." *Museum Worlds: Advances in Research* 4: 4–17.

Kintigh, Keith W., and Jeffrey H. Altschul. 2010. "Sustaining the Digital Archaeological Record." *Heritage Management* 3 (2): 264–74.

Labrador, Angela M. 2012. "Ontologies of the Future and Interfaces for All: Archaeological Databases for the Twenty-First Century." *Archaeologies: Journal of the World Archaeological Congress* 8 (3): 236–249.

Law, Matt, and Colleen Morgan. 2014. "The Archaeology of Digital Abandonment: Online Sustainability and Archaeological Sites." *Present Pasts* 6 (1–2): 1–9.

Lipe, William D. 1974. "A Conservation Model for American Archaeology." *The Kiva* 39 (3–4): 213–245.

Lyons, Patrick D., and Arthur W. Vokes. 2010. "The Role of Fee Structures in Repository Sustainability." *Heritage Management* 3 (2): 213–232.

MacFarland, Kathryn, and Arthur W. Vokes. 2016. "Dusting Off the Data: Curating and Rehabilitating Archaeological Legacy and Orphaned Collections." *Advances in Archaeological Practice* 4 (2): 161–173.

Majewski, Teresita. 2010. "Not Just the End Game Anymore." *Heritage Management* 32 (2): 167–188.

Marquardt, William H., Anta Montet-White, and Sandra Scholtz. 1982. "Resolving the Crisis in Archaeological Collections Curation." *Antiquity* 47 (2): 409–418.

McDavid, Carol. 1999. "From Real Space to Cyberspace: Contemporary Conversations about the Archaeology of Slavery and Tenancy." *Internet Archaeology* 6, Special Theme: Digital Publication. http://intarch.ac.uk/journal/issue6/mcdavid/toc.html.

———. 2004. "From 'Traditional' Archaeology to Public Archaeology to Community Action: The Levi Jordan Plantation Project." In *Places in Mind: Public Archaeology as Applied Anthropology*, edited by Paul A. Shackel and Erve J. Chambers, 35–56. New York: Routledge.

Milanich, Jerald T. 2005. "Homeless Collections: What Happens to Artifacts When They Have No Place to Go?" *Archaeology* 58 (6): 57–64.

Morgan, Colleen. 2009. "(Re)Building Çatalhöyük: Changing Virtual Reality in Archaeology." *Archaeologies: Journal of the World Archaeological Congress* 5 (3): 468–487.

Morgan, Colleen, and Stuart Eve. 2012. "DIY and Digital Archaeology: What Are You Doing to Participate?" *World Archaeology* 44 (4): 521–537.

Norris, Pippa. 2001. *Digital Divide: Civic Engagement, Information Poverty, and the Internet Worldwide*. New York: Cambridge University Press.

Orser, Charles E., Jr. 1996. *A Historical Archaeology of the Modern World*. New York: Plenum.

Purser, Margaret. 1999. "Ex Occidente Lux? An Archaeology of Later Capitalism in the Nineteenth-Century West." In *Historical Archaeologies of Capitalism*, edited by Mark P. Leone and Parker B. Potter Jr., 115–41. Contributions To Global Historical Archaeology. Boston: Springer.

Reynolds, John. 2016. "Illinois State Museum Reopens to Public After Nine-Month Shutdown." *The State Journal-Register*. Accessed September 12, 2017. http://www.sj-r.com/news/20160702/illinois-state-museum-reopens-to-public-after-nine-month-shutdown.

Richards, Julian D., Tony Austin, and Catherine Hardman. 2010. "Covering the Costs of Digital Curation." *Heritage Management* 3 (1): 255–263.

Richardson, Lorna. 2013. "A Digital Public Archaeology?" *Papers from the Institute of Archaeology* 23 (1): 1–12.

Singleton, Theresa A., and Mark Bograd. 2000. "Breaking Typological Barriers: Looking for the Colono in Colonoware." In *Lines that Divide: Historical Archaeologies of Race, Class, and Gender*, edited by James A. Delle, Stephen A. Mrozowski, and Robert Paynter, 3–21. Knoxville: University of Tennessee Press.

Trimble, Michael K., and Eugene A. Marino. 2003. "Archaeological Curation: An Ethical Imperative for the Twenty-First Century." In *Ethical Issues in Archaeology*, edited by Larry J. Zimmerman, Karen D. Vitelli, and Julie Hollowell-Zimmer, 99–112. Walnut Creek, CA: AltaMira Press.

Tringham, Ruth. 2010. "Forgetting and Remembering the Digital Experience and Digital Data." In *Archaeology and Memory*, edited by Dušan Borić, 68–104. Barnsley: Oxbow Books.

———. 2013. "A Sense of Touch—the Full Body Experience—in the Past and the Present of Çatalhöyük, Turkey." In *Making Senses of the Past: Toward a Sensory Archaeology*, edited by Jo Day, 177–195. Center for Archaeological Investigations, Southern Illinois University Carbondale, Occasional Paper No. 40. Carbondale: Southern Illinois University Press.

10

"Free for the Taking"

Archaeology and Environmental Justice in Setauket, New York

CHRISTOPHER N. MATTHEWS

About 100 meters north of the Silas Tobias archaeological site in Setauket, New York, the New York State Department of Environmental Conservation (DEC) has posted a sign that says "Closed Area." The sign adds that "taking clams or other shellfish from this uncertified area is prohibited" and warns that "violations are punishable by fine, jail sentence or both" (Figure 10.1). The sign was posted in the late 2000s to warn people that Conscience Bay was no longer safe for clamming due to pollution. The primary pollution sources are runoff from surrounding lands and waste from boats, waterfowl, pets, and a local sewage plant. The pollutants include high levels of bacteria, fecal coliforms and pathogens, suspended solids from sediment runoff, large debris, and trash (i.e., floaters), phosphorus and nitrogen from fertilizers, and petroleum compounds from nearby roadways (Cashin Associates 2009, 3–5, 3–8). In other words, the pollutants are directly connected to the transformation of the region into a densely populated suburban environment. The DEC has posted warning signs like this one throughout Long Island's coastal communities, indicating the widespread effects of the region's rapid suburban growth on the water and its native species (McCaffrey 2019; Cashin Associates 2009).

The sign in Figure 10.1 caught my attention because the archaeology at the Silas Tobias site shows that the use of the local waters in Conscience Bay was very much a way of life for the residents of the site in the past. At least as early at 1823, members of the Tobias family lived in a small home on the west shore of the bay. The family occupied the home until the 1890s, producing an archaeological record of three generations on the site. The

Figure 10.1. "Closed Area" sign adjacent to the Silas Tobias archaeological site, Old Field, New York. Photo by Christopher N. Matthews.

Tobiases were a mixed-heritage family of color whose origins likely connect to Native Americans from southern New England and Long Island and to people of African descent. In 2015, archaeologists from Montclair State University identified architectural debris associated with the former Tobias home and an artifact-rich midden behind the house. This midden stood out because it consisted of a thick layer of very dark soil and abundant shells, a characteristic more commonly associated with precontact sites in the region (Salwen 1962; Ceci 1980; Bernstein 2006). However, artifacts in the midden show that it was created over the course of the nineteenth century, much later than other shell midden sites in the region. The midden is clear evidence that the Tobias household used Conscience Bay as a source of food in the 1800s. Obviously, due to contemporary pollution, members of the Setauket community can no longer use the bay and its resources for food. Understanding this environmental change and its effects on people of color in the area is the focus of this chapter.

This study has two goals. First, it examines this juxtaposition of the past and present life of shell fishing and other uses of natural resources in order to understand the meaning of shellfish for the Tobias family and other families of color. Second, this study looks at how this local history is part of a larger struggle by people of color to survive in the environment of Setauket. I also consider the struggles of the current community to fend off the latest environmental and social threat—gentrification. I contend that gentrification is a part of a long history of racist assaults on Setauket's community of color that has persisted and evolved over the last 100 years. In order to connect this research with the larger discourse of environmental racism and justice, I consider some of the key ideas in the field of environmental justice and their connections to archaeology. I then turn back to Setauket to illustrate how the issues of environmental racism and environmental justice relate to archaeological interpretations.

Environmental Justice as an Archaeological Concern

The concept of environmental racism derives from a broader interest in environmentalism that reaches back to the nineteenth-century conservation movement (Chapman 2018; Lumley and Armstrong 2004; Tober 1981; Judd 1997). Early environmentalism in the United States was driven by a negative reaction to industry and urban growth. Nineteenth-century Romantics believed that preserving natural environments was essential "to people's physical and spiritual health," which derived from "the restorative effects of 'wildness' on the human spirit" (Chapman 2018). It became common for governments and cities to set aside lands as wilderness or urban parks for the sake of health and restoration. Early efforts in environmental conservation also led to the professionalization of archaeology in the United States. Beginning with the American Antiquities Act of 1906, archaeologists were expected to be credentialed and to serve the same sense of the greater good that conservationists had adopted (King 1998; Harmon, McManamon, and Pitcaithley 2006; Matthews 2012; Trigger 1989). While environmental conservation has become a dynamic and far-reaching field that seeks to address problems related to pollution, land use, food and medical safety, endangered species, and climate change, the focus of archaeology has remained comparatively static in its seemingly myopic concentration on material culture, the past, and the preservation of the archaeological record. However, the parallels between environmentalism and archaeology remain clear, and the time for an articulation of an "archaeological

justice" movement inspired by the environmental justice movement has
come (Little and Shackel 2014).

Understanding environmental racism is a major part of the environmental justice movement. Environmental racism is the practice of disproportionately releasing environmental contaminants and poisons in areas
where those most affected are underprivileged racial minority populations.
The concept of environmental racism is typically credited to racial justice
activist Benjamin Chavis, who coined the term in 1982 while protesting
a hazardous waste landfill in North Carolina (Holifield 2001, 83). Chavis
(1994, xii) said that environmental racism was the result of the "deliber-
ate targeting of communities of color for toxic waste facilities, the official
sanctioning of the presence of life threatening poisons and pollutants for
communities of color, and the history of excluding people of color from
leadership of the environmental movement." Environmental racism thus
points both to specific racist acts and practices of exclusion that exploit the
vulnerability of people of color for the benefit of the white majority.

Environmental racism became more widely acknowledged in the 1990s
as the practice helped coalesce a diverse group of activists working on a
broad range of environmental and social problems. A profound statement
issued by the First National People of Color Environmental Leadership
Summit expanded environmental concerns to include hazardous waste
disposal, military occupation, Native American self-determination, uneven infrastructural development, issues related to zoning and land use,
city planning and real estate, and urban crime and blight (Connell 2011).
As Holifield (2001, 79) writes, "activists have drawn on the legacy of the
civil rights and social justice movements to reunite environmentalism with
the spiritual and cultural traditions of people of color and the problems of
the inner city." Environmental racism has thus evolved to become part of
an effort for environmental justice, which, as defined by the United States
Environmental Protection Agency, seeks to "ensure that all people, regardless of race, national origin or income, are protected from disproportionate
impacts of environmental hazards" (quoted in Holifield 2001, 80).

There are many examples of environmental racism and justice, but the
recent (2014–present) water crisis in Flint, Michigan, is very poignant.
Flint is a deindustrialized midwestern city with a majority African American population. Flint has been racialized as a "Black city" since the 1990s,
when the majority of the white population moved away in search of better
jobs (Pulido 2016b). This demographic change and racialization matters
because the levels of lead in Flint's municipal water were high enough to

cause rashes, burning eyes, and Legionnaire's disease and lead poisoning in children. These health issues affected Black residents disproportionately. City and state officials knew about this issue for two years before they took action to do any substantive remediation (Pulido 2016b). These efforts to clean the water came after scientists and activists publicized the crisis in the press, suggesting that the response might have come even later without this pressure (Kennedy 2016). This sort of poisoning and the severely delayed reaction that happened is highly unlikely (and indeed has not happened) in communities that are whiter and more affluent. Because Flint was a poor Black city, the state government abandoned it. As Flint's congressional representative Dan Kildee stated, "There's a philosophy of government that has been writing these places off" (quoted in Pulido 2016b, 5). Lacking a powerful voice in the halls of state power, poor communities of color seem disproportionately likely to suffer from the pollution others create.

According to Laura Pulido (2016b; see also Pulido 2015, 2016a), ignoring environmental contamination in places like Flint is an example of "racial capitalism" that has close ties to the production and racialization of poverty. Racial capitalism is the enrichment of some communities (which are usually white) through policies and practices that impoverish others (who are usually nonwhite). It is also tied to the creation of "surplus populations" (Pulido 2016b, 8). Surplus populations have value, "if one can call it that[,] [because of] their general expendability. This disposability allows both capital and the state to pursue policies and practices that are catastrophic to the planet and its many life forms because much of the cost is borne by 'surplus' people and places" (Pulido 2016b, 8; see also Gilmore 2008; Harvey 1989; Márquez 2013). Racism is the key element of a world view that sees people of color in Flint and many other places as disposable surplus populations.

Environmental justice theory highlights the intersectional framework whereby race and class dovetail both with each other and with how capitalist structures are built and reproduced. In a capitalist system, wealth requires a surplus, whether it be objects or human beings, who exist in the minds of capitalists to provide "potential" value. Until the time comes when they might be called on to work, "surplus populations have zero value to capital" (Pulido 2016b, 11), and thus they are left out of the calculations capitalists and their allies make. Pulido (2016b) argues that many of the residents of Flint, who are both poor and Black, fit the description of a surplus population in the United States, where neoliberal capitalists act for their own benefit and ignore surplus populations and objects until they need them for their profit-making ventures. Environmental justice activists argue that the places where "surplus" populations live are "surplus places" where capitalists can dump the by-products and waste that their production and accumulation creates (also see Voyles 2015).

Archaeologists can learn a great deal from the broader discourse of environmental justice. As people who do research on environmental impact, many cultural resource management archaeologists are positioned to provide commentary on how exploitation of the environment has contaminated historic and archaeological sites (Shackel and Palus 2006). However, for the most part environmental justice activism has not found a footing in contemporary archaeological practice. One possible reason is that archaeologists are positioned in the "cultural" side of managing the environment rather than "natural resources" side. The perception that this separation exists means that archaeologists do not feel that it is their job to assess and comment on environmental contamination.

An example of this division of labor can be found in the environmental and archaeological studies of the United States Radium Corporation site in Orange, New Jersey. Famous for the tragic story of the radium girls, young female technicians who were poisoned by exposure to toxic radium at the factory from 1917 to 1926, the factory closed in 1927 following several legal settlements with former employees. As a result of the deaths of radium factory workers, family members filed lawsuits that established an important precedent that allows employees to sue corporations for abuses of their labor force, including exposing workers to contaminants (Moore 2017). In 1983, the EPA declared the factory a superfund site. It was fully remediated and was opened to new use in 2006. In addition, the state of New Jersey commissioned work to evaluate the environmental impacts of the factory that included two surveys to assess the cultural resources of the site above and below ground (see Grossman 1996; Boesch 1998). These reports concluded that the United States Radium site had a "high potential for intact Native American archaeological deposits in locations adjacent to the former wetlands in the northwest portion of the surveyed area."[1] While the initial report by Grossman (1996) assessed the integrity and potential historical significance of the standing structures that remained from the radium factory, neither archaeological study notes that the site is dangerously polluted or refers to its powerful connections to the labor movement and environmental history. Clearly, the division between cultural and environmental assessments in this case is profound. Current cultural resource management practices do not focus on understanding the full historical importance of sites. In this case, this is not the fault of the consulting archaeologists since their scope of work was restricted from the outset. Instead, the management system that determined that archaeology should focused on prehistory and architectural assessment and that other environmental researchers should focus on remediation and recovery is to blame. This system means that the significant environmental history of a site like the United States Radium factory is caught in the interstices and thus remains unaddressed.

I suggest that we can use one of our other key archaeological tools to overcome the separation of natural and cultural resources—the way we describe the long-term histories of the human occupation and uses of the landscape (Hodder 1987; Ashmore and Knapp 1999; David and Thomas 2010). In the case of the United States Radium site, this would have meant making an effort to understand how ancient Native American and modern industrial uses of the site coexist within the narrative of the site's significant history. In the case of Flint, this could be a critical historical examination of the industrialization and deindustrialization of the city that focuses on how a racialized poor community's struggle for clean water is part of the way the public should understand industrial sites. Industrial history does not end with the closing of plants and factories, especially when the residue of industrial production and the negative social changes wrought by fast capitalism (McGuire 2008, 5–6) continue to be factors for those who live in and near the former industrial places. Telling the story of the how the past shapes the present is equally useful in rural places and small towns.

Because an interest in the history of places and landscapes is a core feature of archaeology, it could be a foundation for building an archaeological justice movement. Environmental justice advocates count on such material histories to understand exactly what effects contaminants have had and what sort of environmental remedies and restoration are needed in a given place. In the following sections, I use a long-term history approach to document environmental racism and displacement in Setauket, New York. The purpose is to show how people of color have suffered the fate of being perceived as a surplus population and currently face perhaps a final displacement from their ancestral home.

Archaeology and Environmental Justice in Setauket

Given what we know about how the environment is a locus for understanding the struggles of minority people in the United States, it is appropriate to examine environmental contexts and relations in the archaeology of minority communities and the experiences of environmental racism those communities have had. In what follows, I use insights from the archaeology of the Native American and African American community in Setauket to examine the relationships among the environment, culture, and power in five historical moments. The first relates to how free people of color used the environment productively in the nineteenth century, which has been documented archaeologically. The second relates the story of an environmental struggle and catastrophe in the early twentieth century that was also captured in the archaeological record. A third moment is the 1940–1960s, the childhood years of elders living in the community today. They tell stories about the efforts they made to continue to use the environment productively. A fourth moment is the late 1960s, when a small, racially mixed, working-class community was displaced to make room for a new highway and commercial district. The last moment is the period since the 1960s, especially since 2004, a period when suburban development in Setauket has displaced the last remaining members of the descendant community. These moments relate the long-term struggle of the community of color in Setauket to resist displacement from access to resources and spaces they needed to remain in their ancestral home.

Environmental Relations in Nineteenth-Century Setauket

The Silas Tobias home site is located on the western shore of Conscience Bay in what is known as Old Field Village, an incorporated municipality that before 1927 was part of Setauket. The site is on an undeveloped, wooded lot between Old Field Road and the waterfront. A deed filed with Suffolk County indicates that in 1823, Silas Tobias sold a half-acre lot with a dwelling house to Abraham Tobias for $30. There is no preceding deed on record, so it is not known how Silas Tobias came to be the grantor. A 1797 map shows a house in the area of the site, so it may be that Silas Tobias occupied the lot but did not have the formal title. Maps from 1837, 1873, and 1896 show a house in the location of the Silas Tobias archaeological site, and the latter two maps identify a house as the home of "S. Tobias." Because of the date, the S. Tobias identified on the maps is likely a descendant of the Silas Tobias whose name is on the 1823 deed. No house is shown in the location on maps published in 1909 and 1917. This matches up with the deed history of the property, which indicates the "heirs of Abraham Tobias" sold the lot in 1893 to Edward Ostrom, a local white landowner. These

Table 10.1. Shells from the Silas Tobias site sorted by species type

Type	Weight (g)	%
Soft-shell clam	42,456.7	71.2
Hard-shell clam	6,268.6	10.5
Scallop	10,248.5	17.2
Mussel	38.5	0.1
Whelk	112.2	0.2
Oyster	367.7	0.6
Other	41.1	0.1
Total	59,533.3	99.9

documents indicate that the site was home to the Tobias family for most of the nineteenth century.

Archaeology at the Tobias site included a shovel test pit survey of the entire lot and excavation of eleven one-meter by one-meter test units. These excavations identified architectural features that indicate a small frame house facing Old Field Road that sat on stone and brick piers. A brick chimney built on a stone foundation was situated along its north side. The home sat on a raised section of the lot that now stands about four feet above the shore of Conscience Bay. This elevated position protected the home from occasional high water and pushed any rain runoff away to the Bay. On this elevated section behind the house there is a dense midden consisting of shells, faunal remains, and a wide range of nineteenth-century domestic artifacts (including ceramics, glass, buttons, nails, and other hardware) (Figure 10.2). The date range of ceramics in the midden run from the late eighteenth to the late nineteenth centuries, roughly matching the documents associated with the Tobias occupation. The contents of this midden provide evidence of how the Tobias family interacted with their local environment to collect food and related resources.

Shells make up the majority of collected data from the midden deposit. The sheer number of the collection and the fact that the shells range from whole shells to tiny fragments made counting them an unreasonable task. Instead, the shells were sorted by species and weighed. The results of this analysis are presented in Table 10.1, which shows that the vast majority were soft-shell clam, *Mya arenaria*. Soft-shell clams are a locally available species found in sandy or muddy bottoms of bays and estuaries, including Conscience Bay. The other shellfish species recovered, except for whelk, are also

TOBIAS EU9 level A2 ¼"

Figure 10.2. *Top*, East wall profile of excavation unit 5 at the Tobias site, showing the dense shell-midden layer; *Bottom*, Sample artifacts from the backyard midden at the Tobias site. Photos by Christopher N. Matthews.

common in estuary waters like those of Conscience Bay. The assemblage of shells indicates that the bay was a key food source for the Tobias family, and the consistency of species throughout the midden suggests that the family used their own shoreline for generations.

The faunal collection is quite diverse. It consists of specimens related to mammals, turtles, birds, and a variety of fish species. Domestic mammals are represented by cattle, sheep, and pig. There is no evidence of standardized butchery traces, such as saw marks, and there is a quite a bit of the nonmeaty parts of the animals (such as phalanges and skull and mandible fragments) in the collection. This suggests that the Tobias family raised and butchered the animals themselves. If that was the case, it would explain the fence mentioned in the deed. There are also bones from snapping turtle and smaller mammals, including rabbit and opossum, that indicate that the family trapped or hunted to supplement their diet. The bird species are both domestic and wild and include chicken, goose, and duck. The collection also includes a large number of fish vertebrae, which, along with the water birds and shells, suggests the use of the nearby shoreline for wild food resources.

An analysis of botanical remains from the Silas Tobias site shows that the household also made use of wild plants for food, medicine, and household applications (McKnight 2017). This analysis confirmed that the backyard midden had the highest concentration and diversity of botanicals remains. Species identified include

1) Amaranth/pigweed, which can be consumed as a leaf vegetable and used as a dye and as a medicinal and ornamental plant.
2) Bedstraw (Galium), which has stems and leaves that can be used as bedding material or mattress stuffing. The young shoots of Galium are edible as a potherb or a fresh green, and its seeds can be ground as a coffee substitute. Galium is also used medicinally and as a fiber dye.
3) Huckleberry, a wild edible fruit.
4) Cherry, another wild edible fruit, although it was also cultivated in the nineteenth century.
5) Sumac, the fruit of which can be used as medicine, to produce a dye, or to make a tea or jelly (McKnight 2017, 9–10).

There is one other important piece of foodways evidence from the Tobias site: the remains of two eel-spear heads (Figure 10.3). Eel spears are typically long-handled wooden shafts with wrought-iron heads that are

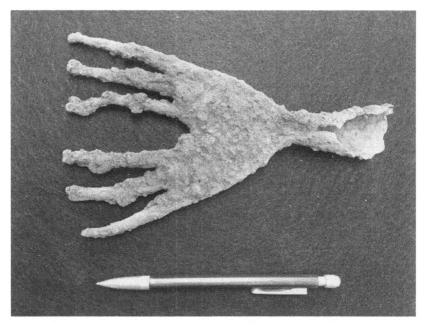

Figure 10.3. Iron eel spearhead recovered from the Silas Tobias site. Photo by Christopher N. Matthews.

used to capture and hold slippery eels by piercing their thick skin. The style of eel spears at the Tobias house would have had a central spoon blade that is missing from the recovered example in Figure 10.3. The spoon blade would have impaled the eel and the tines on each side would have held the eel's body. The tool was designed to capture the eel and keep it alive so that it could be sold fresh (Bryant 1985).

Eel spearing is another example of how the Tobias family exploited the local environment for food resources. Eel spearing also has deep resonance in Setauket because of the William Sidney Mount's painting titled *Eel Spearing at Setauket* (1845), which depicts a woman of color standing in the front of a small skiff ready to plunge an eel spear of the same type as the one found at the Tobias site into the water. Documents related to Mount's painting and to his patron note that the scene is set on Conscience Bay looking east across the water toward Strong's Neck (Green 1999). This vantage point would have been close to where the Tobias family lived. It is likely that Mount knew the Tobias family since he lived in nearby Stony Brook and had painted many other people of color from the area in other works. There is thus a distinct possibility that the woman in the painting and the eel spear she is holding were both from the Tobias household.

While there is ample evidence that the Tobias family actively exploited their local environment for subsistence and perhaps for trade, other artifacts found at the site include the remains of common ceramic and glassware vessels and nails and other iron implements. This shows that the family did not rely on the local environment exclusively and that they had the freedom to combine naturally available resources with goods from the market at will. In fact, it may have been their direct access to natural resources, such as eels, clams, and fish, that provided resources they could exchange for market goods such as ceramics, bottles, and nails.

Since the time the Tobias family left the site in the 1890s, the lot has been unused and the family has largely been forgotten. In 1900, the lot was joined with another across Old Field Road to form a larger property. This new property was owned by Frank Melville, a prominent white businessman from New York City who chose Old Field for his summer residence. He purchased and remodeled a mansion that still stands across the road from the Tobias site. Melville brought a new way of life to the area. He was not interested in exploiting the natural environment for its resources; he sought property for leisure and as an expression of wealth. This new way of living is still the norm in Old Field, which, according to the 2010 census, is one of the most expensive places to live on Long Island (City-Data.com 2018). Maintaining this high status, however, has come with an environmental cost since it is the pollutants that come from new construction, lawn fertilization, pets, and automobiles that have damaged the local waters and their wildlife.

The Struggle with Water on Lake Street

In 1938, a Category 3 hurricane known as the Long Island Express swept across Long Island. Its center passed a few miles east of Setauket. The storm did considerable damage in the area and caused as many as 100 deaths after it made landfall on Long Island. It remained an intense storm as it crossed over the island before moving into New England, where winds and flooding killed another 600 people in five states. In and around Setauket, the effects of the storm were powerful. In Northport, located west of Setauket on the north shore of Long Island, there were no deaths but the *Northport Journal* reported that "trees fell like match sticks" and that "uprooted trees, washouts, and flooded cellars" caused substantial property damage. It also reported that boats were "piled up at the head of the harbor" and "private docks [were] destroyed."[2]

Reports of the hurricane's effects closer to Setauket are not available, but we have evidence in the archaeological record at the Jacob and Hannah Hart site on Lake Street, which archaeology teams from Hofstra University and Montclair State University excavated in 2011 and 2015. The Hart site is the location of the former home of Jacob and Hannah Hart, who settled there in 1888. The Harts, another family from Setauket's Native and African American community, lived in the home, where they raised twelve children. Both Harts lived at the site until their deaths; Hannah died in 1922 and Jacob followed in 1931. In the 1930 census, only Jacob and his youngest son, Ernest, were recorded as living at the home. Ernest was listed as the sole resident in the 1940 census. Descendants believe that he remained in the home until the 1938 hurricane struck but left soon after.

The Harts' property included a frame house with an attached kitchen ell that stood on a stone foundation. The home also had a series of brick pathways and stone-covered surfaces and a spring-fed well for drinking water about ten meters west of the house. Another ten meters farther, the property reached the edge of the creek that feeds the millpond just downstream. The creek would have provided cool air, occasional food and medicinal resources, and a lovely place for children to play. In all, it seems to have been a small, yet tidy and well-apportioned household and property.

Further research on the site and the family, however, suggests a different interpretation. Evidence from archaeology shows that the site was quite a difficult place to live for the Harts, in large part because of a constant battle with groundwater. The sense that the site was waterlogged was obvious to archaeologists, who quickly encountered groundwater during excavation, sometimes just a few inches below the ground surface. Although the water created very difficult conditions for the excavation, we thought that the high water table was caused by the silting in of the millpond downstream after the mill closed. Furthermore, we assumed that this silting had occurred since the Harts left the site, since who would live in such a wet place?

Two elders who remember when the Harts still lived on the site told me that they remembered a well under the home that the Harts accessed by lifting the floorboards. Since there is no archaeological evidence for such a feature under the house, I think they remember that the family could lift their floorboards to show that there was standing water under the house. In the local newspaper, editors published an article that praised Jacob Hart for pulling weeds growing in the millpond downstream from his home, noting that this effort beautified the village (Green 1999, 66). Because of the trouble with water at his home, it is more likely that Hart was clearing

Figure 10.4. Buried stone and brick surfaces at the Jacob and Hannah Hart site, Setauket, New York. Photo by Christopher N. Matthews.

plant growth from the pond so that the water would have better flow away from his property. The struggle with groundwater is likely why the family laid brick and stone pathways at the site. These pathways connect the front and side doors of the home to the street front and provide a paved path to the well west of the house (Figure 10.4). Stone, especially, is not easily accessible on Long Island, which consists mostly of a sandy subsoil (see Figure 10.2). Thus, the use of stone for a pathway suggest a strong desire to pave the ground, a desire that resulted from dealing with groundwater that created a slippery and muddy surface.

The Harts' struggle with water came to a head in 1938 because of the hurricane. At this point, Ernest Hart was the only one living in the house, so it is likely that he experienced the storm on his own. Since he was living there in 1940, we know that the home survived, although it was probably damaged. A 1948 document signed by three of Jacob and Hannah Hart's daughters relinquished any interest in the property and noted that the home had been abandoned and torn down. It is likely that the storm led Ernest to move away. Those who knew him recall that he moved to Bridgeport, Connecticut, where he lived for several years before returning to Setauket to live in a small house on his sister Lucy's lot on Christian Avenue.

While this documentary trail provides fragmentary evidence of damage to the property, archaeological evidence suggests that the site was seriously impacted by the 1938 storm. Two stratigraphic layers over the whole of the excavated western yard section of the site tell the landscape history of the site since 1938. The uppermost layer is a thick jumble of roots and soil that was virtually impenetrable. The best tool to remove the layer was a large pair of root clippers that could be used to cut the root mat out of the ground. Almost no artifacts were found in this upper layer other than a Pepsi bottle from the 1970s. Below this root mat was a very gritty, gray sand that in some places was as much as six inches thick. This layer also had almost no artifacts. Below this we encountered a buried surface with the brick and stone pathways mentioned above and an abundance of domestic artifacts from the late nineteenth and early twentieth centuries. This stratigraphic profile (Figure 10.5) indicates that gray sand buried the ground surface the Hart lived on and that the plants from the surrounding swampy environment subsequently overtook the site.

Based on this evidence, I believe that the gray sand washed in and over the site as a result of flooding caused by the hurricane. Its consistency across the yard area of the site shows that this was a major flood event. In the areas where the house stood there is virtually no sand, indicating that this flood deposit was introduced to the site and was not natural to it. The fact that this layer of sediment was then buried by an accumulation of thick plant growth suggests that the site was abandoned after the flood. Ernest Hart likely faced the choice of either trying to repair a broken house situated on a flood-prone property or leaving and trying to start a new life elsewhere. The evidence suggests that he chose the latter.

Property records and historic maps suggest that the Harts' home was the only structure in the area to be destroyed by the storm. Houses from

Figure 10.5. Stratigraphic profile from the side yard of the Jacob and Hannah Hart site showing flood deposit (gray layer) overlaying cultural deposits. Photo by Christopher N. Matthews.

the same era of nineteenth-century construction located immediately next door are still in good condition. In fact, these houses have the added value of being in a historic district and of having an association with prominent names from Setauket's past. The same could have been true for the Harts' house if it had survived. This loss has another characteristic: the Harts were the only people of color living in that area in 1938. Thus, we have to consider that their long-term struggle with groundwater problems, which ultimately left their home vulnerable to the hurricane, may reflect one way that people of color were mistreated in Setauket. It was only the Harts who lived in such miserable conditions, and even Mr. Hart's effort to publicly show his struggle by clearing the millpond were misunderstood by the white community. That no one seemed to notice that the family were in a losing battle against groundwater speaks volumes about how those in power related to those most vulnerable in the community.

Building a Community on the Land

By the 1930s, people of color had built a small enclave along a stretch of Christian Avenue in Setauket. This neighborhood grew up around the

Bethel AME Church and Laurel Hill Cemetery, two of the community's prominent historic landmarks. In the 1940s and 1950s, this enclave grew to be the home for several dozen people of color who had moved there from other parts of Setauket and surrounding towns. They opened an American Legion hall in 1949 that has become an important landmark of the community. From oral histories we also learned that members of the community enjoyed an intimate relationship with the land. In 2005, Pearl Hart, who was born on Christian Avenue in 1925 and lived her whole life there, recalled that

> the springtime meant getting our gardens planted for the fall, with harvest in the fall. The foliage in this area was beautiful. The laurel bushes all in bloom made this place another world. I readily understand our cemetery's name being Laurel Hill. The wildflowers along the road, the roses, the buttercups, added to the beauty. During the summer it was great to walk Christian Avenue. The road was narrow allowing the tree branches from each side of the road to reach each other forming a canopy or shield from the hot sun. It was just beautiful. So nice and cool. . . . The month of August was a time the harvesting of fruits and vegetables, which we canned for the winter. Also, the summer meant getting the family together to enjoy the great outdoors. We had the most delicious food[,] including fish and clams from the bay and a special dessert for our August work, blueberry pie. The berries were plentiful then.[3]

This memory opens an understanding of the relationship between the community, the land, and the bay. Pearl Hart's younger brother Robert Lewis also remembers walking on deer trails, pathways, and bridle paths through the woods with siblings, friends, and adults in the 1950s and 1960s. For Lewis, remembering the past landscape invokes memories of him and his aunt, Lucy Hart Keyes, walking down to "Mahoney's Lot" to collect "pails and pails" of wild blueberries. They would then follow animal trails to reach West Meadow Creek, where they played in the water and along the shore and gathered beach plums and crabs. The area along the creek where they went was in the vicinity of a private beach that was used by a new gated community running down to the shore from Mt. Grey Road. While Robert remembers going to school with kids who lived in that neighborhood, he never saw white families collecting blueberries, plums, or crabs.

These stories describe how the community of color enjoyed access to freely available resources as recently as the 1960s and that they collected those abundant foods from the formerly undeveloped lands adjacent to their neighborhood. They also show that this use of the landscape was mostly their own practice; they knew other families in the area who did not do the same sorts of activities.

The Contamination of Chicken Hill

At roughly the same time that the community developed on Christian Avenue, another working-class community developed across town in a neighborhood known as Chicken Hill. This area was first developed around 1900 to provide housing for the mostly Eastern European immigrants who worked in Setauket's rubber factory (Stern 1991). A set of short streets was laid out near the factory where small frame houses were built and rented to factory workers. When the rubber industry fell on hard times in the 1910s, the factory closed and the neighborhood become a mixed-race community of working-class families. The 1940 census recorded seven white and seven "Negro" households whose members rented homes along the two blocks of Jersey Avenue on Chicken Hill. Local families constituted many of the non-white households, although one family had moved from Virginia and one from Connecticut. The white families consisted of two U.S.-born families, two families from Lithuania, two from Poland, and one from Russia. Sixteen working people of both races were laborers, four women of color did housework, three men worked as handymen, one man worked as a truck driver, and one man was a boat captain. In essence, regardless of skin color, the people of Jersey Avenue lived very similar working-class lives.

Today the streets where the homes of Chicken Hill stood are the site of a series of commercial strip malls along a highway bypass constructed in the 1960s. Ethel Lewis recalled when this highway was built and how environmental concerns were used to get people to leave Chicken Hill:

The water was bad. That's what they said. That was the reason why they decided to move the people out and convert the buildings. . . . They tried to use the whole area for development . . . no homes at all, just . . . stores, office buildings. . . . They had to get out and find homes all over. That was a big human saying for a while: "We don't know where to go. Where are we going to go?" That shouldn't have been allowed. They shouldn't have put them out until they did have somewhere to go. They told them that the water wasn't clean enough and it would start a disease over there and the whole town would be an epidemic. I daresay [the water] was bad. . . . What about other areas that just got street water? Theirs is new, just put in. Why couldn't . . . they have been similar. It was watered, Setauket water developed a name.[4]

It appears that the water in Chicken Hill came from old sources such as wells that had become contaminated with pollution, probably bacteria. The sources of the contamination are not recorded, but it was likely partly the result of the crowded and low-quality living conditions in the neighborhood. Yet as Mrs. Lewis notes, other parts of Setauket were modernized with new municipal "street" water sources that provided safe water. Although an epidemic was avoided, the impact of the contaminated water was still felt, as residents of Chicken Hill were displaced and no accommodations were made to rehouse them. While displaced white families could move to new housing in Setauket and elsewhere without facing restrictions or difficulties because of their race, people of color on Chicken Hill had fewer options.

The Encroachment of Suburbia

The final moment of environmental struggle for the Native American and African American community in Setauket dates from the 1970s to the present. Once people were pushed out of Chicken Hill, the only place left for people of color to live in Setauket was along Christian Avenue. In the 1960s and 1970s, a growth in population there that began after the demolition of Chicken Hill created a community with as many as forty-two households occupying thirty-two lots on Christian Avenue, including adjacent parts of Mud Road and Locust Avenue. For a few years, this was a good period for the community. The population was robust and many families had the resources to own their homes. However, both their neighborhood and the world around them was changing fast. One of the most pronounced changes to Setauket since the 1960s has been a substantial growth in the population that has led to development and gentrification. The local and regional population increased more than tenfold during the period 1940 to 1980: the combined population of the three villages of Setauket, Old Field, and Stony Brook grew from 2,135 in 1940 to 27,160 in 1980 and the population of the larger township of Brookhaven grew from 32,117 in 1940 to 365,015 in 1980 (Long Island Regional Planning Board 1982). This growth precipitated a transformation in Setauket from a predominantly rural village to a suburban environment. The impact of this change has been profound on the original residents.

For one, as we have seen, the pollution of the local waterways has eliminated the traditional practice of clamming and other shoreline collecting practices. In 1935, Ethel Lewis's three-year-old son Howard would run down the road to the bay, pail in hand, to collect clams; no child would do that today.[5] As new homes replaced fields and forests, sediment runoff increased. New housing developments also require roads, waste facilities, and storm drains, all of which lead to further runoff and an increase in the leeching of contaminants into the soil and water, especially bacteria.

Suburban development in Setauket has also brought new economic and social challenges for the Native American and African American community. Like clamming and other water-based labor that provided a supplemental income to families in the community, the undeveloped lands surrounding their neighborhood provided them with "free for the taking!" huckleberries, blueberries, cherries, and raspberries. The pears, apples, and peaches that children stole from orchard trees on neighboring farms are now all gone or inaccessible, since the farms have been redeveloped into private property.[6] Additional costs have come with the installation of new water utilities that have replaced the water pump near Bethel AME Church that served residents for a generation.

Additionally, as the population has grown, local government has become more invasive. Homeowners are no longer permitted to make substantial repairs to their homes without hiring or being a licensed contractor. When they renovate, they need a permit. They also need to keep their homes up and have them inspected in order to obtain a certificate of occupancy. Certificates and permits cost money, of course. A growing population also means more school buildings, teachers, and administrators, all of which are paid for through property taxes. Fortunately for students, the Three Village school district is very high performing, but a quality education is typically the result of a large school budget paid for with higher taxes. As a result, Setauket has become a very exclusive, affluent suburban community. Higher living costs have pushed poorer people out of the village; many have chosen to find more affordable homes elsewhere. There are now fewer than ten families of color living on Christian Avenue, and most of these are older people whose children have left Setauket. The prospects for the longevity of the Black community are slim because of the adverse effects of the gentrification of the village.

The consequences of suburban gentrification were felt directly in 2004 when a historic home on Christian Avenue that stood across the street from Bethel AME Church was torn down. The home was built in the late nineteenth century and in the 1930s was moved from Old Field to Christian Avenue. It was owned by a member of the Native American and African American Calvin family, which has roots in the village that date to at least the 1840s. By 2004, however, the owner no longer wanted to keep it and a contractor bought the property, then tore down the small house and replaced it with a modern suburban colonial. The family who purchased the new house was not from the community and the house has been sold multiple times since. Both its style and size and its role as a suburban investment rather than a long-term home have eroded key aspects of the traditional neighborhood. The only positive result of this demolition and rebuilding was that it spurred the community to form an independent historical society, the Higher Ground Intercultural and Heritage Association. Higher Ground successfully petitioned to establish the Bethel–Christian Avenue–Laurel Hill historic district in 2005 and have solicited researchers to contribute to their preservation efforts. Higher Ground has been my host and research partner in Setauket since 2009.

Discussion and Conclusion

This string of stories stretching from the beginning of the nineteenth century to the present provide a view of the long-term relations with the environment among members of Setauket's Native American and African American community. Some of this history has been positive, for example the way people of color had free access to locally available food and medicinal resources that they consumed directly or exchanged for other goods in the market. Other moments have been difficult as people have faced environmental hazards such as a high water table, hurricanes, contaminants, pollution, and, most recently, development and gentrification. Regrettably, each moment of positive relations with the environment has been followed by something negative. The final result was always displacement. All of the families of color in Old Field had left by the 1930s, the time when Old Field was separated from Setauket and became an extremely wealthy village. In at least one case, a former nonwhite resident of Old Field took their home with them, resituating it on a lot on Christian Avenue. This home was torn down in 2004 to make room for a suburban house that a contractor built to be resold. Thus, a struggle with displacement and erasure moved with the families even as they left to start over in new places. In other cases, families of Native American and African American descent were restricted to living in suboptimal environments. An example is the Harts, who lost a fight against rising groundwater on Lake Street. This also applies to the residents of Chicken Hill, who lost their homes because their landlords and village officials chose not to monitor their drinking water until they used poor-quality water as a reason for moving them out. In each case, these struggles are evidence that people of color in Setauket were victims of environmental racism.

A response to this racism must be forthcoming for this research to be useful. What can be done now? How can these stories be a base for practicing archaeological justice? The first step in a response to a problem is always recognition and understanding. To that end, the research I have presented is designed to illuminate the long history of struggle of the community of color in Setauket to survive, I hope in a way that will show that food security, drainage, and pollution are concerns that we all share and are all responsible for. It is easy to miss the point that there are environmental consequences to fertilizing a lawn or failing picking up after a pet. It is also likely that most Setauket residents today do not realize that these environmental losses are unevenly distributed depending on the history, status, and race of a community. That is the premise of environmental justice activism—that corruption of the environment often has an uneven impact on different people and groups. Environmental justice also asks allies in the fight against environmental racism, who should include collaborators such as archaeologists, to be aware that the use of the environment as a racist strategy is tied to the deep histories of racism that communities have fought against for generations. Thus, the goal cannot be simply cleaning up the mess. The solution has to be restorative so that a community can resume its positive relationship to the environment. Even though it is not possible for people of color to return to a way of life similar to that of the Tobiases on Conscience Bay, we can recognize now that their descendants are leaving Setauket as a result of new forms of environmental racism that reproduce an environmental assault against people of color in the village that has been ongoing for generations. Addressing this struggle through the lenses of archaeology and justice requires an appreciation of the ways that people contribute to their community beyond paying taxes. In support of the community of color in Setauket, we need to develop creative ways to recognize their particular historical role and significance so that their story is seen as part of the life and landscape of the village. We also need to know more about their experience and survival of colonialism, slavery, racism, and displacement. Learning these stories will show us how people of color in America have struggled against and resisted their destruction. We also need to recognize that the forces that displace and marginalize vulnerable communities like this one have also benefited many others. The groups that have benefited need to understand that Setauket will become a better place if it makes space in both its historical narratives and its present-day geography for the Native American and African American community of color that has lived there for generations. Archaeological justice involves reconnecting histories that have become separated over time, including the histories of people who are imagined as belonging to distinct white and black communities. Regardless of the method, the goal of archaeological social activism is to promote justice in communities through the lens of heritage so that those who are most vulnerable are recognized and given the resources they need to persist.

Notes

1. Deputy State Historic Preservation Officer Dorothy P. Guzzo to Mr. John Prince, Remedial Project Manager, New Jersey Remediation Branch, United States Environmental Protection Agency, January 17, 1997. On file, New Jersey Historic Preservation Office, Trenton, NJ, HPO-A97-93.

2. "No Northport Casualties in Hurricane Wednesday," *Northport Journal,* September 23, 1983, 1.

3. Read into the record at the hearing to establish the Bethel-Christian Avenue-Laurel Hill historic district in 2005.

4. Transcript of interview with Ethel Mae Lewis, May 4, 1987. On file at Three Village Historical Society, Setauket-East Setauket, NY.

5. Transcript of interview with Ethel Mae Lewis.

6. Transcript of interview with Ethel Mae Lewis.

References Cited

Ashmore, Wendy, and A. Bernard Knapp, eds. 1999. *Archaeologies of Landscape: Contemporary Perspectives.* New York: Blackwell.

Bernstein, David J. 2006. "Long-Term Continuity in the Archaeological Record from the Coast of New York and Southern New England, USA." *The Journal of Island and Coastal Archaeology* 1 (2): 271–284.

Boesch, Eugene. 1998. "Subsurface Archaeological Investigation of the U.S. Radium Site Study Area—Tasks 6 and 7." Prepared for Malcolm Pirnie, Inc. On file, New Jersey Historic Preservation Office, Trenton, NJ.

Bryant, Nelson. 1985. "Outdoors: Art of Spearing Eels." *New York Times,* February 4, 1985, C11.

Cashin Associates. 2009. *Conscience Bay and Setauket Harbor Storm Water Manage-*

ment Plan. Submitted to Town of Brookhaven. Hauppage, NY: Cashin Associates, P.C. Accessed May 16, 2018. https://www.brookhavenny.gov/DocumentCenter/View/146/ Conscience-Bay-and-Setauket-Harbor-Stormwater-Management-Plan—March-2009-PDF.

Ceci, Lynn. 1980. "Locational Analysis of Historic Algonquin Sites in Coastal New York: A Preliminary Study." Research Report 19. Proceedings of the Conference on Northeastern Archaeology 7. Accessed May 16, 2018. https://scholarworks.umass.edu/anthro_res_rpt19/7.

Chapman, Ann E. 2018. "Nineteenth Century Trends in American Conservation." *National Park Service.* Accessed May 16, 2018. https://www.nps.gov/nr/travel/massachusetts_conservation/nineteenth_century_trends_in_%20american_conservation.html.

Chavis, Benjamin F., Jr, 1994. Preface. In *Unequal Protection: Environmental Justice and Communities of Color,* edited by R. D. Bullard, xi–xii. San Francisco, CA: Sierra Club Books.

City-Data.com. 2018. "Old Field, New York." City-Data.com. Accessed August 22, 2018. http://www.city-data.com/city/Old-Field-New-York.html.

Connell, Robert. 2011. "National People of Color Environmental Leadership Summit." In *Green Culture: An A-to-Z Guide,* edited by Kevin Wehr, 301–303. Los Angeles: Sage Publications.

David, Bruno, and Julian Thomas, eds. 2010. *Handbook of Landscape Archaeology.* New York: Routledge.

Gilmore, Ruth Wilson. 2008. "Forgotten Places and the Seeds of Grassroots Planning." In *Engaging Contradictions: Theory, Politics, and Methods of Activist Scholarship,* edited by Charles Hale, 31–61. Berkeley: University of California Press.

Green, Theodore A. 1999. "The Hart-Sells Connection." In *William Sidney Mount: Family, Friends, and Ideas,* edited by Elizabeth Kahn Kaplan, Robert W. Kenny, and Roger Wunderlich, 63–67. Setauket, NY: Three Village Historical Society.

Grossman, Joel. 1996. "Archaeological and Historical Sensitivity Evaluation of the U.S. Radium Facility Tasks 1, 2, 3, 4, and 9." Prepared for Malcolm Pirnie. Inc. On file, New Jersey Historic Preservation Office, Trenton, NJ.

Harmon, David, Francis P. McManamon, and Dwight T. Pitcaithley. 2006. *The Antiquities Act: A Century of American Archaeology, Historic Preservation, and Nature Conservation.* Tucson: University of Arizona Press.

Harvey, David, 1989. *The Limits to Capital.* Chicago: University of Chicago Press.

Hodder, Ian, ed. 1987. *Archaeology as Long-Term History.* Cambridge: Cambridge University Press.

Holifield, Ryan. 2001. "Defining Environmental Justice and Environmental Racism." *Urban Geography* 22 (1): 78–90.

Judd, Richard W. *Common Lands, Common People: The Origins of Conservation in Northern New England.* Cambridge: Harvard University Press.

Kennedy, Merit. 2016. "Lead-Laced Water in Flint: A Step-by-Step Look at the Makings of a Crisis." *The Two Way,* April 20. Accessed May 16, 2018. https://www.npr.org/sections/thetwo-way/2016/04/20/465545378/lead-laced-water-in-flint-a-step-by-step-look-at-the-makings-of-a-crisis.

King, Thomas F. 1998. *Cultural Resource Laws and Practice: An Introductory Guide*. Walnut Creek, CA: AltaMira.

Little, Barbara J., and Paul A. Shackel. 2014. *Archaeology, Heritage, and Civic Engagement: Working toward the Public Good*. New York: Routledge.

Long Island Regional Planning Board. 1982. *Historical Population of Long Island Communities, 1790–1980, Decennial Census Data*. Hauppauge, NY: Long Island Regional Planning Board, Hauppauge, NY.

Lumley, Sarah, and Patrick Armstrong. 2004. "Some of the Nineteenth Century Origins of the Sustainability Concept." *Environment, Development and Sustainability* 6 (3): 367–378.

Márquez, John. 2013. *Black-Brown Solidarity: Racial Politics in the New Gulf South*. Austin: University of Texas Press.

Matthews, Christopher N. 2012. "Gilded Ages and Gilded Archaeologies of American Exceptionalism." *International Journal of Historical Archaeology* 16 (4): 717–744.

McCaffrey, Brian M. 2019. "Water Quality Trends for Conscience Bay: 2018." Setauket, NY: Storm Water Management Program, Setauket, NY.

McGuire, Randall H. 2008. *Archaeology as Political Action*. Berkeley: University of California Press.

McKnight, Justine. 2017. "Report on the Analysis of Flotation Samples Collected from the Silas Tobias Site (10353.000057), Setauket, Long Island, New York." Prepared for Christopher Matthews, Montclair State University. On file, Montclair State University.

Moore, Kate. 2017. *The Radium Girls: The Dark Story of America's Shining Women*. New York: Source Books.

Shackel, Paul A., and Matthew M. Palus. 2006. "The Gilded Age and Working-Class Industrial Communities." *American Anthropologist* 108(4): 828–841.

Pulido, Laura. 2015. "Geographies of Race and Ethnicity 1: White Supremacy vs White Privilege in Environmental Racism Research." *Progress in Human Geography* 39 (6): 809–817.

———. 2016a. "Geographies of Race and Ethnicity II: Environmental Racism, Racial Capitalism and State-Sanctioned Violence." *Progress in Human Geography* 41 (4): 524–533.

———. 2016b. "Flint, Environmental Racism, and Racial Capitalism." *Capitalism Nature Socialism* 27 (3): 1–16.

Salwen, Bert. 1962. "Sea Levels and Archaeology in the Long Island Sound Area." *American Antiquity* 28 (1): 46–55.

Stern, Marc J. 1991. "The Social Utility of Failure: Long Island's Rubber Industry and the Setauket Shtetle, 1876–1911." *Long Island Journal* 4 (1): 15–35.

Tober, James A. 1981. *Who Owns the Wildlife? The Political Economy of Conservation in Nineteenth America*. Westport, CT: Greenwood Press.

Trigger, Bruce. 1989. *A History of Archaeological Thought*. Cambridge: Cambridge University Press.

Voyles, Traci Brynne. 2015. *Wastelanding: Legacies of Uranium Mining in Navajo Country*. Minneapolis: University of Minnesota Press.

indigenous

11

Engaging Archaeology as Social Justice for Navajo Communities

KERRY F. THOMPSON AND ORA V. MAREK-MARTINEZ

Economic development has long been a concern on reservation lands (Champagne and Goldberg 2005). The lack of economic development on reservations is a factor in the perpetuation of extreme poverty. Instead of keeping money circulating in reservation communities, the fact that most necessary goods and services such as groceries, retail shops, and laundromats are located off the reservation moves most of the money out of reservation economies quickly (Miller 2013). It is not possible for most reservation residents to build equity in their homes because there is no housing market and thus their homes have no market value. For many Americans, home equity can be the key to greater economic gains like starting a business; it is often a homeowner's most valuable asset. The relationship between owning a home, having access to running water and electricity, and economic development is poorly understood and/or articulated. Residential development on tribal trust land can be a lengthy, complicated, and adversarial process. On the Navajo Nation, individuals who seek to lease land to build homes on bear the primary responsibility both for working through the complicated lease process and for the cost—in both time and money—of assembling the proof that a legal survey, an archaeological inventory, an environmental protection agency assessment, and a biological survey of the land in question have taken place. As archaeologists who have worked on the Navajo Nation for individual and large-scale housing developments, we have witnessed the struggle for tribal member homeownership and suggest that it is intimately intertwined with economic development. We propose that tribal governments, who govern lands where residential development is onerous and complicated for tribal members, engage communities to approach residential development with a holistic approach in which modern needs are balanced with the protection of cultural resources.

The Navajo Nation

The Navajo Nation government has created policies based on western-based ideologies about land use and ownership. These laws have created many of the inequities in home ownership and economic development opportunities for tribal members that we have observed. In her ten years of experience with the Navajo Nation and the Navajo Region Bureau of Indian Affairs (BIA), Marek-Martinez has observed that federal government bureaucrats and lawyers who were located far away from tribal lands crafted these policies without tribal input and then presented them to the Navajo Nation to implement and regulate through the BIA's oversight of tribal lands and land use policy. These policies provide one-acre parcels of land with sole or joint (between a married couple) ownership to any adult Navajo tribal member. However, one-acre parcels are an affront to the cultural practices of the Navajo people, who have historically practiced collective use of the land based on family, or k'é, relations. The development of the current system is rooted in the settler-colonial history between the United States and the Navajo Nation, as formed through the assimilationist policies and programs that have regulated land use for tribal lands held in federal trust. Relationships between tribes and the United States were often directed toward acculturating and assimilating tribal peoples in order to end the perceived dependency of tribes on the U.S. government (Deloria and Lytle 1983). Consequently, efforts to mimic western perceptions of land ownership on tribal lands results in a hostile and difficult housing situation that subjects tribal members to substandard and often dangerous living conditions—if they have homes at all. On the Navajo Nation, many tribal members view the cultural compliance process as it is currently implemented as unnecessary and prohibitive of progress. The process has been codified, and although provisions exist to engage with local communities, all authority and decision-making capacity rests with a central government official. The Navajo Nation's reliance on western ideas of centralized power and authority has removed the Navajo people from the decision-making process about what is appropriate on their land.

Federally recognized American Indian tribes with reservation lands typically occupy more tribal trust land than any other kind of land.[1] Tribal trust land is held in trust by the United States on behalf of American Indian tribes. Tribal nations thus occupy and use tribal trust land but do not own it in the same sense that the average American citizen may own their own land. On the Navajo Nation, homeowners do not own the land on which their homes are built and in some instances, the leased land with the home and any improvements can revert to tribal ownership (Navajo Land Department 1993).

As a category of federally defined land, tribal trust land is subject to both federal and tribal rules and regulations governing development. Our primary concern here is the work that falls under the purview of archaeologists. Navajo citizens are required to secure archaeological surveys to obtain permission to build a home on reservation land and install utilities. The traditional disciplinary goals of site preservation, data collection, and furthering knowledge of the past that are important to the archaeological community are secondary, if resources are available to address them at all. On the Navajo Nation, and perhaps in Indian Country in general, it is challenging for archaeologists to implement current practices in the discipline that seek to include and address myriad public interests because building a life and achieving a desired *quality* of life take priority.

Housing availability and housing conditions are persistent problems for the Navajo Nation. Of the 43,907 occupied housing units on the Navajo Nation and on off-reservation trust land, twenty-one percent lack plumbing facilities, compared to 0.4 percent of occupied housing units in the United States overall. Sixteen percent of Navajo homes lack kitchens, compared to 0.9 percent of U.S. homes overall.[2] Most archaeologists who work in a project-driven enterprise are completely unaware of these inequities. In order to practice archaeology that engages Navajo communities, however, projects and research must take into account these and other pressing needs that often take priority over knowledge about the past and for which archaeological skills can be useful.

The Path to a Lease

In theory, the path to both a homesite and a business site lease begins with an application and fee at the agency level, but in practice, most people have built a home first out of need and completed the paperwork later. The local chapter government requires the consent of people who have active grazing permits in the area where a person wishes to build and final approval from the chapter's grazing official. An archaeological inventory is required in order to protect eligible cultural resources from the impacts of residential and business development. The lack of archaeological inventories for these homesites creates a significant obstacle for lessees who apply for home construction and improvement grants and utility lines through their local governments. A lease cannot be finalized and does not legally exist until all of the compliance work is done. A homesite lease is often the first piece of paperwork that is needed to apply for anything else a lessee might need like a water line, power line, or assistance funds. Today there is an application fee, a fee for the lease itself, a fee for the biological assessment, the cost of an archaeological survey, and the cost of a land plat survey.

Because people typically choose where to build based on kin relationships rather than compliance concerns, if an archaeologist locates an archaeological site or a Traditional Cultural Place/Property (TCP), the applicant must select another location and the process must begin again.[3] Since a lessee must obtain a review of the area by both biological and environmental protection agencies, if their chosen area is located in a sensitive zone, the applicant must select a new location and the process begins again. For lessees who have built before completing the paperwork, an archaeological site or biologically sensitive zone can often mean that they will never have utilities installed on their property.

The process for a business site lease is similarly complicated and can be more onerous in other ways. However, the Business Regulatory Office of the Navajo Nation's Division of Economic Development will often pay for the same costly services that homesite lessees pay out of pocket as an incentive to attract certain kinds of businesses to the Navajo Nation. In many cases, business owners will not engage in any construction on Navajo Nation lands because they are aware of the undeveloped nature of the land and the associated costs of infrastructure development. Lack of business opportunities can be divisive for the community and are prohibitive of economic growth on the Nation.

In 2016, the *Arizona Republic* published a series of articles that provide insight into the housing challenges the tribe faces.[4] Although the series has been criticized for exaggerating the housing crisis on the Navajo Nation, it adequately conveys that there is a real and ongoing crisis. The challenges to building a home on the Navajo Nation are relevant to any archaeological, scholarly, or intellectual endeavor in a social justice framework. Whether we are proposing an archaeological project or discussing better management of cultural resources, we always come up against the same obstacle— we cannot reasonably expect people struggling in various stages of this homesite lease process to have the same level of interest in cultural resource management issues that we have. If we assume the interest is there, people who haul water and wood and care for livestock have enough to do to make their day-to-day lives work, let alone build a satisfactory quality of life that includes time for cultural resource issues. Therefore, the implementation of a community-based management system for cultural resources and the cultural landscape may provide the flexibility and infrastructure needed to engage local communities, particularly livestock owners, homeowners, and potential entrepreneurs, in the archaeological process. Sharing the authority to manage cultural resources that are important to the Navajo public may make it more likely that communities will begin to engage in a Navajo-style archaeology—that is, an archaeology that works for and with the Navajo people.

Archaeology and Infrastructure Development

Infrastructure on the Navajo Nation is built by three entities: the Navajo Tribal Utility Authority (NTUA), the Indian Health Service (IHS), and the Navajo Nation Division of Transportation (NNDOT). NTUA is a tribal nonprofit enterprise that provides water, power, phone lines, and some solar panels. Most recently, NTUA has also provided internet access. The Indian Health Service also builds water lines and other water infrastructure. A homesite lease does not guarantee that a home will have access to running water and power unless a lessee has thought about and planned for the logistics and cost of installation before beginning the process. Utility lines are installed often at an added expense to the lessee and only if the home is within reach of an existing water or power line *and* the proposed lines have been cleared through the same biological, archaeological, and environmental protection processes as the homesite lease itself. The NTUA is primarily responsible for maintaining and repairing utility lines. Those who choose to live remotely may rent or buy solar panels for electricity, but they will likely have to haul their own water from one of the wells located across the Navajo Nation or from nearby border towns.

The installation of water lines and systems in very remote areas is an issue of concern to the IHS. Through a regulatory compliance agreement between the IHS and the Navajo Nation, the lines have to be maintained by the Navajo Nation. The Navajo Nation's tribal utility company, NTUA, is not managed by the tribal government, but is a nonprofit entity that the Navajo Nation operates. NTUA is not fully equipped to maintain all remote water lines and systems, and as a result many of the installed systems are falling into disrepair. Importantly, NTUA is not itself the Navajo Nation. It is operated *by* the Navajo Nation and this distinction exempts it from the regulatory compliance agreement the IHS has with the Navajo Nation. What has happened as a result is the creation of a system that makes it difficult, if not impossible, to identify who is accountable for certain parts of the Nation's infrastructure. This is stressful and time consuming and diminishes the quality of life for people who unknowingly got caught in the middle.

Roads

The Navajo Nation Project Management Program in the NNDOT has taken over the BIA Navajo Region Division of Transportation's responsibility to maintain and build roads. It has done so by entering into a government-to-government contract with the Federal Highway Administration that enables it to receive direct funding. The Division of Transportation receives funding to offer technical assistance to the NNDOT that varies from year to year.

All entities responsible for infrastructure development are, of course, bound by the same cultural resource management laws and policies as would-be home builders and business owners are on the Navajo Nation. In our experience, most infrastructure projects are initiated, planned, and staffed by people who typically see archaeology as an expensive and unnecessary regulatory obstacle. Conducting archaeology on tribal lands without community input usually results in a complete rejection of the archaeological process and of the potential value of archaeology for protecting cultural resources and the cultural landscape. A former elected official in Thompson's home community stated outright that he did not lobby for road improvement or paving funds primarily because of the archaeological work the process would inevitably involve. On the Navajo Nation, new road construction costs around $1,000,000 per mile before the costs for archaeological and other environmental studies are factored in. These studies are usually budgeted at 1 percent of the overall construction costs per the Bureau of Indian Affairs–Indian Reservation Roads Program and 25 CFR Part 170 (U.S. Department of the Interior, Indian Affairs n.d.). Nevertheless, the Navajo government and public often single out archaeological studies as the most cost prohibitive and time consuming element of road building (Vock 2017; Yurth 2010a and 2010b). That stigma reinforces negative stereotypes of and associations with archaeology. The result is the destruction of cultural resources and the traditional cultural landscape.

We have observed that some communities request that archaeological and environmental studies be omitted from the development process. During her time as a manager for the Navajo Nation, Marek-Martinez requested funding each year from the Navajo Tribal Council. In some cases, council delegates related concerns from their constituents about archaeological and environmental studies and would entertain thoughts about not funding the departments responsible for these studies. These types of perceptions and comments have created a binary opposition between protecting the cultural landscape and improving the quality of life for Navajo citizens. Some communities are looking for ways to record and safeguard their local histories but do not necessarily include archaeological sites as part of their concern. In Navajo world view, culture, language, and philosophies are embedded in the landscape and the Navajo way of life is dependent upon the landscape. This creates a resistance to any activities that disturb the ground, including infrastructure development activities that could prove beneficial for Navajo communities that have been initiated without consulting with the appropriate people, namely local elders and traditional knowledge holders.

The Navajo Nation attempted to address some of these issues by mandating ethnographic interviews and presentations at affected chapter houses and with the local community, including elders and traditional knowledge holders. In practice, however, the industry standard became a stop at the local chapter government to speak with chapter personnel about grave locations and to ask whether they knew anything about cultural places, sacred areas, plant- or herb-gathering areas, or other areas that need to be protected. This type of interaction has excluded an entire population of knowledgeable individuals and any type of local community participation in the archaeological process. Unfortunately, this seems to have reinforced long-held negative perceptions of archaeologists and archaeology in general.

Today, archaeology is bureaucratic and is intertwined with federal and tribal regulations and centralized and local political differences. Infrastructure development and the implementation of western-based policies that guide the Navajo Nation's development policies have created a haphazard approach to residential, commercial, and infrastructure development on the Navajo Nation. Local communities awaiting infrastructure that will support economic development opportunities are caught between political agendas and the economic aspirations of outside forces that usually drain resources from tribal lands.

Discussion

The slogan of the Navajo Nation Division of Natural Resources is "Land, Water, Power and Quality of Life." The Navajo Nation Division of Natural Resources oversees the archaeological compliance work on the Navajo Nation. We think that while critiquing one's government is necessary and healthy, it is unproductive in the absence of suggestions for solutions. Responsible Navajo Nation citizenship and social justice entails bringing problems into the light in order to help find solutions. So how do we achieve balance among quality of life, cultural resource management, and protecting our cultural landscape within the confines of federal and tribal regulations?

In 2009, Thompson volunteered to do archaeological inventories of homesites for people in her community and adjacent communities. Later, in the period 2011 to 2013, Thompson and a colleague obtained permission from the Navajo Nation to bring Northern Arizona University undergraduate and graduate students to these reservation communities to do archaeological inventories for homesite leases. They taught the students archaeological survey skills and worked with them on writing the requisite reports. Thompson quickly found that this volunteer work was an opportunity to teach students more than archaeological survey skills and report writing. Topics such as the history of tribal trust land status and the realities of reservation life were discussed in the field and in the classroom. Thompson, her colleague, and their students were able to complete homesite surveys for approximately 125 residents of the Navajo Nation with no money other than the $40 class fee each student had already paid to Northern Arizona University as part of their enrollment in an archaeology class. Any assistance in alleviating the bureaucratic burden that archaeology has become was welcomed in the communities where Thompson and her students worked. The project was halted when the Navajo Nation General Leasing Regulations of 2013 altered the homesite lease process to include both a biological assessment from the Navajo Nation Department of Fish and Wildlife and an assessment from the Navajo Nation Environmental Protection Agency. An additional fee and added requirements made archaeology part of a larger reporting requirement for lessees.

For someone unfamiliar with how the Navajo Nation bureaucracy operates, this volunteer approach presents significant challenges. Thompson began working in the community she is from and was able to leverage her family connections to make this volunteer project work and expand beyond her home chapter. Although the need is great throughout the reservation, there is sufficient, and deserved, suspicion of researchers unaffiliated with the Navajo Nation who propose archaeological work in many communities. While they make up the smallest percent of total archaeologists in the Southwest, there are Navajo archaeologists with whom academic archaeologists can collaborate and work. Archaeology on the Navajo Nation cannot be solely an academic enterprise; it has to (and can) provide immediate, tangible benefits for the quality of life of communities and their individual members.

We suggest that with community discussion and engagement, for example, a field school could be built around a road that a community has indicated it would like to see paved or otherwise improved. Admittedly, the archaeology is one piece of a large puzzle in something as large as a road but we believe that with planning it could work, especially if it used the resources the departments and initiatives of Northern Arizona University offer. In working with the Navajo Nation Heritage and Historic Preservation Department, we frequently come back to students because they are an opportunity to make reservation life less opaque to a larger American public. Stereotypes about Native Americans abound in American society and towns like Flagstaff on the border of reservations are no different. In the early days of Thompson's academic appointment at Northern Arizona University, it was not uncommon to encounter anthropology students who didn't know how close they were to two Native American nations and were unaware of the issues Native American communities face nationally and locally. Today, we teach a course at Northern Arizona called Indigenous Perspectives in Anthropology and we are reviving an existing course titled Applied Indigenous Archaeology. Engaging students in archaeological work on a reservation could provide real-world experience that dovetails with the scholarly work with which we engage in the course. Students in those courses learn archaeological skills and engage in discussions about oppression, power, and privilege. They also have the opportunity to learn about and interact with communities that many of them would never have otherwise. The students do not even have to be exclusively anthropology and archaeology students, as much of the fieldwork can be used for majors in earth and social sciences. This interdisciplinarity also presents education majors with an opportunity to create meaningful, locally situated lesson plans and experiences for K–12 students on and off the Navajo Nation. We think the key is to focus on reciprocal activities where the benefit for the Navajo community is tangible and makes progress towards a better quality of life for community members and the NAU students acquire the knowledge and experience entailed in a community-based archaeology project.

Focusing on Indigenous perspectives in our archaeological approach to this issue can lead to a collaborative, community-based project that builds capacity for planning for development in communities in ways that are appropriate and sustainable (Atalay 2008, 2012; Colwell-Chanthaphonh et al. 2010; Wilcox 2009). The task undertaken by the former Navajo Nation Archaeology Department to train tribal members and other Native Americans in archaeological methods was very successful in training and eventually staffing tribal and local federal agencies with Navajo archaeologists. This approach in a Navajo community may alleviate the expense associated with permitting requirements and build capacity so the community is a part of the overall tribal archaeological process. It also indigenizes archaeological processes to create a unique Navajo approach to heritage management. This project should include a public archaeology component in which non-Native students are also provided with educational opportunities to work on tribal lands and see the everyday realities of tribal members. Becoming aware of the realities of contemporary Native American communities is an experience that will challenge notions of Otherness and illuminate the continued oppression of Native American people. A plentiful literature relates to the collaboration and partnership between archaeologists and Native American communities that discusses the challenges—and the rewards and enrichment—of such an experience for both Native and non-Native students (e.g., Silliman 2008; Teeter, Martinez, and Kennedy-Richardson 2013). Gonzalez and colleagues (2006) explain the importance of a reciprocal approach to working with tribal community members during archaeological field schools by implementing a "ritual blueprint" (403) in the field school as a way of integrating tribal world views in archaeological practice and interpretation. This approach also trains the next generation in collaborative and Indigenous archaeology. The framework used in Thompson's volunteer project could be expanded to include a community-based approach that is integrated with a Navajo ritual blueprint where university students and local communities teach and learn from one another, build community capacity, and train future generations of tribal members and archaeologists in a respectful and ceremonial manner.

We have seen the difference made when communities receive much-needed infrastructure. We encourage these communities, and other Native communities, to participate in planning and in the archaeological process in an equitable manner on projects on their communal land base. Each Navajo Nation chapter has the ability to create community land use plans for a period of five or ten years. Many of these plans can be used to guide archaeological studies that include the Anthropology Department at Northern Arizona University, local chapters, and community members. Building these types of collaborative relationships is an important part of an Indigenous archaeological research process (see Atalay 2006, 2007; Croes 2010; Gonzalez et al. 2006; Silliman 2008; Watkins 2008) that serves to benefit all parties. Instead of the cost of these studies being the responsibility of the individual homeowner or business owner, all parties can co-manage investigations and conduct work that benefits tribal communities and helps train community members and university students in archaeological practices at no cost to the owner for the archaeological survey. Supporting Navajo communities, documenting Navajo heritage, and teaching future archaeologists do not have to be mutually exclusive endeavors and may in fact work together to further the discipline of archaeology's goals of sharing power.

Notes

1. The Navajo Nation consists of trust lands, allotment lands, and fee lands that total close to 17 million acres. All of these land classes are subject to compliance with federal and tribal Cultural Resource Management policies and regulations.

2. U.S. Census Bureau, 2005–2009 American Community Survey, accessed August 1, 2017, https://www.census.gov/programs-surveys/acs/.

3. Per the Navajo Nation Heritage and Historic Preservation Department's Cultural Resource Compliance Section, archaeological sites or Traditional Cultural Places/Properties located within 200 feet of the homesite location will be moved so the boundary of the homesite location and the site or TCP boundary are 200 feet from one another.

4. "To Build a Home: The Navajo Housing Tragedy," *Arizona Republic,* December 14, 2016.

References Cited

Atalay, Sonya. 2006. "Indigenous Archaeology as Decolonizing Practice." *American Indian Quarterly* 30 (3–4): 280–310.

———. 2007. "Global Application of Indigenous Archaeology: Community Based Participatory Research in Turkey." *Archaeologies: Journal of the World Archaeological Congress* 3 (3): 249–270.

———. 2008. "Multivocality and Indigenous Archaeologies." In *Evaluating Multiple Narratives: Beyond Nationalist, Colonialist, and Imperialist Archaeologies,* edited by Junko Habu, Claire Fawcett, and John M. Matsunaga, 29–44. New York: Springer.

———. 2012. *Community-Based Archaeology: Research with, by, and for Indigenous and Local Communities.* Berkeley: University of California Press.

Champagne, Duane, and Carole Goldberg. 2005. "Changing the Subject: Individual versus Collective Interests in Indian Country Research." *Wicazo Sa Review* 20 (1): 49–69.

Colwell-Chanthaphonh, Chip, Thomas J. Ferguson, Dorothy Lippert, Randall H. McGuire, George P. Nicholas, Joe E. Watkins, and Larry J. Zimmerman. 2010. "The Premise and Promise of Indigenous Archaeology." *American Antiquity* 75 (2): 228–238.

Croes, Dale. 2010. "Courage and Thoughtful Scholarship = Indigenous Archaeology Partnerships." *American Antiquity* 75 (2): 211–216.

Deloria, Vine, Jr., and Clifford M. Lytle. 1983. *American Indians, American Justice.* Austin: University of Texas Press.

Gonzalez, Sara, Darren Modzelewski, Lee M. Panich, and Tsim Schneider. 2006. "Archaeology for the Seventh Generation." *American Indian Quarterly* 30 (3–4): 388–414.

Miller, Robert J. 2013. *Reservation "Capitalism": Economic Development in Indian Country.* Lincoln: Bison Books, a trade imprint of University of Nebraska Press.

Navajo Land Department. 1993. Homesite Lease Policy and Procedure. Accessed August 1, 2017. http://dinehbikeyah.org/docs/homesite/HSL_Policies&Procedures.pdf.

Silliman, Stephen W., ed. 2008. *Collaborating at the Trowel's Edge: Teaching and Learning in Indigenous Archaeology.* Tucson: University of Arizona Press.

Teeter, Wendy G., Desiree R. Martinez, and K. Kennedy-Richardson. 2013. Cultural Landscapes of Catalina Island. In *California's Channel Islands: The Archaeology of Human-Environment Interactions,* edited by Christopher S. Jazwa, and Jennifer E. Perry, 410–437. Salt Lake City: University of Utah Press.

U.S. Department of the Interior. Indian Affairs. N.d. "Tribes Served by the Navajo Region." Accessed July 7, 2020. https://www.bia.gov/regional-offices/navajo/tribes-served.

Vock, Daniel C. 2017. "In Navajo Nation, Bad Roads Can Mean Life or Death." *Governing the States and Localities,* July. Accessed April 23, 2020. https://www.governing.com/topics/transportation-infrastructure/gov-navajo-utah-roads-infrastructure.html.

Watkins, Joe. 2008. "The Repatriation Arena: Control, Conflict and Compromise." In *Opening Archaeology: Repatriation's Impact on Contemporary Research and Practice,* edited by Thomas Killion, 168–176. Santa Fe: School for Advanced Research Press.

Wilcox, Michael V. 2009. *The Pueblo Revolt and the Mythology of Conquest: An Indigenous Archaeology of Contact.* Berkeley: University of California Press.

Yurth, Cindy. 2010a. "Where's the Tar? Paved Roads an Elusive Goal on Navajo Nation Land." *Navajo Times,* February 11.

———. 2010b. "Archaeologist: Departmental Infighting Hinders Paving." *Navajo Times,* February 26.

feminism!

Conclusion

Beyond Archaeology as Science
Activist Archaeology for Social Action

JOE WATKINS

At dinner in a Basque café in Reno, Nevada, in 1993, I was privileged to have a conversation with Alison Wylie. We discussed ethics, opportunities, and numerous other topics. At one point in our discussion, Alison brought up Janet Spector's work at Inyan Ceyaka Atonwan, or Little Rapids, an archaeological site on the Minnesota River. I left the dinner yearning for more information on Spector's work.

Spector's 1993 book *What This Awl Means: Feminist Archaeology at a Wahpeton Dakota Village* documented her research and the results of excavations at Little Rapids and offered a glimpse into feminist archaeology, one facet of what might be considered to be activist archaeology. Activist archaeology is an approach to using archaeology and/or archaeological methods that attempts to influence social change, or, as Stottman (2010, 8) defines it, "[using] archaeology to affect [*sic*] change in and advocate for contemporary communities, not as the archaeologist sees it, but as the community itself sees it." Spector used her work to add people back into the past, thereby allowing others to better recognize that the past has an impact on the future and on those whose ancestors created it.

In many ways, the concept of using archaeology to effect change, or at least to advocate for it, is late in coming. Most archaeologists are taught that archaeology should be an objective scientific approach to investigating the past. However, as Bruce Trigger noted in 1980, science is rarely objective: "problems social scientists choose to research and (hopefully less often) the conclusions that they reach are influenced in various ways . . . (among them) . . . the attitudes and opinions that are prevalent in the societies in which they live." (662)

Defining Activist Archaeology

In this chapter, I explore some approaches within archaeology that might be considered activist archaeology. This exploration will not necessarily be chronological. I examine a few aspects of practicing archaeology that have an activist bent. I do not practice all of these approaches and therefore am not up to date with the most current literature on many of these topics. I recognize my limitations, but I do not intend this chapter to be a compendium of current research related to such topics. Instead, I want to describe some of the ways archaeologists are approaching their practice as a way of influencing (or at least trying to influence) social change.

One of the earliest approaches to evaluating the impact of archaeology on contemporary populations is the archaeological work in Annapolis of Mark P. Leone, Parker B. Potter, and Paul A. Shackel (Leone and Potter 1984; Leone, Potter, and Shackel 1987). Their work in the Archaeology in Annapolis program involved a critical approach to archaeology as a way of pointing out how "archaeological interpretations presented to the public may acquire a meaning unintended by the archaeologist and not to be found in the data" (Leone, Potter, and Shackel 1987, 24). Their work identified how black history is presented separately from white history and noted that history in Annapolis, which has been written almost exclusively by white people, ignores slavery. This history glosses over foundational relationships between these two groups, thereby preventing black people from using slavery as a reference point in comparing their present with their past. One result of the Archaeology in Annapolis program was that it explicitly changed the narrative the public received.

Building on the works of Leone in Annapolis, feminist approaches to archaeology contributed to some of the earliest approaches to activist archaeology, as noted by the 1993 publication about Spector's work at Little Rapids. Conkey (2003, 868) argues that archaeology fell behind much of the feminist and gender anthropology that characterized the 1970s because of the combination of the purportedly objectivist approach that scientific archaeology prioritized and the relatively small number of women archaeologists in visible, respected positions.

Conkey and Gero (1997, 412) felt the need to push for "an explicitly feminist inquiry in archaeology, one that is committed to changing the way archaeology is practiced, the way it is presented, and the nature of archaeological interpretation." While gender studies may have initially developed to reject the equation of human behavior with the behavior of men, feminist archaeological studies have introduced sociopolitical topics as a way of injecting social activism into archaeology. Feminist archaeology includes a sociopolitical agenda that intends to integrate the social and political aspects of feminism with the scientific examination of the remnants of past cultures. In addition, Conkey and Wylie (2007) note the impact that "doing archaeology as a feminist" has had on the discipline.

Indigenous Archaeology and Community-Based Participatory Research

George Nicholas defines Indigenous archaeology as

> an expression of archaeological theory and practice in which the discipline intersects with Indigenous values, knowledge, practices, ethics, and sensibilities, and through collaborative and community-originated or -directed projects, and related critical perspectives. Indigenous archaeology seeks to (1) make archaeology more representative of, responsible to, and relevant for Indigenous communities; (2) redress real and perceived inequalities in the practice of archaeology; and (3) inform and broaden the understanding and interpretation of the archaeological record through the incorporation of Aboriginal worldviews, histories, and science. (Nicholas 2008, 1660)

Colwell-Chanthaphonh et al. (2010, 233), write that "Indigenous archaeology is the attempt to introduce and incorporate different perspectives of the past into the study and management of heritage—to accommodate the diverse values for archaeology that exist in our pluralist democracy." Many other authors have written about and described Indigenous archaeology, including Atalay (2006, 2012), Colwell-Chanthaphonh (2009, 2012), Ferguson (1996), Nicholas (2010, 2014), Silliman (2010), and Watkins (2000, 2003). Edited volumes approaching the topic include Colwell-Chanthaphonh and Ferguson (2007), Kerber (2006), Silliman (2008), and Smith and Wobst (2005). All these works look at how Indigenous archaeology can be a way of influencing how archaeology can be made more relevant to contemporary American Indian and other Indigenous communities. The activism is not merely an academic enterprise; it often influences government policies and the agencies that interact with and impact Indigenous people and communities.

The relationship between the U.S. government and its Indigenous groups (American Indians or Native Americans) is defined by a series of laws and regulations that outline the special relationship that has arisen from the federal government's responsibilities to the tribes based on the various treaties it made with the early tribal nations. Supreme Court Justice John Marshall compared this "trust responsibility" to the relationship between a trustee and a ward because the federal government has a fiduciary responsibility to the tribes (see D'Errico [2000] for a more detailed discussion of the history of the concept of tribal sovereignty in Indian law). This special government-to-government relationship deals with interactions between federally recognized tribes and federal agencies, which act as the representatives of the federal government. (Tribes that are not federally recognized may have standing in some states [California, for example] that is nearly equivalent to the standing of federally recognized tribes.)

In the United States, the primary law that influences how federal land managers and project officials take the impacts of federal actions on historic properties into consideration is the National Historic Preservation Act of 1966 (NHPA). This law established that material manifestations of the past are important to *all* of the United States and are worthy of protecting. The law requires federal agencies to consult with tribes at various points in the historic preservation process. Consultation, in this circumstance, involves gathering opinions and perspectives from the tribes about specific actions to be undertaken, licensed, or permitted by a federal agency. As Thomas King notes, a "mélange" of other cultural resources laws (King 2011, 406–410) are also part of historic resource protection.

The executive branch of the federal government has also provided guidance in the form of Executive Order 13084, Consultation and Coordination with Indian Tribal Governments (issued May 14, 1998); Executive Order 13175, Consultation and Coordination with Indian Tribal Governments (issued November 6, 2000); and the presidential memorandum Tribal Consultation: Memorandum for the Heads of Executive—Departments and Agencies (issued November 5, 2009).

Federal agencies also provide their own guidance, such as Consulting with Indian Tribes in the Section 106 Process of the Advisory Council on Historic Preservation (updated August 22, 2005), Departmental Regulation 1350-002, Tribal Consultation, Coordination, and Collaboration of the Forest Service (issued on January 18, 2013), and the Secretarial Order 3317, Department of the Interior Policy on Consultation with Indian Tribes (issued December 1, 2011).

Those memoranda and policy statements provide guidance about federal agency interactions with tribal nations, but those interactions are more often conducted at individual agency program levels with individuals who may or may not be familiar with tribal culture. Thus, interactions between tribes and the agency can vary considerably, as can the level and quality of interaction between tribes and agencies that have different (but similar) programmatic needs.

In 1992, the National Historic Preservation Act was amended to give tribes the option of taking over the functions of state historic preservation officers on tribal lands. Tribes saw this as an opportunity to participate in the heritage preservation system, and in 1996, twelve tribes formally took over some historic preservation authorities and responsibilities. The program has continued to grow, and as of the end of June 2020, 195 tribes were participating formally in the national historic preservation program with their own tribal historic preservation officers.

Giving tribes the option of taking over the management of historic resources on tribal land was a landmark decision because it tacitly recognized that tribes should manage their own histories. Still, despite the opportunities the act gave the tribes, issues remain.

It is difficult for tribes to find the mechanisms for interjecting their values into the existing historic preservation system, since the laws under which they operate hinder full integration of any nonwestern ideologies. Often, tribal programs are charged with aspects of heritage preservation that extend beyond the NHPA's definitions of heritage. For example, after the Native American Graves Protection and Repatriation Act (NAGPRA) was passed in 1990, some tribes began managing materials that belong to or are related to their cultures beyond those the NHPA defines. The duties of tribal heritage managers often extend beyond place-based heritage and involve graves protection issues, repatriation of cultural materials, preservation of language and culture, and other broad aspects of tribal heritage.

In addition, tribes are often more interested in protecting particular places that go beyond the general history-based significance inherent in the NHPA. For example, tribes have pushed for the construction of a special class of locations known as traditional cultural properties (or places) known as TCPs.

TCPs, first described in the National Park Service's Bulletin 38 (Parker and King 1998, 1), are properties that are "eligible for inclusion in the National Register [of Historic Places] because of its association with cultural practices or beliefs of a living community that (a) are rooted in that community's history, and (b) are important in maintaining the continuing cultural identity of the community." While these locations require a physical space that can be physically defined, they need not be associated with "real" people or "real" events. I place "real" in quotation marks because such properties may relate to locations associated with tribal cultural heroes, tribal origin locations, or other such events that might not be deemed "real" to those who are not tribal members. The Garden of Eden might be one such property; the value ascribed to it would be based on associations or values that not all people would accept. Thomas King (2003) offers a much more detailed discussion of traditional cultural properties in American cultural resource management.

Archaeologists talk as if tribal historic preservation officers are special, but they tend to treat them as if they were versions of state historic preservation officers. There is and should be a difference. Darby Stapp and Michael Burney's 2002 book *Tribal Cultural Resource Management* offers a perspective on the management of cultural resources through a tribal lens. Thompson and Marek-Martinez (this volume) more pointedly discuss how the Navajo Nation has used archaeology and heritage management in tribal programs to expand ideas of social justice on the reservation.

Ian McNiven (2016) wrote of the theoretical challenges of Indigenous archaeology as it is currently practiced. He called for "setting a theoretical agenda for Indigenous archaeology that challenges a series of dichotomies and dualisms that underpin and privilege Western perspectives and Eurocentrism and mask insights into cultural difference and variability past and present" (36). He also noted setting such an agenda would help the discipline move beyond its current state.

But not all archaeologists have viewed Indigenous archaeology as positive. Robert McGhee (2008, 579) wrote about the "significant amount of academic energy invested in professing the urgent need for developing an Indigenous archaeology in North America, and indeed throughout the world." McGhee argued that those who call for Indigenous archaeology do so based on "the emotions and political reactions of scholars to Aboriginal communities that are socially and economically marginal, and that conceive of this situation as the result of historical mistreatment at the hands of Western society" (593)" As Colwell-Chanthaphonh and colleagues (2010, 230), note, McGhee

> pits science against religion, scientists against Indians—a simplistic dualism with science as a pure objective positivist pursuit and Native peoples as ecology-spiritual subjectivists. McGhee's arguments depend on this false essentialized dichotomy, and when framed as

unrestrained Aboriginalism versus impartial science, naturally the scientific community is going to be swayed to the latter.

Other archaeologists responded to McGhee in a series of articles in *American Antiquity*. Croes (2010, 215) wrote: "Overall, McGhee's article does outline pitfalls that can occur in 'Indigenous archaeology,' but I must advocate that archaeologists do, and should, approach [archaeology] as a true 50/50 partnership with tribes, to the mutual benefit of both sides." Wilcox (2010, 225) drew attention to the epistemic problem of McGhee's thesis, noting

> If the scientific study of the past (defined by McGhee) leads to an archaeology that refuses to acknowledge (much less explain) the presence of contemporary Indigenous Peoples, then we must question the objectivity of that field—especially if that particular archaeological practice supports the marginalization of Indigenous interest in favor of its own.

Silliman (2010, 219) commented that "by arguing that essentialism, Aboriginalism, and primitivism ground Indigenous archaeology, McGhee loses sight of the fact that this branch deals more with the opposites of those: postcoloniality, respectful dialogue between various stakeholders of which archaeologist are only one, and activist, multivocal histories." He emphasized that the recognition "that Indigenous people share some commonalities in their histories, struggles, and rights in the cauldrons of colonialism" serves not to "essentialize or universalize worldviews, cultural practices, or histories, but rather encourages a contextual understanding of those within a political and historical reality that needs attention in the contemporary world."

While Indigenous archaeology continues to be politically charged to some and not politically charged enough for others, its practitioners recognize that the archaeology of contemporary living communities with Indigenous bases (wherever located) requires the involvement of those communities if the discipline is to become better informed.

As archaeology programs on tribal lands continue to grow, there is an increasing tendency for such enterprises to involve the community more fully. One such community-based participatory project involving a researcher from the University of Washington (Sara Gonzalez) and the tribal historic preservation office of the Confederated Tribes of Grand Ronde (Briece Edwards, Grand Ronde deputy tribal historic preservation officer) has been developed as a way of using archaeology to increase the capacity of the Grand Ronde Historic Preservation Office to identify, record, and protect tribal heritage on the reservation.

Gonzalez, Kretzler, and Edwards (2018) present the community-based participatory research program carried out on the Grand Ronde reservation. The Field Methods in Indigenous Archaeology (FMIA) program of the Department of Anthropology at the University of Washington contributes to the needs of the Grand Ronde reservation while at the same time offering tribal community members an opportunity to learn about the sometimes-murky field of archaeology.

The Grand Ronde reservation is composed of a community known as the Confederated Tribes of Grand Ronde. In the 1850s, the federal government removed twenty-seven western Oregon bands and tribes to the Grand Ronde Reservation. More than twenty-seven bands and tribes that spoke at least eight languages and maintained an array of cultural practices created a reservation community that was galvanized by the widespread adoption of Chinuk Wawa, a pre-reservation regional lingua franca, as the reservation language (Zenk and Johnson 2010, 458–459). Chinuk Wawa not only resolved communication difficulties between those reservation groups, it also emerged as a symbol of Grand Ronde identity during twentieth-century pressures to assimilate.

This is the historical context of the Grand Ronde historic preservation office. It is responsible for identifying and protecting Grand Ronde heritage on the tribe's 14 million acres of ceded lands, including the approximately 15,000 acres the tribe manages directly. The Field Methods in Indigenous Archaeology program supports the tribal historic preservation office in two ways: 1) it helps define its tribal historic preservation plan by using cultural protocols to structure field practice and foster respectful relations with and to tribal heritage; and 2) it recovers a maximum amount of information from places while minimizing physical and thus spiritual disturbance (Gonzalez, Kretzler, and Edwards 2018, 92–95).

The FMIA's six-week residential field school offers tribal and nontribal undergraduate and graduate students training in community-based participatory research and archaeological and ethnographic methods. The field school reframes archaeological research as a respectful and reciprocal exchange of knowledge. It also shows students how to work with and for a tribal nation as they train to become members of the research team.

These sorts of programs exemplify the benefits of providing training to tribal members so they can participate in the field aspects of archaeology and they serve the needs of tribes related to managing the impacts *after me!*

of federal programs on tribal heritage and places of importance. A group of archaeologists working in British Columbia believe that there might be another benefit of tribal involvement in archaeology. Archaeologists David M. Schaepe, Bill Angelbeck, and John R. Welch, in conjunction with mental health clinician David Snook, have developed the idea that archaeology might be used as occupational therapy to help alleviate cultural stress and historical trauma. Cultural stress is a result of events that have taken place during a person's lifetime, while historical trauma is the cumulative emotional and psychological wounding that has happened across generations, emanating from massive group trauma experiences. The idea is that the harm done in the past continues to play out across generations into the present. In this way, the past is continually a part of the present and (occasionally) a foreshadowing of the future.

Conditions that derive from historical trauma often include depression, self-destructive behavior, suicidal thoughts and gestures, anxiety, low self-esteem, anger, and difficulty recognizing and expressing emotions. BigFoot and Braden (2007), Brave Heart and colleagues (2011), Brave Heart and DeBruyn (1998), and Brown-Rice (2013) discuss the scope and impact of historical trauma and unresolved grief due to the holocaust that has affected Native American people.

The work of Schaepe and colleagues (2017) with three Coastal Salish communities has led them to believe that community-directed studies of ancestral places can improve individual and communal health and well-being. They believe that confirming connections among people, places, objects, knowledges, ancestries, ecosystems, and world views is a potential way for individuals and communities to cultivate identities, relationships, and orientations that are foundational for health and well-being. They believe that archaeology practiced as place-focused research can counteract cultural stress, a pernicious effect of colonialism that is pervasive among Indigenous peoples worldwide.

This "archaeology as therapy" developed "as a result of community-based archaeology . . . mixing the discipline of archaeology with community-based needs . . . to bring relevance to archaeology and capacity and recovery to communities encumbered by centuries of colonialism" (Schaepe et al. 2017, 515). They also recognize that it is important to define methods of addressing community-based needs that avoid inflicting harm or re-traumatizing participants and to ensure that support systems and precautions are established as aspects of this practice. They encourage practitioners to adopt principles and practices of community-based therapy and social work and to ensure that applicable fields of "therapy" and community care are provided by community helpers (e.g., Fletcher 2003; Poonwassie and Charter 2001).

Indigenous archaeology is also finding its place and utility in Japan, where Japan's Indigenous population, the Ainu, have been working to connect their history to the ancient past. The contemporary Ainu are an Indigenous people of Japan who have lived mostly on the northern island of Hokkaido, on the northeastern part of Honshu Island and on what is now the Russian-held Kuril Islands and Sakhalin Island. Historically, the Ainu have experienced hardships and racism at the hands of the majority Japanese, including long-term colonization by the Japanese, government policies of assimilation, community relocation, the spread of disease, decreasing population, and discrimination (Siddle 1996). They were moved off their lands and onto lesser productive plots so that Japanese farming enterprises could use the more productive lands.

According to Hirasawa and Kato (2014, 35), mainstream archaeological research in Japan has focused on the history of state formation based primarily on the dominant population. This tendency is particularly marked in parts of Japan's main island of Honshu, where ancient burial mounds are located and ruins of large settlements from the Yayoi period (300 BC to AD 300) are found. However, the characteristics of archaeological research in Hokkaido tend to differ from those of Honshu because Hokkaido experienced a transition from the Jomon and post-Jomon periods (when subsistence depended on hunting and gathering) to the Ainu culture period. Accordingly, archaeology in Hokkaido can be seen as a type of research that has a history linked to ethnic group formation.

In 2008, the Japanese government recognized the Ainu as Japan's Indigenous population. However, the Ainu do not have any legally recognized individual or collective Indigenous rights; they are merely Japanese citizens. The fundamental philosophy of Japan's constitution is to guarantee individual rights and equality under the law, but it does not always agree with the recognition of collective or Indigenous rights (Nakamura 2014).

Furthermore, the Ainu do not have an institution of representation, although the Japanese government tacitly recognizes the Ainu Association of Hokkaido as a de facto representative body of in terms of national issues of impact to the Ainu. Although the Ainu Association of Hokkaido is the largest Ainu organization, membership is voluntary and less than half of the total Ainu population are members. Most of the Ainu who participate in the revitalization of their cultural practices do so in local Ainu organizations that are primarily social clubs where language, songs, and dances are practiced, learned, and taught. The highlight of each year is the Shakushain Festival in Shin-Hidaka, Hokkaido.

The Shakushain Festival is observed to memorialize the contribution of Shakushain to the Ainu fight for freedom and identity. Every year in the third week of September, Ainu honor Shakushain for his effort to organize Ainu resistance movements against the Japanese in the late 1660s. In the afternoon, Ainu groups from local organizations perform songs and traditional dances connected to Ainu tradition. This and other initiatives mobilize Ainu youth and offer them lessons on Ainu history and culture and their importance for maintaining a communal identity.

Since 2007, Hirofumi Kato of the Center for Ainu and Indigenous Studies at Hokkaido University in Sapporo, Japan, has been using Indigenous techniques and archaeology to help the Ainu better understand the earlier parts of their unwritten history (Kato 2010, 2014a, 2014b, 2017). The Ainu remain loosely affiliated and lack a mechanism whereby individuals can document any degree of Ainu "blood." The identity of those who openly participate in Ainu culture is tied to that culture's development in Hokkaido.

Kato (2014a, 28) has stated that "a viewpoint based on Indigenous archaeology is indispensable for the practice of archaeology in Hokkaido" and has called for greater involvement of the Ainu in developing research protocols that will influence how archaeologists interact with Ainu communities. He wrote, "In the past, researchers have studied reconstruction and interpretation regarding the history of Indigenous people based on objective and scientific methods without input from these individuals. Even from a global perspective, the rights of Indigenous communities to their historical and cultural heritage are legally guaranteed in only a limited number of cases" (22–23). Thus, the growth of Indigenous archaeology in Hokkaido echoes many of the issues Indigenous groups everywhere face and reflects the growing focus of archaeologists who recognize the political underpinnings of much of the archaeological enterprise as it relates to nonstate populations.

The Archaeology of Mass Graves

The use of archaeology and archaeological methods to study of mass graves and the "disappeared" directly relates to the idea of archaeology as an activist enterprise. Archaeologists have provided expertise and technology

234 · Joe Watkins

in investigations of mass grave sites in numerous situations (see Haglund 2001; Haglund, Connor, and Scott 2001; Jankaukus 2009; Owsley 2001; Rosenblatt 2010; and Sigler-Eisenberg 1985).

Michael "Sonny" Trimble and Susan Malin-Boyce (2011, 518–516) discuss some of the lessons learned from working at three mass grave sites in Iraq in the period 2004 to 2007. With the development of the Mass Graves Investigation Team of the Regime Crimes Liaison Office of the U.S. Embassy in Baghdad, the research conducted was similar to many field operations carried out by cultural resource management archaeologists in the United States, with the exception of the danger involved in traveling to and from the field sites and the need to maintain a chain of custody so that the materials could be used by the Iraqi High Tribunal in any war crime proceedings or prosecutions.

Excavated materials provided information about the people who were interred in the mass graves. For example, clothing types were used to identify probable ethnicity and sex and age categories (adult or subadult). Religious objects, personal jewelry, and documents (including identification) were also recovered. Evidence of restraints, blindfolds, and gags were also noted with the remains. Schuldenrein et al. (2017) note that the geoarchaeological methods used at these and other twentieth-century mass grave sites in Iraq contributed to the conviction of Saddam Hussein on charges of genocide for trying to annihilate the Kurdish people in 1988 and can provide a model for addressing atrocities in the future.

In the United States, a team of archaeologists formed Forensic Archaeology Recovery in response to the September 11, 2001, attacks on the World Trade Center in New York City. It is a nonprofit organization whose goal is to "provide technical assistance for locating and recovering evidence in cold cases dedicated to children and the elderly."[1] Forensic Archaeology Recovery enlists trained archaeologists to respond to large-scale disaster scenes and to help in the investigation and recovery of unfound persons when considerable time has passed since disappearance. Adhering to protocols determined by the authorities who have jurisdiction, members of the organization enter recovered materials into a valid chain of custody that can lead to victim identification. In this way, archaeologists are making a difference at crime scenes and in disaster response and are providing closure to the relatives of people who are missing or are unaccounted for in disaster situations.

Archaeologists and archaeological methods are useful in other similar situations. In 2013, a research team from the University of South Florida

(USF) began excavating a cemetery area at the Arthur G. Dozier School for Boys known as Boot Hill. The site was established as the Florida State Reform School on January 1, 1900, in Marianna, Florida. In 1914, it was known as the Florida Industrial School for Boys. The school operated under various names until it closed on June 30, 2011.

Throughout the operation of the boys' school, numerous children and employees died at the facility, sometimes under curious circumstances. Most notorious, however, was a dormitory fire that claimed the lives of at least eight children and two employees of the school in the early morning hours of November 18, 1914. Requests from family members to learn about missing loved ones and from the state of Florida as an act of accountability (Kimmerle, Wells, and Jackson 2012) led the USF team to exhume graves at Boot Hill Cemetery so they could identify the dead to the extent possible.

Using ground-penetrating radar and other archaeological field methods in combination with archival research and interviews of former employees, inmates, and families, the USF research team estimated that there were nearly 100 deaths during the time the facility was in operation. They located fifty burials in the area of Boot Hill. In total, as of January 2016, the USF research team had found fifty-one individuals buried in fifty-five graves, of which three were victims of the 1914 fire (Jackson 2016, 160).

The excavations and exhumations at the Boot Hill burial site were technically precise and painstaking. Team members used ground-penetrating radar and other equipment to help in the process, but human labor was used throughout to clear brush, remove impediments, dig trenches, and locate bodies. The research team used archaeological, bioarchaeological, and forensic methods to recover and document individual items or fragments found in or near graves, such as teeth, bone, coffin handles, and nails.

Throughout all this, the information archaeologists uncovered sometimes elicited "feelings of anger and frustration" in the living people, families, and communities that were engaged in confronting their relationship to the past. At other times there were feelings of relief and gratitude, "shared in the form of overwhelming displays of happiness, joy, tears, and hugs" (Jackson 2016, 161).

The methodological questions archaeologists pose during investigations into the archaeology of the contemporary past often uncover or make visible what has previously been left out or ignored (see Buchli and Lucas 2001; Wilkie 2001). Archaeological tools and methods enable investigators to invite discussion about graves, building remains, tools, bone fragments, and soil samples.

The research at Boot Hill contributed to discussions of racial and social inequity in Florida specifically and in the South in general. It underscored the significant impact and implications of plantation and chattel slavery, convict labor practices, and segregation as practiced in the United States and the "lifeways of people who lived and worked during America's transition from legalized slavery to legalized segregation to integration and Civil Rights, regardless of race" (Kimmerle et al. 2012, 128).

Ultimately, an ad hoc committee of stakeholders that included representatives of state agencies and families of the boys buried at Dozier, USF faculty members, an interfaith organization, and others was established that developed four major goals for the reburial and memorialization efforts:

> 1) shed light on the past; 2) bring justice to families of victims by acknowledging those that died; 3) educate current and future generations about systems, processes, and people that created and sustained an institution that considered some lives *throwaway;* and 4) facilitate dialog between groups and within communities about present issues/concerns and future plans and next steps with respect to Dozier. (Kimmerle et al. 2012, 130, italics in original)

The Undocumented Migration Project

One of the most recent programs to use activist archaeology and its methods is the Undocumented Migration Project (http://undocumentedmigrationproject.com), which Jason De León developed at the University of Michigan. The project uses anthropology, archaeology, and forensic science to document the clandestine migration of people from various countries. In the United States, it has focused on the border between the United States and Mexico.

The project looks at the impact of "prevention through deterrence," the U.S. government policy of funneling people through the desert in southern Arizona. In a blog post for Wenner-Gren's website *Sapiens,* De León, García, and the Undocumented Migration Project (2016) wrote about the ways the United States has used "'hostile' geographic conditions, rattlesnakes, and ultimately, the risk of dehydration and death to deter migrants, essentially outsourcing border enforcement to nature." While the United States Border Patrol catches some immigrants as they walk through the area, other migrant people die along the way.

De León uses forensic methods and experimental research to determine the impact of carrion feeders and other animals on the remains of migrants who die in their struggle to reach their desired goals. For example, he dressed a pig carcass in human clothing and recorded the results. Within three weeks, the remains had been so heavily impacted by animals that nearly everything—including identification that had been placed in the clothing—had disappeared or had been spread widely about the area.

He also talks about implementing "the archaeology of 24 hours ago" as a way of using the materials left behind by the hundreds of thousands of immigrants who try to cross into the United States illegally from Mexico as windows into the migrants' viewpoints. To De León, the Undocumented Migration Project serves as a counter to the message that the migrants crossing into the United States illegally are tied to drug trafficking or drug smuggling that permeates the media and political broadcasts. His goal is to use his work to draw attention to the humanity of the anonymous individuals who have died.

Discussion

Generally, archaeology has been portrayed as an objective science devoted to explaining cultures of the past through the materials left behind. In spite of this definition of the field, however, archaeology has never been apolitical. It has been depicted as the handmaiden of colonialism (Lewis 2013) and as a tool of nationalism (Kohl 1998). Individual archaeologists who practice archaeology may try to maintain objectivity, but personal and social biases all too often creep into the discipline, ranging from the subjects archaeologists choose to research, the locations where they conduct their research, the interpretations of the materials they encounter, and the syntheses they use to report those materials.

In 1919, Warren K. Moorehead, the "dean of American archaeology," wrote that "the American field is rapidly diminishing. I estimate that in twelve to fifteen years all the major archaeological problems will be solved" (quoted in Robinson 2018, 103). At that time, a horde of archaeologists was studying the "great questions" of archaeology—chronologies, culture histories, and so forth. The first generation of archaeologists in the United States developed the basics and it was left to those who followed them to flesh out the finer points. And yet archaeology continues to move forward, refining notions that have formed the foundations of the discipline.

New technology has helped, to be sure. Advances in dating methods, geophysical exploration techniques, computational capabilities, and mDNA research have contributed to archaeologists' abilities to create finer and finer distinctions with the information we bring out of the field. New discoveries add to the information we have, pushing some of the limits of our knowledge concerning the initial peopling of North and South America and the basics of the cultures those human populations created. However, even while technology enables archaeologists to refine their ideas, the academy lags behind in working with people with vested interests in the past and the heritage of the present.

American Indian tribes involved in tribal historic preservation programs have created a basis for moving forward. As historic preservation programs stand now, they are stymied by the structure of the current program under which they operate. The federal government currently requires only that the impact of federal undertakings on cultural resources be *considered,* thus allowing development to proceed forward, regardless of the importance of the resource. For example, the Dakota Access Pipeline was built on private property and therefore did not fall under the purview of the National Historic Preservation Act. As a result, a site that is known to be sacred to the Standing Rock Sioux was not protected. It is often up to individual archaeologists to advocate for protecting cultural resources, sometimes outside the existing system. This is a form of activism.

Archaeologists employed by tribal programs also might be seen to be activists, especially to outsiders who might believe the archaeologists are working for the benefit of the tribe at the expense of archaeology as a discipline. Forward-looking archaeologists who work in the field of cultural resources management might also be seen as activists if they take the approach that the resources that are important to communities should be protected rather than merely excavated.

The most basic component of activist archaeology involves taking into consideration the wishes of the communities that have ties with the materials archaeologists uncover. Those materials may be artifacts from an archaeological site that can provide information about a culture of the past, or they might be more recent materials that benefit from the use of archaeological methods to recover special information that might otherwise be lost, such as forensic investigations of mass burials or missing persons. At this time, the opportunities for a more activist archaeology are endless, relying only on someone's imagination to move them forward.

Marshall (2000, cited in Hirasawa and Kato 2014) notes that communities are rarely monocultural and seldom (if ever) of one mind. They also remind us that using cultural resources in whatever form (excavation, interpretation, display) should begin with a consideration of which communities stand to benefit and gain value from the historical narratives that emerge from the interpretation of archaeological sites and artifacts.

Is it time to stop trying to be objective scientists searching for "the truth" or "the past" in archaeological deposits? Do we owe it to the people we study to do archaeology only for their benefit at the expense of every other thing we have been taught? These are questions that we should be asking ourselves every day. Our answers should be easily justifiable, at least to ourselves.

The academy is perhaps the last bastion of freedom in terms of the practice of archaeology. With few restrictions in place regarding research, archaeologists in academic positions are less encumbered by restrictions (unless the subjects of their research happen to be on public land or their research requires a federal permit). Archaeologists in the academy should be more aware of the possibility that their students who complete the bachelors, masters, and doctorate degrees in archaeology are not likely to find academic positions teaching archaeology. Speakman et al. (2017), who examined the prospects of obtaining a faculty position in anthropological archaeology at BA/BS, MA/MS, and PhD institutions in the United States and Canada, concluded that "only about 1 in 5 US/Canada-derived anthropological doctorates is successful in obtaining a faculty position in a US or Canadian anthropology department" (9).

Given this finding, it is highly unlikely that the recent graduates will find jobs teaching archaeology or doing research that is unencumbered by federal guidelines of one sort or another. It seems highly likely that recent graduates will find work in some area of cultural resource or heritage resource management. Will they become activist archaeologists? Perhaps.

Entry-level archaeologists employed by cultural resource management firms—even those who have learned new ideals in community archaeology courses or ethics classes—are not likely to be in positions to initiate conversations with community members. It is usually the field director or principal investigator who has the authority or viewpoint that community involvement is beneficial to carrying out the project under contract and who recognizes the benefit to archaeology that derives from community involvement. And this is where we must rely, in large part, on the archaeologists whose job it is to teach not only archaeological methods, regional chronologies, and various techniques but also about the ways that archaeology can have an impact on contemporary populations. It ultimately might be up to the academy to teach people that activist archaeology can be good archaeology.

This is not to say that archaeologists who practice activist archaeology do not have influence. Archaeologists who work for tribal programs initiate social change nearly every day as they work to provide the tribal perspective in the archaeology they practice. Archaeologists who run community-based programs and field schools create examples that will influence young archaeologists and their future careers. Managers of cultural resource firms employ the majority of practicing archaeologists in the United States (at least), and they have the opportunity to create public programs that involve communities of all sorts.

Hopefully this is not the last word on activist archaeology. As Stottman (2010, 15) wrote, "As activist archaeologists, we consciously connect the past with the present; and although we may not save the world, in some small way, we can change it."

Note

1. "Mission & Vision," Forensic Archaeology Recovery, accessed April 23, 2020, http://forensicarchaeologyrecovery.org/mission-vision.

References Cited

Atalay, Sonya. 2006. "Guest Editor's Remarks: Decolonizing Archaeology." In "Decolonizing Archaeology," special issue, *American Indian Quarterly* 30 (3–4): 269–279.

———. 2012. *Community-Based Archaeology: Research with, by, and for Indigenous and Local Communities.* Berkeley: University of California Press.

BigFoot, Delores, and Janie Braden. 2007. "Adapting Evidence-Based Treatments for Use with American Indian and Native Alaskan Children and Youth." *Focal Point* 21 (1): 19–22. Accessed April 23, 2020. https://www.pathwaysrtc.pdx.edu/pdf/fpW0706.pdf.

Brave Heart, Maria Yellow Horse, and Lemyra M. DeBruyn. 1998. "The American Indian Holocaust: Healing Historical Unresolved Grief." *American Indian and Alaska Native Mental Health Research* 8 (2): 60–82.

Brave Heart, Maria Yellow Horse, Josephine Chase, Jennifer Elkins, and Deborah B. Altschul. 2011. "Historical Trauma among Indigenous Peoples of the Americas: Concepts, Research, and Clinical Considerations." *Journal of Psychoactive Drugs* 43 (4): 282–290.

Brown-Rice, Kathleen. 2013. "Examining the Theory of Historical Trauma among Native Americans." *The Professional Counselor* 3 (3): 117–130. Accessed April 23, 2020. http://

tpcjournal.nbcc.org/examining-the-theory-of-historical-trauma-among-native-americans/.

Buchli, Victor, and Gavin Lucas, eds. 2001. *Archaeologies of the Contemporary Past.* New York: Routledge.

Colwell-Chanthaphonh, Chip. 2009. *Inheriting the Past: The Making of Arthur C. Parker and Indigenous Archaeology.* Tucson: University of Arizona Press.

———. 2012. "Archaeology and Indigenous Collaboration." In *Archaeological Theory Today,* 2nd ed., edited by I. Hodder, 267–291. Cambridge, UK: Polity.

Colwell-Chanthaphonh, Chip, and T. J. Ferguson, eds. 2007. *Collaboration in Archaeological Practice: Engaging Descendant Communities.* Lanham, MD: AltaMira Press.

Colwell-Chanthaphonh, Chip, T. J. Ferguson, Dorothy Lippert, Randall H. McGuire, George P. Nicholas, Joe E. Watkins, and Larry J. Zimmerman. 2010. "The Premise and Promise of Indigenous Archaeology." *American Antiquity* 75 (2): 228–238.

Conkey, Margaret. 2003. "Has Feminism Changed Archaeology?" *Signs* 28 (3): 867–880.

Conkey, Margaret, and Joan Gero. 1997. "Program to Practice: Gender and Feminism in Archaeology." *Annual Review of Anthropology* 26: 411–438.

Conkey, Margaret, and Alison Wylie. 2007. "Doing Archaeology as a Feminist." *Journal of Archaeological Method and Theory* 14 (3): 209–358.

Croes, Dale R. 2010. "Courage and Thoughtful Scholarship = Indigenous Archaeology Partnerships." *American Antiquity* 75 (2): 211–216.

De León, Jason, Eduard "Lalo" García, and the Undocumented Migration Project. 2016. "A View from the Train Tracks: U.S. Policy Is Effectively Hiding the Suffering of Undocumented Immigrants." *Sapiens,* February 16. Accessed April 23, 2020. https://www.sapiens.org/culture/prevention-through-deterrence/.

D'Errico, Peter. 2000. "Sovereignty." In *The Encyclopedia of Minorities in American Politics,* vol. 2, edited by Jeffrey Schultz, Kerry L. Haynie, Anne M. McCulloch, and Andrew Aoki, 691–693. Phoenix, AZ: Oryx Press.

Ferguson, T. J. 1996. "Native Americans and the Practice of Archaeology." *Annual Review of Anthropology* 25: 63–79.

Fletcher, Christopher. 2003. "Community-Based Participatory Research Relations with Aboriginal Communities in Canada." *Pimatziwin: A Journal of Aboriginal and Community Health* 1 (1): 27–62.

Gonzalez, Sara L., Ian Kretzler, and Briece Edwards. 2018. "Imagining Indigenous and Archaeological Futures: Building Capacity with the Confederated Tribes of Grand Ronde." *Archaeologies: Journal of the World Archaeological Congress* 14 (1): 85–114.

Haglund, William D. 2001. "Archaeology and Forensic Death Investigations." In "Archaeologists as Forensic Investigators: Defining the Role," special issue, *Historical Archaeology* 35 (1): 26–34.

Haglund, William D., Melissa Connor, and Douglas D. Scott. 2001. "The Archaeology of Contemporary Mass Graves." In "Archaeologists as Forensic Investigators: Defining the Role," special issue, *Historical Archaeology* 35 (1): 57–69.

Hirasawa, Yu, and Hirofumi Kato. 2014. "Cultural Heritage and Archaeology at the Shiretoko World Natural Heritage Site." In *Indigenous Heritage and Tourism: Theories and Practices on Utilizing the Ainu Heritage,* edited by M. Okada and H. Kato, 33–38. Sapporo: Hokkaido University Center for Ainu and Indigenous Studies.

Jackson, Antoinette. 2016. "Exhuming the Dead and Talking to the Living: The 1914 Fire at the Florida Industrial School for Boys—Invoking the Uncanny as a Site of Analysis." *Anthropology and Humanism* 41 (2): 158–177.

Jankaukus, Rimantas. 2009. "Forensic Anthropology and Mortuary Archaeology in Lithuania." In "Highlights in Physical Anthropology: Eight Invited Reviews," special issue, *Anthropologischer Anzeiger* 67 (4): 391–405.

Kato, Hirofumi. 2010. "Whose Archaeology? Decolonizing Archaeological Perspective in Hokkaido Island." In *Indigenous Archaeologies: A Reader on Decolonization Reader on Indigenous Archaeologies,* edited by Marge Bruchac, Siobhan Hart, and H. Martin Wobst, 314–321, Walnut Creek, CA: Left Coast Press.

———. 2014a. "Indigenous Heritage and Community-Based Archaeology." In *Indigenous Heritage and Tourism: Theories and Practices on Utilizing the Ainu Heritage,* edited by M. Okada and H. Kato, 17–32. Sapporo: Hokkaido University Center for Ainu and Indigenous Studies.

———. 2014b. "The Hokkaido Sequence and the Archaeology of the Ainu people." In *Encyclopedia of Global Archaeology,* edited by Claire Smith, 3428–3435. London: Springer.

———. 2017. "The Ainu and Japanese Archaeology: A Change of Perspective." *Japanese Journal of Archaeology* 4: 185–190.

Kerber, Jordan, ed. 2006. *Cross-Cultural Collaboration: Native Peoples and Archaeology in the United States.* Lincoln: University of Nebraska Press.

Kimmerle, Erin H., E. Christian Wells, and Antoinette Jackson. 2016. "Report on the Investigation into the Deaths and Burials at the Former Arthur G. Dozier School for Boys in Marianna, Florida." Submitted to the Internal Improvement Trust Fund and the Florida Department of Environmental Protection. Florida Institute for Forensic Anthropology and Applied Sciences, University of South Florida. Tampa.

King, Thomas F. 2003. *Places that Count: Traditional Cultural Properties in Cultural Resource Management.* Walnut Grove, CA: AltaMira Press.

———. 2011. "Cultural Resource Laws: The Legal Mélange." In *A Companion to Cultural Resource Management,* edited by Tom King, 405–419. West Sussex, UK: Blackwell Publishing.

Kohl, Philip L. 1998. "Nationalism and Archaeology: On the Constructions of Nations and the Reconstructions of the Remote Past." *Annual Review of Anthropology* 27: 223–246.

Leone, Mark P., and Parker B. Potter Jr. 1984. *Archaeological Annapolis: A Guide to Seeing and Understanding Three Centuries of Change.* Annapolis: Historic Annapolis.

Leone, Mark P., Parker B. Potter Jr., and Paul A. Shackel. 1987. "Toward a Critical Archaeology (with Comments)." *Current Anthropology* 28 (3): 283–302.

Lewis, Herbert S. 2013. *In Defense of Anthropology: An Investigation of the Critique of Anthropology.* New Brunswick, NJ: Transaction Publishers.

Marshall, Yvonne. 2002. "What Is Community Archaeology?" *World Archaeology* 34 (2): 211–219.

McGhee, Robert. 2008. "Aboriginalism and the Problems of Indigenous Archaeology." *American Antiquity* 73 (4): 579–597.

McNiven, Ian J. 2016. "Theoretical Challenges of Indigenous Archaeology: Setting an Agenda." *American Antiquity* 81 (1): 27–41.

Nakamura, Naohiro. 2014. "Realising Ainu Indigenous Rights: A Commentary on Hiroshi Maruyama's 'Japan's Post-War Ainu Policy. Why the Japanese Government Has Not Recognised Ainu Indigenous Rights?'" *Polar Record* 50 (253): 209–224.

Nicholas, George P. 2008. "Native Peoples and Archaeology." In *Encyclopedia of Archaeology*, vol. 3, edited by D. Pearsall, 1660–1669. New York: Academic Press.

———. 2014. "Archaeology, Indigenous." In *Oxford Bibliography of Anthropology*, edited by J. L. Jackson. Oxford: Oxford University Press.

———, ed. 2010. *Being and Becoming Indigenous Archaeologists*. Walnut Creek, CA: Left Coast Press.

Owsley, Douglas W. 2001. "Why the Forensic Anthropologist Needs the Archaeologist." In "Archaeologists as Forensic Investigators: Defining the Role," special issue, *Historical Archaeology* 35 (1): 35–38.

Parker, Patricia, and Thomas King. 1998. *Guidelines for Evaluating and Documenting Traditional Cultural Properties*. Bulletin 38. Washington, D.C.: National Park Service. Accessed April 23, 2020. https://www.nps.gov/subjects/nationalregister/upload/NRB38-Completeweb.pdf.

Poonwassie, Anne, and Ann Charter. 2001. "An Aboriginal Worldview of Helping: Empowering Approaches." *Canadian Journal of Counselling* 35 (1): 63–73.

Robinson, Brian. 2018. "Laying the Foundations for Northeastern North American Archaeology." In *Glory, Trouble, and Renaissance at the Robert S. Peabody Museum of Archaeology*, edited by Malinda Stafford Blustain and Ryan J. Wheeler, 99–116. Lincoln: University of Nebraska Press.

Rosenblatt, Adam. 2010. "International Forensic Investigations and the Human Rights of the Dead." *Human Rights Quarterly* 32 (4): 921–950.

Schaepe, David M., Bill Angelbeck, David Snook, and John R. Welch. 2017. "Archaeology as Therapy: Connecting Belongings, Knowledge, Time, Place, and Well-Being." *Current Anthropology* 58 (4): 502–533.

Schuldenrein, Joseph, Michael K. Trimble, Susan Malin-Boyce, and Mark Smith. 2017. "Geoarchaeology, Forensics, and the Prosecution of Saddam Hussein: A Case Study from the Iraq War (2003–2011)." *Geoarchaeology* 32 (1): 130–156.

Siddle, Richard M. 1996. *Race, Resistance and the Ainu of Japan*. London: Routledge.

Sigler-Eisenberg, Brenda. 1985. "Forensic Research: Expanding the Concept of Applied Archaeology." *American Antiquity* 50 (3): 650–655.

Silliman, Stephen W. 2010. "The Value and Diversity of Indigenous Archaeology: A Response to McGhee." *American Antiquity* 75, (2): 217–220.

Silliman, Stephen W., ed. 2008. *Collaborating at the Trowel's Edge: Teaching and Learning in Indigenous Archaeology*. Tucson: University of Arizona Press.

Smith, Claire, and H. Martin Wobst, eds. 2005. *Indigenous Archaeologies: Decolonizing Theory*. London: Routledge.

Speakman Robert J., Carla S. Hadden, Matthew H. Colvin, Justin Cramb, K. C. Jones, Travis W. Jones, Corbin L. Kling, Isabelle Lulewicz, Katharine G. Napora, Katherine L. Reinberger, Brandon T. Ritchison, Maria Jose Rivera-Araya, April K. Smith, and

Victor D. Thompson. 2017. "Choosing a Path to the Ancient World in a Modern Market: The Reality of Faculty Jobs in Archaeology." *American Antiquity* 83 (1): 1–12.

Spector, Janet. 1993. *What This Awl Means: Feminist Archaeology at a Wahpeton Dakota Village.* St. Paul: Minnesota Historical Society.

Stapp, Darby C., and Michael S. Burney. 2002. *Tribal Cultural Resources Management: The Full Circle to Stewardship.* Walnut Creek, CA: AltaMira Press.

Stottman, Jay M., ed. 2010. *Archaeologists as Activists: Can Archaeologists Change the World?* Tuscaloosa: University of Alabama Press.

Trigger, Bruce. 1980. "Archaeology and the Image of the American Indian." *American Antiquity* 45 (4): 662–676.

Trimble, Michael K., and Susan Malin-Boyce. 2011. "CRM and the Military: Cultural Resource Management." In *A Companion to Cultural Resource Management,* edited by Tom King, 515–533. West Sussex, UK: Blackwell Publishing.

Watkins, Joe. 2000. *Indigenous Archaeology: American Indian Values and Scientific Practice.* Walnut Creek, CA: AltaMira Press.

———. 2003. "Through Wary Eyes: Indigenous Perspectives on Archaeology." *Annual Review of Anthropology* 34: 429–449.

Wilcox, Michael. 2010. "Saving Indigenous Peoples from Ourselves: Separate but Equal Archaeology Is Not Scientific Archaeology." *American Antiquity* 75 (2): 221–227.

Wilkie, Laurie. 2001. "Black Sharecroppers and White Frat Boys." In *Archaeologies of the Contemporary Past,* edited by Victor Buchli and Gavin Lucas, 108–118. London: Routledge.

Zenk, Henry, and Troy A. Johnson. 2010. "A Northwest Language of Contact, Diplomacy, and Identity: Chinuk Wawa/Chinook Jargon." *Oregon Historical Quarterly* 111 (4): 444–461.

CONTRIBUTORS

Christopher P. Barton is assistant professor of archaeology at Francis Marion University. His focus is on developing collaborative archaeology projects that serve underrepresented communities in the United States and Ireland. He is a coauthor of *Historical Racialized Toys in the United States.*

Stephen A. Brighton is associate professor of archaeology and anthropology at the University of Maryland. His area of research concerns the applied methods and theories of Modern World Archaeology to the Irish Diaspora both home and abroad. Brighton has excavated numerous sites in the United States related to Irish and Irish-American laboring families dating from the late 18th to the early 20th centuries. Currently, he is located in the Skibbereen-area of County Cork and focused on understanding post-Famine Irish society and the dynamic and complex history, heritage, and culture of modern Ireland impact on and expression through material culture leading up to revolution, civil war, and the creation of the Republic of Ireland. Brighton is the author of numerous articles on the Irish Diaspora and author of the book *Historical Archaeology of Irish Diaspora: A Transnational Approach*, which presents a new approach to understanding 19th century Ireland and the diasporic experience in becoming Irish American.

Stacey L. Camp is associate professor of anthropology and director of the Campus Archaeology Program at Michigan State University. She previously served as director of the Alfred W. Bowers Laboratory of Anthropology, an archaeological repository serving the ten northern counties of Idaho. Her research examines the archaeology of immigrants living in the late nineteenth- and early twentieth-century western United States.

Kasey Diserens Morgan, a PhD student at University of Pennsylvania, focuses on heritage preservation in Quintana Roo, Mexico, specifically the history of the Caste War of Yucatan or the Maya Social War, a Maya rebellion of the nineteenth century. She is studying the built heritage of the town to understand larger questions of identity, memory, and place and how these concepts have changed over time.

Yamoussa Fane is a historian and technical advisor for Ministère de la Culture in Djenné, Mali. His research interests are local history, tourism, and cultural heritage in Mali.

Tiffany C. Fryer is a Cotsen Postdoctoral Fellow and a lecturer in the Department of Anthropology at Princeton University. She uses historical archaeology and ethnography to better understand how the legacies of the past, particularly violent conflict, form present-day political consciousness and imaginations of the future. Her current research, which is based in Quintana Roo, Mexico, seeks to push the limits of the pragmatic application of archaeological projects and think critically about the sociopolitics of heritage and its interplay with community development through community-organized participatory research.

Daouda Keita is lecturer of archaeology at Université des Sciences Sociales et de Gestion de Bamako. His research focuses on ethnoarchaeology and heritage in the Segou region of Mali.

Nathan Klembara is currently a PhD student at Binghamton University. His focus is on identifying loci for queer analyses in the Upper Paleolithic with particular attention to the Paleolithic burial record. His current fieldwork is concentrated at the open-air Magdalenian site Peyre Blanque.

Ora V. Marek-Martinez is executive director of the Native American Cultural Center at Northern Arizona University, where she is also assistant professor of anthropology. She has worked as a Tribal Historical Preservation Officer for the Navajo Nation. Her research focuses on southwestern archaeology and tribal archaeology with an emphasis in epistemic injustice and decolonizing methodologies.

Christopher N. Matthews is professor of anthropology at Montclair State. He is a historical archaeologist with special interests in race, heritage, inequality, and collaborative community-based research in the mid-Atlantic region. He has led projects in Maryland, New Orleans, and Long Island,

New York. He is the author of *The Archaeology of American Capitalism* (2011) and *An Archaeology of History and Tradition* (2002) and several articles and books chapters.

Bernard K. Means is assistant professor of anthropology at Virginia Commonwealth University. His scholarly pursuits include reconstructing American Indian village spatial and social organizations, the research potential of archaeological collections, and the history of archaeology across the Americas, especially during the Great Depression. Dr. Means is also director of the Virtual Curation Laboratory, which is creating three-dimensional digital models of archaeological and paleontological objects used for teaching, research, and public outreach from northern India and across the Americas. Dr. Means is the author of *Circular Villages of the Monongahela Tradition* (2007), the editor of and a contributor to the *Shovel Ready: Archaeology and Roosevelt's New Deal for America* (2013), and the author of numerous articles.

Vinod Nautiyal is a member of the Archaeology Department of Hemwati Nandan Bahuguna Garhwal University and a visionary in digital archaeology. Nautiyal, an early proponent of 3D modeling and LIDAR, is the author of "Situating Rock Art in the Archaeology of Garhwal Himalaya A Fresh Look" and *Methods and Models for Teaching Digital Archaeology and Heritage.*

Kyle Somerville has joined Environmental Design & Research of Syracuse, New York, as a cultural resources specialist and project archaeologist. He served as the project director for Phases I–III archaeological surveys for a company in Rochester, New York. Kyle earned his PhD in anthropology from the University at Buffalo. He is the author of "A Case Study in Frontier Warfare: Racial Violence, Revenge, and the Ambush at Fort Laurens, Ohio," *Journal of Contemporary Archaeology* (2011).

Moussa dit Martin Tessougue is assistant professor of geography at the University of Social Sciences and Management of Bamako. His research interests are economic geography, population geography, and tourism in Mali.

Kerry F. Thompson is assistant professor at Northern Arizona University and a member and resident of the Navajo Nation. Her primary interests in archaeology and applied archaeology are those that intersect with social justice, inclusion, and equity issues for Native American people; the development of Indigenous perspectives in anthropology and archaeology; and understanding current U.S. cultural resource management laws and policies from a federal Indian law perspective.

Joe Watkins is an American archaeologist and anthropologist, the chief of the Tribal Relations and American Cultures program, and the American Indian Liaison Officer of the National Park Service. He was the director of Native American Studies at the University of Oklahoma until 2013 and has worked as an adjunct in the department of anthropology at the University of Maryland since the fall of 2014. He is a member of the Choctaw Nation of Oklahoma and is currently a senior consultant for Archaeological and Cultural Education Consultants.

Andrew J. Webster is a PhD student at University of Maryland and co-author, with Stephen A. Brighton, of "Archaeological Investigations at the Peter Murray Site, County Cork (Site Number: 16E0241)."

INDEX

Lightning Source UK Ltd.
Milton Keynes UK
UKHW021939090321
380066UK00003B/91